THE TEACHINGS
OF MAIMONIDES

THE TEACHINGS
OF MAIMONIDES

BY
THE REV. A. COHEN
M.A. (Cantab.), Ph.D. (Lond.)

PROLEGOMENON BY
MARVIN FOX

KTAV PUBLISHING HOUSE, INC.
NEW YORK
1968

FIRST PUBLISHED 1927

Library of Congress Catalog Card Number: 68-17310
Manufactured in the United States of America

PREFACE

THIS book is intended to serve a double purpose. It firstly presents a summary of the teachings of Maimonides on Philosophy, Psychology, Religion and Ethics in a systematic classification. Although he earned a great and enduring reputation for his masterly systematisation of the mass of Rabbinic law, he has nowhere left an orderly account of his opinions. They have to be collected and pieced together from the whole field of his compositions. Secondly, the summary is given in the author's words by quotations from his writings. The volume, accordingly, takes the form of an *anthologie raisonnée*.

Despite the existence of English versions of the *Guide*, the *Eight Chapters* and parts of the *Yad*, few readers are likely to have the patience or inclination to go through them from cover to cover. Especially is this so with the first-mentioned work which is acknowledged to be one of the outstanding philosophical productions of the Middle Ages and exerted a deep influence upon the thought of Jewish and Christian theologians. Much in its pages would deter the casual reader. The opening chapters in particular would probably induce him to lay the book aside as being without interest and value.

That is perhaps the reason why so little is known of Maimonides, apart from his name. It is consequently hoped that the present volume may be the means of creating a fuller acquaintance with this eminent Jewish thinker. Much of his teaching is, of course, out of date. There is no longer the necessity to harmonise Revelation with Aristotelian philosophy, which was the urgent theological problem in his day ; but the spirit which animated his mind and pervades his writings is as much needed now as ever before. His philosophy may be antiquated, but his insistence on the supremacy of reason and his emphasis on knowledge as the essential preparation for religious comprehension are of eternal value.

I wish to express my thanks to the Chief Rabbi (Dr. J. H. Hertz) for his kindness in lending me his copy of Lichtenberg's edition of the *Responsa*, to the Librarian of Jews' College (Dr. H. Hirschfeld) for sending me the numerous volumes I required in the preparation of this book, and to the Rev. S. M. Lehrman, B.A., of Manchester, who generously undertook the task of correcting the proofs.

A.C.

Birmingham,

February, 1927.

TABLE OF CONTENTS

THE TEACHINGS OF MAIMONIDES

TABLE OF CONTENTS

TABLE OF CONTENTS

MAIMONIDES' WORKS CITED

Guide=*Guide for the Perplexed.* A complete translation was made into English by Dr M. Friedländer (3 vols., 1881-85). A revised one-volume edition, with the elimination of the notes, was published in 1904 (Routledge). The passages quoted are given in Friedländer's translation.

C.M.=*Commentary on the Mishnah.* Included in the work are three essays : (i) Introduction ; (ii) Introduction to Ḥélek (i.e., Sanhedrin chap. X). An English translation was published in the *Jewish Quarterly Review*, XIX, pp. 28-58. My quotations are from this version, by kind permission of the Editor, Mr C. G. Montefiore ; (iii) *Eight Chapters*, prefaced to the commentary on tractate Abot. The Hebrew text, with an English rendering, was published by Dr J. I. Gorfinkle in 1912. This translation has been drawn upon by the courtesy of Dr Gorfinkle and the Columbia University Press.

Yad=*Yad ha-ḥazakah* or *Mishneh Torah.* The first of the fourteen books was translated into English by E. Soloweyczik (1863) and partly by H. Bernard (1832). The section on Almsgiving was translated by J. W. Peppercorne (1840). The citations in this volume are newly translated.

Responsa=*Kobets Teshubot ha-Rambam*, ed. Lichtenberg (1859). Besides his letters this collection includes some of Maimonides' smaller works, such as *Iggéret Téman*, *Ma'amar Kiddush ha-Shém*, *Ma'amar Teḥiyyat ha-Métim*, his *Ethical Will*, etc.

Ma'amar ha-Yiḥud=the Hebrew translation of *Makalah fi 'l-Tauḥid*, ed. Steinschneider (1847). Despite its title " Essay on the Unity ", it is not, as the *Jewish Encyclopedia* (vol. IX, p. 81) describes, " an essay on the unity of God ". It is a summary of the contents of the first two sections of the *Yad*.

Mitswot=*Kitab al-Fara'id*, in Hebrew *Séfer ha-Mitswot*, " The Book of the Commandments ". The passages cited have been translated from the Arabic edition of M. Bloch (1888).

Millot=*Millot ha-Higgayon*, " The Terminology of Logic ".

PROLEGOMENON

Dr. Abraham Cohen, author and editor of *The Teachings of Maimonides,* was a scholar of established reputation and recognized achievement. Apart from his original works, he made a major contribution to learning through his service as General Editor of the *Soncino Books of the Bible.* In this role as editor he produced scholarly commentaries on all the books of the Hebrew Bible, an achievement which was possible only for a man who had a deep and comprehensive mastery of the vast and complex biblical literature. His equal mastery of rabbinics was demonstrated in his *Everyman's Talmud* and in his contributions to the Soncino edition of the Babylonian Talmud in English. In the present volume Cohen approaches Maimonides in a way which was fully consistent with the scholarship of his day. However, our situation has changed considerably in the more than forty years since the book first appeared. The general cultural, intellectual, and philosophical climate has undergone a major revolution, and the study of Maimonides must now also be viewed in a radically new perspective. An analysis of this new situation in Maimonidean studies and its implications for our understanding of that great thinker will occupy a central place in this Prolegomenon.

To Cohen and to most of his generation Maimonides appeared as a typical medieval philosopher, distinguished from others primarily by his Jewish faith and his incredibly vast and creative rabbinic learning. His problem was understood as the parallel of other medieval thinkers, primarily that of reconciling a revealed religion with the claims of a purely rational philosophy. It was thought that anyone with proper scholarly equipment and interest could find out easily enough just what Maimonides was saying in his various works.

Admittedly, the *Guide of the Perplexed* is a long and difficult book, one which Cohen thinks that, "Few readers are likely to have the patience or inclination to go through . . . from cover to cover."[1] In his view this is not so much a result of the intrinsic difficulty of this book, but rather a consequence of the fact that a work written in the twelfth century poses special problems for a twentieth-century student. It seemed perfectly reasonable to Cohen to alleviate the difficulties by composing the present work which has two objectives. First, it tries to give a systematic picture of the doctrines of Maimonides, presenting them in an orderly and structured pattern, though Maimonides himself had presumably failed to do so. Cohen studied not only the *Guide* but all the other works of Maimonides which had any relevance to philosophical or theological issues. He attempted in this book to bring together from the entire Maimonidean corpus a unified exposition of the system of Maimonides. Second, this book seeks to introduce the student to the thought of Maimonides by presenting him with an anthology selected with discrimination from his various works. The anthology is so structured as to allow Maimonides to speak for himself, with only brief transitional explanations by Cohen.

Given the probability that today's readers are no more diligent or scholarly than those of forty years ago the anthology stands as a contribution of lasting value. It makes available selections from a number of works of Maimonides, including some which are still not available in English. A reader seeking to acquaint himself with the style and direction of Maimonides' thought can surely make an excellent start with the selections in this volume. What we can no longer accept without question is Cohen's version of what Maimonides said and his conception of how the parts of the system (if there is a system) fit together. Here we must give consideration to the effects of Maimonidean scholarship during the last forty years and to newer ways of studying his works.

A major development in the study of Maimonides in the last few decades has been the work of Professor Leo Strauss, whose studies force us to reject the easy certainties about

Maimonides which have long been accepted. In two outstanding essays[2] Strauss laid new foundations for the study of
Maimonides, especially the *Guide of the Perplexed.* Strauss
has emphasized the fact that the *Guide* is an esoteric book,
that is, a book whose surface doctrine hides another very
different set of teachings. In his own introduction to the *Guide,*
Maimonides himself makes this point very clear. He speaks
repeatedly of the "secret" doctrine which must be set forth in
a way which is appropriate to its secret character. Rabbinic
law, to which Maimonides is determined to be faithful, had
prohibited any direct public teaching of the secrets of the
Torah. One was permitted to teach them only in private to
selected students of proven competence, and then only the
"chapter headings" might properly be taught. Abiding by this
ruling, Maimonides intends to offer in his *Guide* no more than
such chapter headings, and to arrange the presentation in such
a way that none but the most highly qualified students will be
able to follow his explanations. For this reason, as he tells us,
even the chapter headings (*i.e.,* his teaching) "are not set down
in order or arranged in coherent fashion in this Treatise, but
rather are scattered and entangled with other subjects that are
to be clarified. For my purpose is that the truths be glimpsed
and then again concealed. . . ."[3] Such an exposition must be
carefully constructed so as to protect the simple-minded from
doctrines which they cannot understand and which would only
harm them, while making the truth available to students who
have the proper personal and intellectual preparation. Maimonides tells us explicitly that he used the following method,
among others. "In speaking about very obscure matters it is
necessary to conceal some parts and to disclose others. Sometimes in the case of certain dicta this necessity requires that
the discussion proceed on the basis of a certain premise,
whereas in another place necessity requires that the discussion
proceed on the basis of another premise contradicting the first
one. In such cases the vulgar must in no way be aware of the
contradiction; the author accordingly uses some device to
conceal it by all means."[4] It is one of the mysteries of our
intellectual history that these explicit statements of Maimoni-

des together with his instructions for how to read his book have been almost universally ignored. This is not the place to consider the reasons. For us it is enough to have been warned by Strauss so that we may exercise appropriate caution and not repeat the mistakes of our predecessors in the study of Maimonides.

Once we begin to read Maimonides in the way that he requires of us we can no longer be comfortable about the ease with which Cohen and most other scholars attributed particular doctrines to him. Only the most painful study makes it possible for us even to hazard an opinion concerning the views of Maimonides, and such an opinion is reliable only if it emerges from a sensitive confrontation with the obstacles and subtleties of the texts. We can best grasp the nature and scope of our problem if we give some consideration to the variety of opinions that recognized scholars have offered with respect to major problems in the interpretation and teaching of Maimonides.

We begin with the question of whether Maimonides was a model of traditional piety or, as some assert, a veiled heretic. That the latter charge is not utterly fantastic can best be understood if we remember the great controversy which arose shortly after his death, and which tore apart major Jewish communities in Europe and the East. In some places his philosophic writings were banned so that it was a serious violation for anyone to study them. Intense feelings built up to a tragic climax in the burning of the *Guide* in a public ceremony in France some thirty years after his death.[5] In a variety of ways the controversy continued for centuries. It is well-known that only a generation ago there were *yeshivot* in eastern Europe where the study of Maimonides' *Guide* was considered *prima facie* evidence of severe heretical tendencies. No doubt, that attitude can still be found in various circles today.

Even when he was not accused of personal impiety there were always those who attacked particular doctrines of Maimonides as contrary to the fundamentals of the Jewish faith. Every student of the *Mishneh Torah* is familiar with the often bitter criticisms of R. Abraham ben David of Posquières, some of which are on theological points. Rabad suggests, for example, that the views of Maimonides on resurrection and the world-to-come are contrary to the established teachings. He even expresses doubt concerning the legitimacy of Maimonides' views on the incorporeality of God.[6] In the same standard editions of the *Mishneh Torah* in which the glosses of Rabad are printed we also find the *Kesef Mishneh* of R. Joseph Karo, the sixteenth century author of the *Shulhan Aruk*. Karo consistently defends Maimonides against the attacks of Rabad, not only with respect to issues in law and jurisprudence, but also in the controversies concerning matters of theology and the fundamentals of faith. This pattern continues through the ages; to one group Maimonides is a heretic or at least propounds heretical views, while to another his teachings are a model of conventional orthodoxy. Nahmanides, in his commentary on the Pentateuch, attacks Maimonides at some points almost without restraint. In a familiar passage, Nahmanides goes so far as to say that certain views expressed in the *Guide* are so far wrong that "they directly contradict the teachings of Scripture so that it is forbidden to listen to them and certainly forbidden to believe them."[7] We know, of course, that the same Nahmanides was often a defender of Maimonides against attacks of the very sort which he himself launched. What is perhaps less known is that Maimonides found another vigorous defender against these attacks in R. Yom Tob b. Abraham of Seville. This great fourteenth-century Talmudist composed a small book, the *Sefer ha-Zikaron,* for the specific purpose of explaining and defending the views of Maimonides which had been criticized by Nahmanides.[8]

Even among recent and contemporary writers the battle continues. Ahad ha-Am represented Maimonides as a pure rationalist who imposed reason on faith and, when necessary, adjusted the norms of rabbinic law in order to force them into conformity with the demands of reason. His famous essay on Maimonides is entitled, "Shilton ha-Sekel" ("The Supremacy of Reason"). This view of Maimonides is strenuously

opposed by Aharon Kaminka who claims that for Maimonides
reason, philosophy, and science were all subordinated "to the
absolute supremacy of his strongly held faith in the truth and
eternity of the Torah of Moses and the talmudic tradition
which derives from it. That faith welled up from the depths
of his heart . . . and it alone can explain the integrity of all
the remarkable achievements of his life."[9] Kaminka presents
peculiar evidence for the complete orthodoxy of Maimonides
and for the claim that while he assimilated philosophy into the
tradition, it never dominated his thinking or his teachings. He
is certain that if Maimonides had deviated in any slight degree
from the norms of rabbinic doctrine this would have been
detected at once and he would not have been accepted as the
unexcelled authority in matters of law and faith. It is characteristic of the blindness or tendentiousness of much Maimonidean scholarship that Kaminka was able to ignore the
mass of familiar animadversions on Maimonides, since to
recognize them would have forced him to abandon his own
thesis. In contrast to Kaminka, Tschernowitz casts serious
doubts on the orthodoxy of Maimonides, asserting that he was
so committed to the primacy of worldly learning that not only
did he make philosophy the judge of what should be an article
of faith, but "with respect to every matter of law with which
he dealt, if there was any contradiction between scientific
knowledge and the traditional view he almost always decided
in favor of science. . . . Maimonides, the philosopher, is clearly
visible behind the walls of his own structure of traditional
Jewish law."[10] Finally, any study of the writings of Leo
Strauss on Maimonides or of some of the more recent work
of Shlomo Pines reveals, between the lines (if not openly),
the conviction that the true views of Maimonides were very
far indeed from conventional orthodoxies. The main purpose
of his esoteric style in the *Guide* is, according to this view, to
make it possible for him to express his heretical ideas without
injuring either the social structure or the naive and useful
faith of simple-minded believers.[11]

    An extension of the controversy over the orthodoxy of
Maimonides emerges in differences over the question con-

cerning his relationship to Aristotle and Aristotelian philosophy. It may seem strange to some to suggest that there is any
question here open to discussion, since it is a commonplace
of the textbooks that Maimonides was completely under the
dominance of the philosophy of Aristotle. The only generally
recognized exception is his stand on the creation of the world
ex nihilo against the Aristotelian doctrine of the eternity of
matter.[12] Yet an examination of scholarly discussion reveals
deep disagreement on this question as well. In one of his
earliest scholarly studies Harry A. Wolfson, among the greatest
historians of medieval philosophy, argues that Maimonides
can only be understood as an Aristotelian. He "is a true
convert to Aristotelian philosophy. To him the thorough
understanding of Aristotle is the highest achievement to which
men can attain." His primary purpose was to show that scriptural and rabbinic teaching was in harmony with the philosophy of Aristotle. "Maimonides was not a rabbi employing
Greek logic and categories of thought in order to interpret
Jewish religion; he was rather a true medieval Aristotelian,
using Jewish religion as an illustration of the Stagirite's metaphysical supremacy."[13] Wolfson concludes that Maimonides'
personal piety should not be questioned. He was without
doubt a meticulously observant Jew, but his personal piety
was in no way derived from or connected with his Aristotelian
philosophic system. Husik goes even further in this direction
with the claim that though the doctrines of Aristotle radically
oppose the teachings of the Hebrew Bible, Maimonides was
a devoted Aristotelian and tried to achieve a harmony between
Greek philosophy and Torah.[14]

This widely accepted interpretation of Maimonides can be
found in a variety of forms and in many places, particularly
in regard to Maimonides' ethics. Because he taught the doctrine of the mean, it is often taken for granted that his ethical
theory was essentially Aristotelian in origin and in its content. For M. Lazarus, in his *The Ethics of Judaism,* and
David Rosin, in his *Die Ethik des Maimonides,* there is no
question as to the almost pure Aristotelianism of Maimonides'
ethics. Their understanding of Maimonides is by far the most

common one. Yet, no less a philosopher than Hermann Cohen differs sharply from them. Cohen's famous and controversial essay, *"Charakteristik der Ethik Maimunis,"* is a major attempt to demonstrate that Maimonides' ethics were completely independent of Aristotle's and that he is, in fact, fundamentally opposed to Aristotle. Cohen holds that if Maimonides' ethics were not independent of Aristotle his doctrine would be self-contradictory, unphilosophical, and could, as a result, have no place in his system. One of the main burdens of Maimonides' thought, according to Cohen, is his battle against materialism. His great achievement is the victory of idealism over materialism, and for this very reason he cannot be thought of as supporting the essentially materialist views of Aristotle. Even Maimonides' doctrine of the mean is thought by Cohen to differ radically from the Aristotelian doctrine. Because Maimonides often used Aristotelian terminology, people have been misled into thinking that he was a follower of Aristotle's philosophy. Cohen claims that this was only a strategem employed by Maimonides in order to gain a favorable hearing for himself. Given the dominance of Aristotle over medieval thought it would have been intellectual suicide to oppose him openly. The trick, which Maimonides mastered superbly, was to sound like an Aristotelian while undermining all the foundations of the Peripatetic philosophy.[15]

These differences concerning the interpretation of Maimonides are not necessarily related to the private commitments or personal views of the scholars in question. We find that Zvi Diesendruck, who was a professor at the Hebrew Union College, a Reform rabbinical seminary, and Yaakov Moshe Charlap, a model of old Orthodox piety in the religious quarter of Jerusalem, both agree with Hermann Cohen that Maimonides was no Aristotelian. They take this position not only with respect to his ethics but include practically the whole of his philosophy. Diesendruck argues that "the entire philosophy of Maimonides is one continuous endeavor to overcome Aristotle in the most essential points. . . . Maimonides differs from him in all matters of importance in metaphysics as well as ethics; in these fields he regards the Aristotelian teachings as erroneous and even dangerous."[16] Though there is no reason to think that Rabbi Charlap knew the work of Professor Diesendruck, he follows a remarkably similar line of argument. Granting that Maimonides incorporated some elements of Greek philosophy into his works, Charlap proclaims as a fact beyond all doubt that these elements were totally transformed and Judaized before Maimonides gave them a place in his writings. The terms Charlap uses for this process of intellectual transformation are the exact terms normally used for the process of religious conversion into the Jewish faith.[17]

As we allow the pendulum to swing again to the opposite extreme we find one more contemporary writer affirming Maimonides' Aristotelianism and with it his complete heresy. Yaakov Becker pictures for us a Maimonides who is strikingly similar to Leo Strauss', though he gives no direct indication that he has studied or been influenced by the work of Strauss. His Maimonides is an esoteric writer determined to set forth in one work two opposed systems of thought. One is to be a system of traditional Jewish beliefs intended for the protection of the untutored masses, while the other is an Aristotelian philosophy which is *the* truth and which contradicts the religious tradition at almost every crucial point. We have here a special version of a "double-truth" theory, with Maimonides hiding his true doctrines from the eyes of the vulgar. In Becker's view, "Maimonides never resolves the contradictions between the Torah of Moses and the philosophy of Aristotle. On the contrary, he expands and deepens them. His war against Aristotle was only apparent. At the profoundest levels of the *Guide of the Perplexed* he continually deepens the abyss between these two world views. He makes absolute distinctions between them, while justifying each as appropriate for different spheres of human life."[18] Becker goes on to show, to his own satisfaction, that for Maimonides the true philosophy was that of Aristotle. His God, like Aristotle's, is in no significant respect the God of the Torah. He is not the creator of the world; he is not the power that sustains the world; there is no providence; and God has no relationship whatsoever to the world. Such is the interpretation of Becker.

What shall we make of such a welter of contradictory opinions about Maimonides? Our first conclusion must be that we can no longer rest easy with the comfortable certainties that characterized the work of Abraham Cohen in this volume, and which seem typical of most other writers on Maimonides. Students of the history of philosophy will rightly point out that this problem of interpretation is not peculiar to Maimonidean scholarship. Many major philosophers have evoked similarly contradictory interpretations. As one example, we need only think of the range of opinions regarding the relationship of Aristotle to Plato. Yet it can be argued (and, I believe, demonstrated) that hardly ever has there been such deep disagreement over so many issues and over so many centuries about the views of a single philosopher. If Maimonides does not differ in kind from other philosophers, he surely differs in degree. The reasons are not difficult to isolate. First, we must consider the effects of his literary style on which we commented earlier. Any esoteric writer is subject (by his own deliberate choice) to wider ranges of interpretation and misinterpretation than a straightforward writer. In the case of Maimonides we must always find out not only what he seems to say, but also whether he is actually saying what he seems to say. We must depend on hints and on our own capacity to construct an ordered system where there appears only to be disorder. It is no surprise that such writing evokes wildly contradictory interpretations.

The problems of interpreting Maimonides are compounded by the range of subject matter about which he wrote, the varying purposes for which he wrote, the diverse styles which he employed, the number of years which separate his earliest and latest works, and the question of the interrelationships of his various works. We can illustrate the nature of our difficulties by considering an example of the problem which faces us when we try to see Maimonides' teaching from the perspective of all the relevant passages in his writings. It is well-known that in his ordering of the commandments of the Torah the number "14" plays a very significant role. His *Sefer ha-Mitzvot* (Book of the Commandments) sets forth a series of fourteen "roots", *i.e.*, general principles for identifying, enumerating, and classifying the commandments. His great legal compilation, the *Mishneh Torah,* is a codification of the commandments divided into fourteen books. Finally, in the *Guide* he informs us that he has "divided all the commandments into fourteen classes."[19] Knowing how careful a writer Maimonides was, it would be reasonable to assume that these three classifications of the commandments into fourteen groups are in some fashion related, if not identical. Yet, a first reading shows them to be quite different from each other, and if there is a relationship it is by no means obvious. In any case, we might expect that scholars would have dealt with the problem and solved it. Instead we find casual discussions and contradictory opinions with little careful attention to the texts. What is most disturbing is that these discussions and opinions are found in the works of men whose scholarly distinction is beyond all question. We find that Isidore Epstein, one of the greatest of Jewish scholars in England, says that the fourteen-fold division of the commandments in the *Guide* is a classification and summarization of the fourteen books of the *Mishneh Torah.*[20] Yet, as we shall see shortly, the differences are very great and very obvious, so much so that no one, least of all a responsible scholar, should be guilty of identifying the two classifications as alternate versions of the same scheme. Other scholars, however they may differ in background and method, tend to treat the three fourteens in a very casual way, though this hardly seems faithful to what we know of Maimonides and his literary method. Isaac Herzog, the late Chief Rabbi of Israel, says of the three fourteens that, "This is, of course, sheer coincidence. There is no sort of logical correspondence between the respective divisions."[21] This is an opinion which Rabbi Herzog repeats in several other studies. The same view is expressed by Irving Levey, a well-known scholar in the Reform movement, when he asserts that, "Mere coincidence has thrown the number 'fourteen' into great prominence in the works of Maimonides."[22] And one of the outstanding contemporary scholars in the field of Jewish philosophy shares this opinion. S. Rawidowicz writes that the only thing these three classifications of the commandments have in common is the number "fourteen," but holds that there is no other significant connection among them, neither in their theoretical foundations nor in their practical consequences.[23]

In contrast with these views we have the analysis of Leo Strauss. He is never willing to believe that there is anything purely coincidental in the writings of Maimonides. Certainly, we should not dismiss as coincidental something as obviously connected as this threefold classification of the same set of commandments into fourteen groups. Strauss argues that it is Maimonides' deliberate plan to give the impression that the three fourteens are essentially the same in order to mislead the casual student. It would appear that he succeeded even with diligent students, as the example of Epstein would testify. Strauss would have us study these three cases carefully, note the precise differences, and from them (and other relevant evidence) determine just what Maimonides has hidden under the outer surface of the fourteens.[24] Unhappily, Strauss does not carry his analysis further, so we do not know his solution to the problem.

For our purposes it might be fruitful to examine the texts somewhat more closely in this case, in order to see how complex and subtle the problem is. In Chapter 35 of Part III of the *Guide* Maimonides sets forth his division of the commandments into fourteen classes. Since he explicitly seems to relate this division to the fourteen books of the *Mishneh Torah* it is natural that we should assume the connection. However, when we study his text carefully we are overwhelmed by remarkable incongruities and inconsistencies. Of the fourteen books in the *Mishneh Torah* only nine are specifically mentioned in the classification in the *Guide*. A discerning student must ask himself why five of the books are omitted, and what principle determined which are omitted and which included. Further, we note that, remarkably enough, the first book of the *Mishneh Torah*, the "Book of Knowledge," is not mentioned, although Maimonides seems to view it as the foundation for all that follows in his code. On the other hand, the first three classes of commandments in the *Guide* are each associated with one section of the "Book of Knowledge." If the structures of the classifications were parallel then each class in the *Guide* should be the counterpart of one book in the *Mishneh Torah,* whereas here we find three classes associated each with one section of one book of the *Mishneh Torah.* Sometimes Maimonides refers to the individual sections by their full names, *e.g., Hilkoth Yesodei ha-Torah* (Laws of the Foundations of the Torah). At other times he refers to the content of such a section, but not to its full name. So, for example, he tells us that included in the first class, in addition to the commandments that are listed in *Hilkoth Yesodei ha-Torah,* are *teshuba* and *taaniot* (repentance and fasts). Why does he not refer specifically to the full names of the sections of the Code which bear these titles, *i.e., Hilkoth Teshuba* and *Hilkot Taaniot?* Is he suggesting in the *Guide* that he now wants to include only certain portions of those sections, but not all of them? Or is there some other less compromising explanation? Again we note that two sections of the same book in the *Mishneh Torah* are assigned to two different classes in the *Guide,* and that conversely sections from different books in the former are assigned to a single class in the latter. Thus, the Laws concerning Forbidden Foods are in the thirteenth class in the *Guide* and the Laws concerning Prohibited Sexual Relations are in the fourteenth class, though they are both contained in a single book, *Sefer Kedusha* in the *Mishneh Torah.* (It is worth noting that this book is among those whose names are omitted by Maimonides in this part of the *Guide.*) In turn we find, for example, that the fourth class in the *Guide* includes commandments from, at least, four different books of the *Mishneh Torah.*

In this Prolegomenon I cannot attempt even to suggest a solution to this set of problems. What is important for any serious student is to be aware of the complexity that we must cope with in almost every Maimonidean text. That complexity is multiplied if we try to see the various works of Maimonides and their parts in any kind of intelligible and coherent interrelationship. To ascribe such a problem as the three fourteens to mere coincidence, as some very responsible scholars have done, is a far too simple and far too crude a solution. To assure us that the repetition of the fourteens is deliberate, as Strauss has done, is a necessary first step in taking the texts seriously. The real achievement, however, is to solve the puzzle, to explain what Maimonides had in mind, to account for the similarities, differences, inconsistencies and obscurities which have turned this seemingly simple scheme of classification into a dark and impenetrable mystery. We have here one striking example of the kind of demands that must be made on contemporary students of Maimonides, and we can see why the easy certainties of our anthologist and his colleagues can no longer be ours.

Our grasp of the difficulties which confront us in the effort to understand Maimonides' teachings will be even clearer if we consider some additional problems of interpretation. A question which is central to the thought of Maimonides in the opinion of almost every commentator is the problem of our knowledge of God. There is no doubt that Maimonides considered the true knowledge of God to be a necessary condition for the attainment of the highest human perfection. The very first obligation of a Jew that he records in his *Mishneh Torah,* in the first section of the first chapter of the first book, is that we are commanded to know that God exists and that He is the necessary basis for all else that exists. Similarly, the first commandment listed in his *Sefer ha-Mitzvot* is the commandment to believe in the existence of God. Chaim Heller, in his scholarly edition of the text of that work, suggests that according to the reading in the Arabic text it would be appropriate to render this commandment as speaking of *knowing,* rather than believing, that God exists. This same theme permeates much of the *Guide* and seems to reach its climax in the very last chapter where the true knowledge of God is presented as the ultimate end of man. Philosophers and prophets agree on this, according to what Maimonides says in that last chapter.

Yet there are some very troubling questions which no student can afford to ignore. How can we be commanded to know anything, especially something as arcane and inaccessible as the ultimate truth about the world? If I truly have knowledge of God, and knowledge here clearly means intellectual apprehension, then I have penetrated the secret of the very ground of all being. To strive for this goal may be every man's duty, but it is strange, to say the least, to insist that we are all *commanded* to reach the goal. Immanuel Kant taught us the principle that ought implies can, that is, that whatever a man is truly obligated to do he is able to do. Conversely, we are not obligated to do that which we are incapable of doing. How puzzling then that Maimonides, who often asserts that only a small intellectual elite is capable of achieving true knowledge of the highest matters, should make the highest knowledge of all obligatory for all men. The confusion grows greater if we consider further aspects of the question.

In Part I, Chapter 15 of the *Guide* Maimonides seems to be saying that whoever makes the effort to know God succeeds, and we can properly be commanded to make such an effort. Moreover, in the first two chapters of Part II of the *Guide* Maimonides claims to have presented rational demonstrations of the existence, unity, and incorporeality of God. If these are, in fact, valid demonstrations, as he apparently believed them to be, then they are such that any man should be able to grasp them. For every man is, as a man, endowed with rational powers, which means, among other things, with the power to follow a rational argument. That man is endowed with such intellectual powers in his very nature is established in the very first chapter of the *Guide,* since this is how Maimonides interprets the biblical statement that man was created in the image of God. So far, then, it appears reasonable to command man to know God.

As we continued to study the texts, however, a typical set of Maimonidean contradictions emerges, and our earlier certainties are no longer easily tenable. In the *Mishneh Torah,* in the same first chapter which commands us to know God, we are surprised to discover that Maimonides also says that the genuine truth about God's nature is beyond all human knowledge. Even Moses, who stands above all other men in his capacity to apprehend God, was incapable of truly knowing Him.[25] The point is repeated and elaborated in the *Guide* with a specific reference to this earlier passage in the *Mishneh Torah*. Speaking of Moses' expressed desire to know God fully, Maimonides points out that Scripture tells us that his plea was denied by God who hid from him this ultimate knowledge. "When I say He hid from him, I intend to signify that this apprehension is hidden and inaccessible in its very nature."[26] If Moses could not know God truly, then surely no other man can achieve such knowledge. In fact, Maimonides goes on in the very next sentences to warn that when man has reached his intellectual limits any effort to go beyond is only destructive. So it now appears that we cannot really know God and we are mystified by the commandment which says that we must.

When we consider what Maimonides says, that we *can* know of God our situation seems even less promising. We are told explicitly that we can gain no positive knowledge whatsoever of God. We know Him only through negative attributes. This means that we can only know what He is not, but never what He is. In fact, even when we speak of God as having certain positive qualities we must interpret them negatively. Thus, to say that God is living is only to say that He is not dead. "Of this thing [*i.e.,* God] we say that it exists, the meaning being that its nonexistence is impossible."[27] It is a strange kind of knowledge indeed which is purely negative. In fact, Maimonides seems to be saying that no man is able to fulfill the commandment to know God, which makes us wonder whether there is any meaningful sense in which it can be a commandment at all. Yet there is no doubt that he explicitly and repeatedly records and codifies such a commandment.

Now we are, of course, familiar with the fact that Maimonides considers this kind of knowledge of God to be significant. At least, he certainly says in various places that it is significant knowledge. However, as he develops his theory of negative attributes Maimonides seems to present the paradoxical doctrine which affirms that the less we know about God the more we know about Him, so that our ideal should be to negate everything that is predicated of Him in order to know everything about Him. "Accordingly the negative attributes make you come nearer . . . to the cognition and apprehension of God. . . . Desire then wholeheartedly that you should know by demonstration some additional thing to be negated, but do not desire to negate merely in words. For on every occasion on which it becomes clear to you by means of a demonstration that a thing whose existence is thought to pertain to Him should rather be negated with reference to Him, you undoubtedly come nearer to Him by one degree. . . . On the other hand, the predication of affirmative attributes of Him, is very dangerous."[28] What can we claim to know about the God, whom we are commanded to know, if all we can do is state what He is not? If we deny only *some* positive qualities, then we leave open the possibility that the innumerable remaining positive qualities may properly be predicated of God. If, on the other hand, we deny in principle *every* positive quality, without undertaking the impossible task of identifying and enumerating them, then we would appear to be in danger of the blasphemous heresy that God is nothing. It seems to help little if we call Him by such names as the Holy Nothingness. While there is every reason to think that Maimonides did not want to fall into this trap, it is extremely difficult to find a way out of it.

Conventional commentators try to resolve the dilemma, if they recognize it at all, by appealing to Maimonides' doctrine that we predicate positive terms of God analogically, rather than literally, and that what we can affirm of Him are the so-called attributes of His actions which we see in our own experience. Though Maimonides explicitly introduces the notion of the analogical use of terms with respect to God, it is not very helpful, as he himself seems to recognize in other places. The key to the problem is that a term used as a common predicate for two subjects must be used either univocally or equivocally, that is, it must either have the same meaning in both cases or a different meaning. If I say that God is wise and compassionate and that Mr. Cohen is wise and compassionate, I must determine whether the predicates mean the same thing in both cases. If they do, then I can rightly claim that I understand God's wisdom and compassion on the model of Mr. Cohen's wisdom and compassion. Of human wisdom and compassion I have direct experience, and I can, therefore, justly claim to know something about God, namely, that He is wise and compassionate in the same way that men are. However, this alternative has been explicitly closed to us by the doctrine which denies that I can ever have such positive knowledge of God. For this reason, then, I must say that I use these terms with totally different meanings in the case of God, and meanings which I cannot specify. It follows that when I speak of God as wise and compassionate I am not saying anything intelligible, since I have no idea of what these predicates mean and can put no content into them. Thus, analogy is not much help, and we are back to the negative attributes with which we began. This is acknowledged by Maimonides, although he earlier introduced the idea of analogical terms. He says that, "It has already been demonstrated that anything that we think of as a perfection—even if it existed as pertaining to Him—in accordance with the opinion of those who believe in the attributes, nevertheless would not belong to the species of perfection that we think of, save only by equivocation, just as we have made clear. Accordingly you must of necessity go over to the notion of negation."[29]

The familiar Maimonidean solution to all this is usually taken to be the notion that though we do not know any positive attributes of God we do know His actions or their consequences in the world. We speak of these as if they had been done by God just as a man would have done them. So when there is a great natural catastrophe which harms people and property we speak of God as being angry, since only great anger would move a man to behave in this way. At best this is only a way of speaking, but it adds no illumination and no knowledge. However we may find it convenient to speak, it seems that we have no knowledge of God since in principle this knowledge is beyond us. It is even doubtful whether on Maimonides' own grounds we can properly speak of God's actions, for to speak of His actions leads ultimately to affirming positive attributes and thus to the same compromises of His absolute unity which Maimonides has taken the greatest pains to avoid.

Here again we have seen how difficult it is to gain a clear understanding of the teachings of Maimonides. There is no doubt that he records the duty to know God as the very first commandment. Nor is there any doubt that he repeatedly speaks in many places in his works about the knowledge of God as the true perfection of man. He treats it as an ideal toward which every man should direct his supreme efforts, and identifies the realization of that ideal with the summit of man's self-fulfillment. Even the most casual reader could cite numerous passages from various books to show that this is the teaching of Maimonides. Yet when we examine it in the total context and full development of his own analysis we seem forced to conclude that this ideal is not only impossible, but empty of content and meaning. There are great hazards here. First, there is the serious danger of misunderstanding and misinterpreting Maimonides. Given certain predilections, it is not very difficult to read him in such a way that he turns out to be a crypto-heretic. Considering all that we know of the man and his life, his piety and his meticulous commitment to the law, this hardly seems like a tenable position. However, with some ingenuity it is an interpretation which can certainly be worked out and made plausible. It is just as easy to read the texts in such way that he emerges as a man of unquestioned and conventional orthodoxy. What must be stressed is that no responsible scholarly reading of Maimonides may be so tendentious as to ignore what does not fit into the reader's preconceived scheme. With great effort and with penetrating intellect he must be read as he asked us to read him. Only then can we hope that a reliable and sound understanding will be open to us. In addition to the danger of misinterpreting Maimonides there is the danger which deeply concerned him

that casual readers might misunderstand him and be corrupted
by their misunderstanding. He tried strenuously to avert this
danger by composing his books, especially the *Guide,* in the
way he did. Nevertheless, the hazards are there, and casual
students may well reach destructive conclusions on the basis
of their limited and confused understanding of this great
thinker.

Granted that Maimonides is a difficult and puzzling writer
who demands inordinate efforts of his readers, we certainly
must ask whether for us today that effort is justified. Have
we any reason, apart from purely historical curiosity or anti-
quarian interest, to study Maimonides with enthusiasm today?
Does his thought have any contribution to make to contemporary man? Is there, at least, some element of continuing
relevance to general philosophic concerns or to specifically
Jewish interests? We must recognize and acknowledge without hesitation that much of what Maimonides wrote seems to
have outlived its usefulness to us. In his Preface, and again in
his Introduction, Cohen stresses this point. "The spirit of the
book [*i.e., The Guide*] is immortal, but much of its actual
content is obsolete. . . . It does not answer the perplexities of
the religious mind today."[30] That the science of Maimonides'
twelfth-century world is out of date surely cannot be seriously
questioned. Traditionalists who are reluctant to admit that
anything in Maimonides could be obsolete might take comfort
from the fact that no less a rabbinic authority than Meir
Lebush Malbim faced this issue squarely more than a century
ago. In the introduction to his commentary on the Book of
Ezekiel, Malbim discusses Maimonides' interpretation of the
vision of the chariot in the first chapter. As he puts it, "Maimonides' interpretation has been refuted because the foundations on which he built it have been refuted. The astronomy,
natural science, and ancient philosophy which were the foundations and supports of his interpretation have been completely undermined and destroyed by the scientific research
which has developed in recent generations. This research has

built its astronomy and structured its natural sciences on new foundations which are stronger and more reliable."

We might well argue that not only Maimonides' science, but his philosophy and theology as well are completely obsolete. Recent philosophical developments in the western world, especially logical positivism and linguistic analysis, cast grave doubts on the meaningfulness of many traditional philosophic questions, and on the validity of their solutions. Similarly, the "new theology" claims to cut the ground out from under classical theological concerns and methods. What is left then for a twelfth-century Jewish thinker to teach us today, if his science is wrong, and his philosophy and theology open to the charge of meaninglessness or irrelevance?

One could defend the view that the stance of contemporary philosophy is by no means the last word, and that there is much of continuing value in earlier metaphysical studies. However, it would require far more space than is available in this brief essay to work out such a claim. Abandoning that effort for the present, it will be more fruitful to concentrate on the significance of Maimonides for contemporary thought in the fields of ethics, the philosophy of religion, and especially of Judaism. It seems to me clear that he has much to teach us about these matters which continue to be of interest and value.

We can learn first, and most importantly, from Maimonides an uncompromising and fearless intellectual honesty in all matters having to do with religion. At a time when the forces of closed-minded intellectual timidity have managed to gain a position of some prominence, even in certain Jewish circles, the example of Maimonides is of great interest. While protecting the integrity of the system of Jewish law, he left room for the intellect to develop its own best understanding concerning the fundamental questions of faith. In his interpretation of the Bible he battled against literalist fundamentalism, finding his justification in the long-established tradition of non-literal midrashic interpretation. The Law is necessarily fixed, because the integrity of society demands that the precepts of the Law must be obligatory. But the human effort to grasp the ultimate nature of things must, in Maimonides' view, never be totally constricted or suppressed. We can command patterns of behavior, and we rightly expect men to subordinate their private inclinations to legal norms. It is dangerous and self-defeating to command conformity in the formulation, understanding, or apprehending of ultimate philosophical or theological matters. Here the mind of man must be left free to find its own way. If, by chance, we were to succeed in preventing man from thinking, we would also have succeeded in robbing him of what is essential to his humanity.

It may seem strange to ascribe such intellectual openness to the same Maimonides who set down a rigid dogmatic structure of thirteen obligatory principles of faith, and who was extremely severe in his explicit condemnation of any Jew who denies even one of these principles. How can he be held up as a model of commitment to freedom of thought? The answer is, as usual, that we must look at the principles of faith in the total context of Maimonides' thought, otherwise we are bound to misunderstand their purpose and their force. In the same *Commentary on the Mishnah* in which the seemingly rigid creed is set forth, we find that Maimonides distinguishes sharply between the fixity of the norms of law which regulate our behavior and the flexibility which is proper in the formulation of theoretical principles. "I have said many times that when there are differences of opinion among wise men about principles of faith which do not lead to any definite actions, then it is not proper to issue a fixed decision in accordance with any one view."[31] Maimonides is saying here that the formulations of the practical *halaka* must be fixed and that differences of opinion must be resolved so that men will know what behavior is required of them. On the other hand, what we might call the theoretical *halaka,* the expressions of the principles of faith, do not demand fixity and agreement. So long as we know the law and observe it, we are free to carry on unrestricted speculation about all those complex theoretical matters which are necessarily subject to diverse views. Now it is known that hardly any aspect of Maimonides' thought engendered so much subsequent debate and diversity of opinion as did his creed. Later thinkers attacked individual articles, or the entire formulation. Some denied that there are thirteen principles of faith and substituted some lesser number. Others rejected the very notion of principles of faith since they argued that we can properly make no distinction among the commandments since all are of equal dignity. Even the principle that God is incorporeal was questioned by Rabad in a famous gloss in the *Mishneh Torah*. He disputes Maimonides' contention that the belief in God's incorporeality is one of the essentials of faith. Says Rabad: "Greater and better men than he [*i.e.,* Maimonides] have accepted the doctrine of corporeality based on their reading of various scriptural and aggadic texts."[32] It is clear from the rest of this gloss that Rabad did not himself believe that God is corporeal nor did he want to encourage that opinion in others. He was only denying that the issue could be settled dogmatically, since there is some ground on which to base divergent opinions. We can see then that by his own expressed rules of method Maimonides had to leave such matters open, for there are educated and reasonable men who differ in their understanding and conclusions.

We must try to resolve the apparent contradiction between this commitment to freedom of thought and the fierce uncompromising rigor with which the thirteen principles of faith are presented by Maimonides. The solution lies in the deep concern that Maimonides had for the protection of the social order, and for making available in that order the maximum opportunity for men to achieve the highest and most reliable knowledge of the highest things. Without an ordered society there can be neither the personal security nor the leisure which men need in order to engage in philosophical or theological speculation. Therefore, he insists on the absolutely binding force of the divine law which directs and regulates the behavior of men. Moreover, though the highest human fulfillment is in the attainment of true knowledge, comparatively few men are inclined to the requisite and demanding philosophic activity. Therefore, the unreflective masses must be provided with a set of sound opinions which will guide them in their thinking and confirm them in right action. We should, however, never confuse this utilitarian imposition of opinion or belief as a social necessity with any attempt to restrict thoughtful men in the process of serious inquiry. The latter must not only be allowed, but encouraged, for theirs is the only road to true human perfection. The point is set forth by Maimonides a number of times, of which the following is a typical example. "Just as it behooves us to bring up children in the belief, and to proclaim to the multitude, that God . . . is one and that none but He ought to be worshipped, so it behooves that they should be made to accept on traditional authority the belief that God is not a body; and that there is absolutely no likeness in any respect whatever between Him and the things created by Him; and that His existence has no likeness to theirs. . . . This measure of knowledge will suffice for children and the multitude to establish in their minds that there is a perfect being, who is neither a body nor a force in a body, and that He is the Deity, that no sort of deficiency and therefore no affection whatever can attain Him."[33] This way of imposing belief on the masses has a kind of social utility which justifies it, but it must never be permitted to limit free speculation on the part of those whose intellect leads them to think about these matters. Much later in the *Guide* Maimonides distinguishes sharply between the masses whose beliefs are imposed by tradition and the independent mind of the man of true knowledge and, hence, true piety. He speaks of his desire "to confirm men in the intention to set their thought to work on God alone after they have achieved knowledge of Him, as we have explained. This is the worship peculiar to those who have apprehended the true realities; the more they think of Him and of being with Him, the more their worship increases. As for someone who thinks and frequently mentions God, without knowledge, following a mere imagining or following a belief adopted because of his reliance on the authority of somebody else, he is to my mind outside the habitation and far away from it and does not in true reality mention or think about God."[34] Once we understand the force of such passages we can see that Maimonides was in fact deeply committed to free inquiry and did not consider it desirable to impose dogmatic orthodoxies on all men. For our age nothing less is acceptable, and it would benefit contemporary authoritarian dogmatists greatly if they allowed themselves to be taught by the greatest mind of the Jewish Middle Ages.

Just as we can profit from an imitation of Maimonides' lack of dogmatism so can we learn much from him about the possibilities and the limits of reason in general. We saw earlier that there are some ambiguities with respect to his conception of the role of reason in the solution of crucial human problems. We alluded to one of the typical views earlier when we mentioned the title and content of Ahad ha-Am's essay, "The Supremacy of Reason." This conception of Maimonides as pure rationalist is echoed by Abraham Cohen in his Preface to this volume when he says, "His philosophy may be antiquated, but his insistence on the supremacy of reason and his emphasis on knowledge as the essential preparation for religious comprehension are of eternal value."[35] That Maimonides placed an extremely high value on reason is indisputable, yet it is a mistake to overlook the fact that he also recognized clear limits to reason. This comes out in two ways that are important for our own time.

The first significant lesson is that man cannot limit himself only to that which is rationally certain, for in doing so he finds it impossible to deal with some of the most urgent of human concerns. A widely held view among contemporary philosophers is that we have no ground for belief about any matter unless it is empirically verifiable or rationally demonstrable. Unhappily, most of the deepest issues that require decision on our part are neither verifiable nor demonstrable. Should we then resign from the human community or from all personal and intellectual responsibility because we cannot answer with demonstrative certainty the questions which are before us? The way of Maimonides is worthy of consideration. He did not find reason fully adequate to deal with all basic questions. He recognized clearly that there are matters for which we can find no help in logic or in the natural sciences, matters which cannot be dealt with either by rational metaphysical speculation or empirical inquiry. Yet he did not on this ground abdicate all responsibility. Intellectual honesty requires that we first determine the boundaries of our rational capacity to deal with certain questions. Listen to the clear and unambiguous way in which he presents his position. "All that Aristotle states about that which is beneath the sphere of the moon is in accordance with reasoning; these are things that have a known cause. . . . However, regarding all that is in the heavens, man grasps nothing but a small measure of what is mathematical . . . the Deity alone fully knows the true reality, the nature, the substance, the form, the motions, and the causes of the heavens. . . . And to fatigue the minds with notions that cannot be grasped by them and for the grasp of which they have no instrument, is a defect in one's inborn disposition or some sort of temptation. Let us then stop at a point that is within our capacity, and let us give over the things that cannot be grasped by reasoning to him who was reached by the mighty divine overflow so that it could be fittingly said of him: With him do I speak mouth to mouth."[36]

Reason has its limits and an intelligent man should recognize those limits. But responsible human life often forces us to take a stand on questions for which rational inquiry offers us no certain answers. We are not free to remain neutral or to take no stand, simply because too much is at stake. Neither should we deceive ourselves into supposing that we have taken a stand on the grounds of rational demonstration or scientific evidence when we have not. From Maimonides we can learn how to see our limits, be intellectually honest, and yet commit ourselves when we must, in the full awareness that we have chosen to go beyond reason. It is essential to know why we have done so and to be clear about the ground we have substituted for reason. Maimonides' treatment of the problem of the creation of the world versus the doctrine of the eternity of matter is the best possible model for us to follow. Avoiding every temptation to self-deception, he shows us with remarkable force and clarity how to approach the resolution of such an issue. He can produce no demonstrative evidence for either thesis, yet it is urgent that he take a stand. In this case he does so on purely religious grounds, making clear what those grounds are, why he has chosen them, and above all that should reason ever prove to be adequate to the question he would be ready to give his allegiance to any rationally demonstrated position without being limited by a fixed prior reading of Scripture. Whoever imitates Maimonides will neither abandon rational and empirical evidence, nor will he be so imprisoned by his desire to know all things that he claims certainty without evidence.

There is a second and related lesson to be learned from this aspect of Maimonides' thought. If we are today no longer very much troubled by some of the classical metaphysical problems which deeply occupied him and his generation, we are very much concerned with moral problems that are similar to his. Questions of personal conduct, relations to other men, obligations to society and to the state—such questions are essentially the same today as they were then, in spite of the changes in the conditions and circumstances of our lives. Moral philosophy is perhaps the greatest intellectual failure of western man. Since antiquity our best minds have devoted themselves to the task of creating a rational morality, of finding in reason the grounds of obligation as well as the content of our duty. Our vast literature in the field of ethical theory is one continuing testimony to our inability to cope with the problem by reason alone. Yet we continue to try because the alternative seems to be moral chaos. I consider it to be one of the greatest of all Maimonides' achievements that he saw this problem clearly and without illusions. Maimonides teaches explicitly that morality is not derived from reason and that moral statements are neither true nor false. Yet he does not conclude from this that what is open to us is only moral anarchy. Because he is under no illusions concerning the capacity of reason to deal with moral questions, he sees that a move must be made in another direction. Morality is too important for the individual and for society to allow ourselves the luxury of demanding either rational certainty or nothing. Maimonides frankly acknowledges that we must turn here to tradition, religion, social convention, or something similar. Speaking of the last eight of the ten commandments (the first two being, in his view, rationally demonstrable) he says that, "As for the other commandments, they belong to the class of generally accepted opinions and those adopted in virtue of tradition, not to the class of the *intellecta*."[37] *His* treatment of morality is complex and subtle, and as a faithful Jew he locates its source in the divine commandments. Contemporary Judaism would do well to reflect on the way of Maimonides. Contemporary philosophy would do equally well. It is not my contention that we must adopt the Maimonidean commitment to morality as divine commandment, though this is surely one viable option. It is important that we consider his arguments against the presumed rational foundations of morality, and face with intellectual honesty the need to base our moral rules on some other foundation. Maimonides can save us here from much of the confusion, much of the cant, and much of the self-deception which surrounds current moral discourse.

In this brief Prolegomenon I have tried to suggest both some of the problems and some of the benefits of the study of Maimonides. Readers of Cohen's anthology can get important first insights into the teachings of the great medieval sage. Beginning with these insights, one may hope that they will be led to further disciplined study in the full awareness that they are dealing with one of the most subtle and most rewarding of all great thinkers. In studying Maimonides properly we are engaged in more than a purely historical exercise. We open up valuable perspectives on some of the most aggravated problems of our own time. Moses Maimonides, when properly understood, is both the greatest of the teachers of Torah and a true guide of the perplexed.

29 Elul 5728   MARVIN FOX
                                               Professor of Philosophy
                                               The Ohio State University

Notes

1. Introduction, p. vii.

2. See especially, Leo Strauss, "The Literary Character of the *Guide for the Perplexed*" in *Essays on Maimonides,* ed. Salo W. Baron (Columbia University Press, 1941). Reprinted in Leo Strauss, *Persecution and the Art of Writing* (The Free Press, 1952). See also, Leo Strauss, "How to Begin to Study the *Guide of the Perplexed*" in the Shlomo Pines translation of the *Guide* (University of Chicago Press, 1963). All quotations from the *Guide* in this essay are from the Pines translation.

3. *Guide,* Introduction to the First Part.

4. *Ibid.*

5. For a recent useful study of the controversy, see Daniel Jeremy Silver, *Maimonidean Criticism and the Maimonidean Controversy, 1180–1240* (Leiden, 1965).

6. Glosses on *Hilkot Teshuba,* III, 7; VIII, 2 and 7.

7. Commentary of Nahmanides on Genesis, 18:2.

8. Yom Tob b. Abraham, *Sefer ha-Zikaron,* ed. Moshe Yehuda Blau (New York, 1957).

9. A. Kaminka, "Ha-Emuna v'ha-Bikoret ha-Siklit b' Mif'alo shel ha-Rambam," *Haarez,* No. 4788, (5695) pp. 17–18.

10. H. Tschernowitz (Rav Tzair), "Lu lo Kam k'Moshe," *M'oznayim,* III, Nos. 4–5, pp. 396–397.

11. See the Strauss essays referred to above, N. 2, and Pines' Introduction in his translation of the *Guide.*

12. Cf., below, pp. 50–54.

13. Harry A. Wolfson, "Maimonides and Halevi: A Study in Typical Jewish Attitudes toward Greek Philosophy in the Middle Ages," *Jewish Quarterly Review,* II, 1911–1912, pp. 306, 314.

14. Isaac Husik, *A History of Medieval Jewish Philosophy,* (Philadelphia, 1944) pp. 299–300.

15. Hermann Cohen, "Charakteristik der Ethik Maimunis," *Moses ben Maimon,* Band I (Leipzig, 1908) pp. 85, 102, 109, 111–113.

16. Zvi Diesendruck, "The Philosophy of Maimonides," *CCAR Yearbook,* XLV, 1935, p. 358.

17. Y. M. Charlap, *Mei Marom: Misabib l'Shmona Perakim* (Jerusalem, 5705) pp. 13, 85–86.

18. Yaakov Becker, *Mishnato ha-Pilosofit shel ha-Rambam* (Tel Aviv, 1955) pp. 19–20.

19. *Guide,* III, 35.

20. I. Epstein, "Maimonides Conception of the Law and the Ethical Trend of his Halachah," *Moses Maimonides: Anglo-Jewish Papers in Connection with the Eighth Centenary of His Birth,* ed. I. Epstein, (London, 1935) p. 64.

21. I. Herzog, *ibid.,* p. 143.

22. Irving Levey, "Maimonides as Codifier," *CCAR Yearbook,* XLV, 1935, pp. 368–396.

23. S. Rawidowicz, "Sefer ha-Petiha l' Mishneh Torah," *Metzudah,* (5715) p. 137.

24. Strauss, *Persecution, op. cit.,* p. 63.

25. *Hilkoth Yesodei ha-Torah,* I, 9 and 10.

26. *Guide,* I, 21.

27. *Ibid.,* I, 58.

28. *Ibid.,* I, 60.

29. *Ibid.,* I, 60; cf., I, 54; I, 56.

30. Below, p. 17.

31. *Commentary on the Mishnah, Sotah,* III, 3.

32. *Hilkoth Teshuba,* III, 7.

33. *Guide,* I, 35.

34. *Ibid.,* III, 31.

35. Below, p. viii.

36. *Guide,* II, 24.

37. *Guide,* II, 33.

INTRODUCTION

I : The Origins of a Jewish Philosophy

WHEN the antiquity of the Jewish people is taken into account and the place it has occupied in the realm of religious thought, it is a remarkable fact that an interest in speculative philosophy scarcely manifests itself before the tenth century of the present era. When once that interest was aroused, it developed apace and grew in intensity. The study of philosophy was pursued with ardour and attracted many of the acutest intellects in Jewry. If the story of the Jewish metaphysicians begins late, when once it is commenced, the four centuries that follow are made notable by the names of eminent thinkers who boldly grappled with the riddles of the Universe. They displayed a real aptitude for speculative investigation.

What is the explanation that this aptitude remained dormant so long and displayed itself just at the time that it did ? Malter's theory[1] is that it was not until then that the Jews came into contact with an alien system of thought which conflicted with their own and were compelled to offer a rational defence of their creed or harmonise the two. The premisses from which this conclusion is drawn are hardly correct. Jews had come into close association with the Greeks and Romans in the pre-Christian centuries.[2] Josephus knew of Aristotle.[3] The Talmudic literature records disputations between Rabbis and heathen philosophers.[4] Another cause must be sought.

I

TEACHINGS OF MAIMONIDES

It has often been remarked that the Oriental mind prefers the concrete to the abstract ; and if this were so, it would be sufficient to account for the absence of metaphysical speculation which is directed towards the intangible. But a generalisation of this nature is usually only a half-truth. It is doubtless correct that the Oriental showed preference for the definite as against the indefinite. The proverbs of Eastern peoples supply ample evidence of this tendency. In Rabbinic literature we find " forty " or " sixty " where an undetermined number is intended.

That characteristic is not exclusively typical of the Eastern mentality only, but is general and found all over the world. It is the mark of the undeveloped mind ; so that it is only in comparatively recent times, with the growth of education, that the average person proves capable of thinking in the abstract. We have to search for still another reason to explain the phenomenon that although the Jewish people produced an ethical and spiritual literature, philosophy was an alien importation and not indigenous.

According to primitive psychology, the seat of the intellect was the *heart*. In the language of the Bible a man thinks by " speaking in, or to, his heart ". If he has to commit something to memory, he " lays it upon his heart ". His ideas and plans originate there. The clever man is " wise of heart ", the fool " lacking of heart ". Nowhere in the Scriptures is the heart of an animal mentioned except as a physical organ.

This attribution of intellect to the heart was not peculiar to the Hebrews. In the view of the Indians, the sun of knowledge rises in the ether of the heart. The Persians regarded the heart as the soil from which the thoughts grew in the same way that trees grow from the ground. The idea is found likewise among the early Greeks. An ancient medical work located the "intelligent soul" in the left ventricle of the heart. Homer describes the inert corpse as ἀκήρεος "without heart", in the sense of without consciousness. The use of *cor* in Latin supports the same view.⁵

What lies at the root of this psychological conception is that thinking is grounded in, if not actually identical with, feeling. What we think is what we feel. Our beliefs are determined not by argument and demonstration, but by our likes and dislikes. Our conclusions are arrived at through intuition and not through ratiocination. So long as such a psychology persisted, philosophical research and logical deduction remained an impossibility, or at any rate, a rarity.

The first blow was dealt at this system by Pythagoras (6th cent., B.C.E.) when he located the νοῦς in the brain. As soon as it was believed that the seat of the intellect was in the head and not in the heart, the road was cleared for the momentous discovery that the mind functioned independently of the heart, and that reason was distinct from emotion and truth was absolute. Hence it was that philosophy originated with the Greeks. Aristotle invented the syllogism which is the foundation of abstract reasoning.

Under the influence of the Bible the Jews retained the older psychology. But there were other forces at work which induced them to keep to the concrete rather than wander into the unchartered domain of the abstract. The acute struggle for self-preservation into which the Jewish people was plunged by the crisis of the first century—a crisis both national and religious—compelled the Rabbis to concentrate on the practical and avoid the theoretical. "Not inquiry

3

but action is the chief thing "[6] became the guiding principle. Greek philosophy had not been without its devotees among the Jews. Especially in Egypt it had found many followers, and the consequences had been harmful to their Judaism. The Rabbis consequently regarded it as a menace to the preservation of the Jewish faith.

There is a famous passage in the Talmud[7] which relates : " Four men went up into Paradise, viz. Ben Azzai, Ben Zoma, Aḥer[8] and Rabbi Akiba. . . . Ben Azzai gazed and died ; Ben Zoma gazed and became demented ; Aḥer cut the plants ; and Rabbi Akiba departed in peace ". Whatever it was that these men precisely aimed at, it is clear that they embarked on some speculative search with disastrous effects. Only one out of the four came through unscathed ; and it is noteworthy that it was this Rabbi Akiba who gave utterance to the aphorism : " Everything is foreseen, yet freedom of choice is given ; and the world is judged by grace, yet all is according to the amount of the work ".[9]

This doctrine touches some of the deepest problems in philosophy to which later Jewish thinkers devoted considerable attention. How can free will be reconciled with God's foreknowledge ? How can God be good and just when the righteous experience adversity and the wicked prosper ? And yet on such perplexities as these, Akiba, perhaps the keenest intellect among the Rabbis, has nothing more helpful to say than that we are to accept conflicting dogmas whether they can be harmonised or not ! His purpose, however, is clear : as a *practical rule of living* we must believe that the will is free, that God has foreknowledge and that He governs the world wisely and justly. It is this practical rule which is of primary importance ; the metaphysical problem is only secondary.

This attitude towards transcendental problems is typical of the Rabbis. It is essentially Hebraic. They held that there was sufficient in the daily round of life to absorb all man's thoughts and energies, and no need to try and penetrate the veil which hides from him the mysteries of the Universe. There was the Biblical teaching : " The heavens are the heavens of the Lord, but the earth hath He given to the children of men " (Ps. cxv. 16), which was taken as signifying that the world is man's sphere and he is incapable of comprehending the realms above.[10]   Hence his range of inquiry is limited to τὰ φυσικά " the physical " and he is cut off from all knowledge of τὰ μετὰ τὰ φυσικά " the metaphysical "—what lies beyond the physical.

It was impossible, however, for the Jews to isolate themselves from the currents of thought which were sweeping through the countries of their domicile. The Aristotelian philosophy had reached the Arabs and profoundly influenced their thinkers. The works of the Greek master had been translated into Arabic and were widely read and discussed. These books passed into the hands of Jewish readers and arrested their attention. The predilection of the Jews for medicine was a contributory cause. They had perforce to study the medical works of the Greek physicians—the standard text-books—which were available in Arabic translation. An acquaintance with scientific method was the result and a desire to delve more deeply into the writings of the Greeks. A new field of scholarship was revealed to them. They discovered a world of thought from which they had been hitherto rigorously excluded. Their intellectual acumen, so long restricted in its scope, had a gargantuan meal upon which to feast. They ignored the cautious advice of their predecessors. They ate of the tree of knowledge and their eyes were opened.

The first contact with Greek thought must have proved most disconcerting to them. The very foundations of their faith seemed to be shaken. It was all so different from what had been traditionally handed down from their fathers. The effect might be compared to the shock which the religious world experienced in the middle of the last century when Darwin propounded his theories. It raised similar questions. Just as the perplexed religionist then asked, How does this new teaching accord with the first chapter of Genesis ? the medieval Jew asked, How does this philosophy fit in with the Hebrew Scriptures ?

The problem was somewhat simplified for the latter because he never for a moment doubted the truth of the Bible. The alternatives for him were either philosophy was wrong or the Bible and philosophy agreed. Of the famous Jewish thinkers only two adopted the former alternative. Judah Halevi (born 1086) rejected the Aristotelian philosophy on intuitive rather than rational grounds. It did not satisfy him spiritually. To his ardent, poetical temperament the cold reasoning of Aristotle proved distasteful. It made no provision for the yearning of the human soul for communion with God. On the other hand, Ḥasdai Crescas (1340-1410) vehemently attacked Aristotle on rational grounds. He analysed his system of thought and declared it unsound.

The majority of Jewish philosophers were fervent admirers of Aristotle.[11] They may have criticised his teachings on points of detail, but they accepted his system as a whole. Their problem, accordingly, was to reconcile his philosophy with the teachings of the Bible. The outstanding personality in this School of harmonisation was Moses, the son of Maimon, better known as Moses Maimonides.[12]

II : MAIMONIDES : HIS LIFE AND WORK[13]

The unique place which Maimonides held in the Jewish world of his time is indicated by the fact that the exact hour of his birth has been preserved. He was born in Cordova at 1 p.m. on the eve of Passover, 4895, which corresponds to March 30, 1135. His family was said to trace its descent through Judah the Prince, the compiler of the Mishnah, to the House of David. This genealogy may rest on nothing more substantial than the unbounded hero-worship of his admirers.

He was certainly a member of a scholarly family, and at the conclusion of his *Commentary on the Mishnah* he subscribes himself, " Moses, son of Maimon the Dayyan,[14] son of Rabbi Joseph the Sage, son of Isaac the Dayyan, son of Joseph the Dayyan, son of Obadiah the Dayyan, son of Solomon, son of Obadiah the Dayyan ". His father was a mathematician and astronomer as well as an expert Talmudist, and from him Moses received his instruction in Jewish lore.

In 1148 the town of Cordova fell into the hands of the Almohades, a fanatical sect of Mohammedans, who presented the Jewish and Christian inhabitants with the alternative of apostacy or death. Maimon, to escape forcible conversion or even a pretence of accepting Mohammedanism, fled with his family and for ten years wandered from town to town in Spain. Eventually he decided to leave the country, sailed for Morocco and settled in Fez in 1160.

Throughout this period of stress and wandering, Moses pursued his studies and displayed such conspicuous ability that the father and younger son, David, engaged in commerce while he devoted himself entirely to the accumulation of knowledge. He took up the study of medicine as the ultimate means of earning a livelihood, although his supreme passion was for theology and philosophy. In Fez he made the acquaintance of several Mohammedan scholars who introduced him to Arabic translations of Aristotle and other philosophical works, and aroused in him the interest in metaphysics which influenced the rest of his life.[15]

Unhappily the religious persecution which had made life bitter in Spain spread also to Northern Africa, and under extreme pressure many Jews became pseudo-Mohammedans. Some scholars have alleged that Maimonides was temporarily in this class, but the grounds on which they base their conclusion are far from decisive.[16] When he escaped martyrdom only through the intervention of a Moslem friend, he resolved to continue his wanderings. On April 18, 1165, he with the other members of his family sailed for Palestine, and on May 16 landed at Acco. The Holy Land was at that time in Christian hands.

The Jewish *savant*, Aḥad Ha'am,[17] has put forward the theory that the suffering which Maimonides experienced under Mohammedan fanaticism was the influence which was the turning-point of his intellectual life and made him the rationalist he became. The case is put forcibly as follows : " He was surrounded by lying and religious hypocrisy ; Judaism had to hide from the light of day ; its adherents had to wear a mask whenever they came out of their homes into the open. And why ? Because Mohammed had called himself a prophet, had performed miracles, according to his followers, to win their faith, and by virtue of his prophetic power had promulgated a new Law and revealed new truths, which all men were bound to believe, although they were contrary to reason. This state of things was bound to make a profound impression on a young man like Maimonides, with his fine nature and his devotion to truth. He could not but feel every moment the tragedy of such a life; and therefore he could not but become violently opposed to the source of religious fanaticism —to that blind faith in the truth of prophecy which relies on supernatural ' evidence ', and despises the evidence of reason. It was this blind faith that led the Moslems to force the Jews into accepting the teaching of the new prophet; and it was this that led many of these very Jews, after they had gradually become accustomed to their new situation, to doubt of their Judaism and ask themselves why they should not be able to believe in Mohammed's prophecy, just as they believed in that of Moses. If Moses had performed miracles, then surely Mohammed might have done the same; and how could they decide between the one teaching and the other with such certainty as to pronounce one true and the other false ?

" These impressions, which were constantly influencing Maimonides' development in his childhood and youth, were bound to swing him violently over to the other side, to the side of reason. Ultimately he was led to subject man—and God too, if we may say so—to that supreme ruler : because Judaism could trust reason never to allow any new prophet with his new teaching to work it harm. When once Judaism had accepted the supremacy of reason and handed over to reason the seal of truth, it would never again be difficult to show by rational proof that the first divine religion was also the only divine religion, never to be displaced or altered till the end of time ; and then, even if ten thousand prophets like Mohammed came and performed miracles beyond telling, we should never believe in their new teaching, because one proof of reason is stronger than all the proofs of prophecy ".

Attractive though the argument be, there are two facts which appear to militate against it. The first is that Maimonides cannot be considered to have condemned persecution as an altogether unjustifiable procedure. He admits that it may be necessary in certain circumstances to put a person to death for the opinions he holds.[18] Tolerant though he undoubtedly was to other religions,[19] he maintains that the welfare of Society may compel the adoption of violent methods for the suppression of erroneous beliefs. Was that not a plea which the Mohammedan persecutors could have urged, and probably did urge, in justification of their campaign ?

The second point is that if the theory were correct, Maimonides' logical mind would have forced him to reject Revelation, with regard to which he had not the slightest doubt. If he believed with a firm faith that God had sent the Torah into the world through the medium of Moses, he could not deny the *a priori* possibility of a Revelation communicated through Mohammed ! But Aḥad Ha'am is certainly right with respect to prophecy. The insistence that the genuineness of a prophet must not be tested by the criterion of miracles must be understood as directed against the claims of Christianity and Mohammedanism.

To resume the story of Maimonides' career. His stay in the Holy Land was of brief duration. The Jewish population was small, barely numbering a thousand families, scattered throughout the country. They were poor materially and intellectually, so that the environment was uncongenial to him. He therefore left for Egypt where there were large Jewish communities. He first went to Alexandria, but finally settled in Cairo and there spent the remainder of his life. He practised as a physician and also lectured on philosophical themes. His reputation as a medical practitioner spread and he was appointed physician to the Grand Vizier. It is stated that Richard I of England offered him a similar position but Maimonides declined it.

Besides his professional work there were many self-assumed duties which kept him very fully occupied. From his youth onwards he was engaged upon the gigantic literary works which established his fame as the greatest Jewish scholar of his time. He became the recognised authority on Rabbinic law, and a stream of correspondence flowed to him in which he was asked for his opinion on disputed points of religious dogma and practice. During the last twenty years of his life he was the *Nagid*, the official head, of the Cairo community, and by his broadmindedness did much to narrow the breach between the orthodox Jews and the Karaites who rejected the authority of the Talmud.

His active and honourable career came to an end, after some years of broken health, on December 13, 1204. His death was followed by an extraordinary manifestation of grief in which Moslems as well as Jews participated. His earthly remains were conveyed to the Holy Land and buried in Tiberias, where his tomb is still to be seen.

Maimonides' life is marked by an almost unceasing literary activity. While still in his youth he contemplated a Commentary on the Mishnah, but it was many years before that early ambition was achieved. His first works were an essay on the Jewish Calendar and a small volume on the terminology of Logic, written before he was twenty-three. His unrivalled reputation rests on his magnificent trilogy, *opera magna* in every sense of the term.

The first is *Kitab al-Siraj*, "The Book of Light", a comprehensive Commentary on the Mishnah, written in Arabic. This work, begun when the author was only twenty-three and completed ten years later, in 1168, already displays the characteristics which distinguish all his compositions. We find there a wonderful mastery of a vast realm of knowledge, critical insight, analytical power, independence of judgment, clearness of exposition and a gift for systematisation.

He regarded the Rabbis as the heirs of the Prophets, and although he emphasised the point that not every statement of every Sage was to be venerated as the acme of wisdom, yet beneath the surface of their teachings is to be discovered a deep well of truth. He classified students of Rabbinic literature into three groups : "The first class is, as far as I have seen, the largest in point of their numbers and of the numbers of their compositions ; and it is of them that I have heard most. The members of this class adopt the words of the Sages literally, and give no kind of interpretation whatsoever. With them all impossibilities are necessary occurrences. This is owing to their being ignorant of science and far away from knowledge. . . . They think that in all their emphatic and precise remarks the Sages only wished to convey the ideas which they themselves comprehend and that they intended them to be taken in their literalness. And this, in spite of the fact that in their literal significance some of the words of the Sages would savour of absurdity. . . .

" The second class of reasoners is also numerous. They see and hear the words of the Sages and accept them in their literal significations, thinking that the Sages meant nothing but what the literal interpretation indicates. They consequently apply themselves to showing the weakness of the Rabbinical statements, their objectionable character, and to calumniate that which is free from reproach. They make sport of the words of the Sages from time to time, and imagine themselves more intellectually gifted and possessed of more penetrating minds, whereas they (peace to them !) are deceived, shortsighted, ignorant of all existing things, and consequently unable to comprehend anything. . . . They are more stupid than the first class, and more steeped in folly. . . .

" The third class of thinkers is (as God liveth !) so very small in numbers that one would only 'call it a class in the sense that the sun is termed a species (although it is a single object). They are the men who accept as established facts the greatness of the Sages and the excellence of their thoughts, as found in the generality of their remarks, where each word points a very true theme. . . . They know that they (peace to them !) would not talk absurdities to one another. And they are convinced beyond doubt that their words have both an outer and an inner meaning, and that in all that they said of things impossible their discourses were in the form of riddle and parable " (C.M., Introd. to Ḥélek).

This extract discloses his method of approach not only to the literature of the Rabbis, but also to the Bible. He contemplated writing a treatise on the passages of the Talmud and Midrash which when read superficially have little or no meaning, but on a correct interpretation convey deep philosophical instruction. This intention was not carried out.

A great deal of the contents of the *Siraj* is nothing more than an exposition of Jewish law as codified in the Mishnah and has no bearing on Maimonides' system of thought. But he incorporated in it three Introductions which are of first-rate importance for this purpose. There is firstly the General Introduction —frequently but incorrectly described as " Introduction to *Zera'im* ".[20] It is in reality an introductory essay on the transmission of the Oral Law from the time of Moses down to the age of the Rabbis. In the course of it he dwells at length on Prophecy and the Prophets and expounds his thoughts on man's place in the Universe. He prefaced his Commentary on the tenth chapter of Sanhedrin, known as *Ḥélek*, with an essay on the principles of the Jewish Faith. And before commenting on the ethical tractate Abot, he added *Eight Chapters* in which he explained his views on ethics. These Introductions are invaluable sources from which to derive a knowledge of Maimonides' teachings.

His second great work is the *Mishneh Torah* " Deuteronomy ", or *Yad ha-ḥazakah* " The Strong Hand ".[21] It occupied ten years in compiling and was finished in 1180. It is a monumental digest of Biblical and Rabbinic law composed in Hebrew. The historian Graetz wrote of it : " It is impossible to give the uninitiated an idea of this gigantic work, in which he collected the most remote things from the vast mine of the Talmud, extracting the fine metal from the dross, classifying all details under their appropriate heads, showing how the Talmud was based on the

Bible, bringing its details under general rules, combining apparently unconnected parts into one organised whole, and cementing it into a work of art. . . . The Talmud resembles a Dædalian maze, in which one can scarcely find his way even with Ariadne's thread, but Maimonides designed a well-contrived ground-plan, with wings, halls, apartments, chambers, and closets, through which a stranger might easily pass without a guide, and thereby obtain a survey of all that is contained in the Talmud. Only a mind accustomed to think clearly and systematically, and filled with the genius of order, could have planned and built a structure like this ".[22] In the opening two sections he gives a résumé in popular style of his teaching on theology, cosmology and ethics.

The third and most famous of all his works was an Arabic treatise entitled *Dalalat al-Ḥa'irin*—in Hebrew *Moreh Nebuchim*, " Guide for the Perplexed ". Through its translation into Latin, Maimonides' name spread to the Christian world and his ideas influenced the medieval theologians. It was written for, and sent in parts to, his favourite pupil, Joseph ibn Aknin, and was completed in 1190.

The purpose of the book is explained by Maimonides in his Introduction : " The object of this treatise is to enlighten a religious man who has been trained to believe in the truth of our holy Torah, who conscientiously fulfils his moral and religious duties, and at the same time has been successful in his philosophical studies. Human reason has attracted him to abide within its sphere ; and he finds it difficult to accept as correct the teaching based on the literal interpretation of the Torah, and especially that which he himself, or others derived from those homonymous,[23] metaphorical, or hybrid expressions. Hence he is lost in perplexity and anxiety. If he be guided solely by reason, and renounce his previous views which are based on those expressions, he would consider that he had rejected the fundamental principles of the Torah ; and even if he retains the opinions which were derived from those expressions, and if, instead of following his reason, he abandon its guidance altogether, it would still appear that his religious convictions had suffered loss and injury. For he would then be left with those errors which give rise to fear and anxiety, constant grief and great perplexity.

" This work has also a second object in view. It seeks to explain certain obscure figures which occur in the Prophets, and are not distinctly characterised as being figures. Ignorant and superficial readers take them in a literal, not in a figurative sense. Even well informed persons are bewildered if they understand these passages in their literal signification, but they are entirely relieved of their perplexity when we explain the figure, or merely suggest that the terms are figurative. For this reason I have called this Book *Guide for the Perplexed* ".

In this culminating work of his life Maimonides carries out the main purpose of his career—to reconcile philosophy and religion as taught in the Hebrew Scriptures. The latter was a Revelation from God and must necessarily be true. The former, apart from details, was proved by reason and must also be true. Truth cannot contradict truth ; they must agree. If therefore the words of Scripture conflict with philosophy, there can be only one conclusion, viz., they have been wrongly understood. Find the correct interpretation and the contradiction must disappear. The inevitable consequence of such a method was that the Bible was twisted and its meaning distorted to make it fit into a system which was utterly alien to it.

Every opinion, Maimonides insisted, had to be checked by its correspondence with the truth as revealed in the Scriptures. To illustrate his uncompromising attitude, the following may be taken as an example : " Many declare that there was no actual voice at the Revelation on Sinai, only the soul of Moses our Teacher was possessed by the higher intellectual ideas, and understood and listened by the way of true reason, i.e., meditation of the Godly thoughts, in a manner it is impossible to grasp. And if the Scriptures had not repeatedly declared, ' he heard a voice speaking ' I would have accepted that theory " (*Responsa* II, 23d). Still more characteristic was the position he took up on the question of the eternity of matter. He strenuously opposed Aristotle on the point ; but he confesses that had that theory been indisputably proved he would have been able to harmonise it with the Bible. Since it was an unproved and unprovable proposition he declined to accept it, and rested content with the plain Scriptural teaching that matter was created.[24]

The *Guide* is unquestionably Maimonides' masterpiece. " The spirit of the book is immortal, but much of its actual content is obsolete " has been truly said of it. It does not answer the perplexities of the religious mind to-day. Nevertheless it is a noble plea for the exercise of reason and the value of knowledge in the realm of religion.

Apart from a number of treatises on medical and allied subjects, he composed a work on the enumeration of the Biblical commandments and several essays. He also left an extensive correspondence on a variety

of topics which is a necessary source for the elucidation of his opinions.

Maimonides was not a stylist.[25] He aims always
at clearness rather than elegance. He had no
appreciation of poetry and little sense of literary form.
He piles up synonyms unnecessarily, and repeats the
same words again and again, or presents the same
thought in different phrases. His sentences are often
long and involved because of the insertion of
parentheses to qualify a statement which appeared
to him too definite. But he achieves his purpose by
his meticulous care for clarity. Where he is difficult
to follow the cause is the abstruse nature of the theme
he treats. He takes the greatest pains to simplify
the subject by concrete examples and analogies. In
this respect he compares favourably with other Jewish
philosophers.

III : Maimonides' System of Thought

In the same way that a phrase is liable to misinterpretation when taken out of its context, so the
teachings of Maimonides are apt to be misunderstood
if removed from their place in his system. A modern
theologian, e.g., remarks that the " misconception of
the term ' knowledge of God ' as used in the Bible
led the leading medieval thinkers of Judaism,
especially the School of Maimonides, . . . into
the error of confusing religion and philosophy, as if
both resulted from pure reason. It is man's moral
nature rather than his intellectual capacity, that
leads him 'to know God and walk in His ways'".[26]
Justification of this criticism could easily be found if
Maimonides' statements on the " knowledge of God "
are taken separately. He does lay the greatest
emphasis on intellectual perfection as a pre-requisite

for " knowing God ". But in his system it is quite evident that the knowledge of God is based on moral perfection. The latter is the essential preparation for the acquisition of the former, and it is going too far to assert, as Kohler does, that the Biblical phrase " knowledge of God " has no relationship to intellectual capacity.

Also from the ethical side Maimonides has been sharply criticised by a modern ethicist for having adopted Aristotle's doctrine of the Mean. "It is astonishing", writes this critic,[27] "that Maimonides should have failed to note the infinite divergence between the Aristotelian and the Jewish moral doctrine so completely as to intermingle the two. Thus it came about that he could speak of the Aristotelian virtues of ' the Mean ' in the same breath, as it were, with the divine pattern of true, real ethics, the inner profound reason for ethical conduct ". Here, too, there is justification for the stricture if Maimonides' treatment of the virtues and vices according to the criterion of the Mean is divorced from his system. But when it is viewed from its place in the system, it takes on another aspect and fits in perfectly without doing violence to the Jewish ethical ideal.

It is essential, therefore, to keep constantly in mind the fact that Maimonides constructed a complete system of thought which embraces God and the Universe in its entirety. To have accomplished this is his supreme achievement. No Jewish philosopher before or after him has commanded such a comprehensive field, although some of them may have dealt more penetratingly with particular problems. Only a master-mind could have carried out such a design, and whether his conception of the Universe be correct or not, whether his solution of metaphysical problems be sound or fallacious, nothing can detract from the greatness of the man's intellect.

One may fittingly apply to Maimonides what has been said of the Greek thinkers : " The modern physical philosopher is apt to dwell exclusively on the absurdities of ancient ideas about science, on the haphazard fancies and *a priori* assumptions of ancient teachers, on their confusion of facts and ideas, on their inconsistency and blindness to the most obvious phenomena. He measures them not by what preceded them, but by what has followed them. He does not consider that ancient physical philosophy was not a free enquiry, but a growth, in which the mind was passive rather than active, and was incapable of resisting the impressions which flowed in upon it. He hardly allows to the notions of the ancients the merit of being the stepping-stones by which he has himself risen to a higher knowledge. He never reflects, how great a thing it was to have formed a conception, however imperfect, either of the human frame as a whole, or of the world as a whole ".[28]

In this sympathetic spirit let us view a brief outline of Maimonides' conception of the Universe. First and last it is bound up with the idea of God, the Creator of all that exists, the First Cause, the Life of the Universe—in the sense that it is by His will that the Universe continues in existence—a God Who is a Unity in the absolute signification of that term. He is incorporeal and perfect in every respect ; His qualities differ from those of man not merely in degree but in kind. With the development of the intellect this truth becomes more clearly recognised, and then one hesitates to attribute positive qualities to God. The higher the intellectual progress of man, the more he says what God is not rather than what He is. God does not become, through this process of elimination, nothing else than a mere negation. " That human descriptions are inadequate to express the nature of God does not mean that God has no nature. When we deny that the human mind can know what God is, we are re-asserting the fact that God is non-human ; but each negation of inadequate conceptions of God's being reaffirms the fact that He exists. Existence in the case of God is not an accident ; it is identical with His essence. The more we negate the attribute the more we affirm the essence, and we are left finally with the idea of God as absolute existence ".[29]

What purpose God had in creating the Universe it is impossible to say. It was due to His will which is incomprehensible to the finite mind. The Universe is constituted, as Aristotle taught, of two elements— matter ($\H\lambda\eta$) and form ($\epsilon\hat{\iota}\delta o s$). It is essential to understand exactly what is to be understood by the term " Form " because it plays an all-important part in Maimonides' philosophy. An object consists of a basic substance, but it is not this substance which in itself makes the object what it is, because the object may change although the matter remains the same. For instance, a piece of copper is dug from the earth and converted into an urn. It is afterwards melted down and made into a statue. It is again melted down and minted into coin. Throughout the series of changes the same matter persists, but in each case it is used for a different purpose, a different *idea* is attached to it. The combination of matter and idea brings the object into being. The idea is not destroyed in the process of change ; it is simply replaced by another. The technical term for this idea is " form ". It is the cause of the essential properties by which a thing is what it is ($\tau\grave{o}\ \tau\grave{\iota}\ \mathring{\eta}\nu\ \epsilon\hat{\iota}\nu a\iota$).

According to this theory, " matter as such is an unreal or merely potential factor, which becomes a definite, concrete reality only through the idea or the ideal purpose. The idea of the purpose is not in itself real either ; it becomes so only when it is realised in matter ".[30] Maimonides mentions that " Plato and his predecessors called substance the female and form the male " (Guide, I, 17). He is probably alluding to the passage in the Timæus where Plato says, " We may liken the receiving principle to a mother and the source or spring to a father ".[31] Their union produces the object.

The Universe as created by God comprises three strata. First there are the Intelligences or Angels which consist of form without matter. They are the medium through which God acts upon the world of matter and gives it the form it needs. This corporeal world must be thought of as a globe of solid formation, containing nine Spheres one within the other. They consist of matter and form which are fixed and not liable to change. They might be subject to destruction, if God so will it, but they are unalterable in their constitution. They each revolve in a direction and at a speed determined by the Intelligences. The sun, moon and stars are attached to these various Spheres. Since they are transparent and colourless orbs, man is able to view all the heavenly bodies from his place on earth. The innermost Sphere holds the Moon. The outermost Sphere is divided into twelve sections, and from the figure reflected by the stars in each section, it is given a distinctive name, e.g., Ram, Bull, etc. These are known as the twelve signs of the Zodiac.

In the centre of the globe, fixed and immovable, is the earth. Both the earth and all it contains are constituted of form and matter ; unlike the Spheres, however, these are not constant but in a state of flux. The forms are continually changing.

Matter is constructed of four elements—fire, air, water and earth. The four elements are present in all matter but in different proportions, and upon the proportion depends the nature of a piece of matter. If the element of fire preponderates, as it does in animate beings, the quality of warmth is conspicuous. When the element of earth is greatest, the preponderating characteristic is hardness and dryness, as in stone. Destruction consists in the rearrangement of the elements into different proportions, the elements themselves being indestructible.

Though the Universe is thus divisible into strata and capable of various subdivisions, it is "one individual being". Just as the human body is a single entity, despite its numerous limbs and organs, through the action of the heart, so the Universe with all its distinct parts and elements is one harmonious whole through a controlling force, viz., God.

It has already been pointed out that the will of God determined that in the sublunary Sphere matter and form shall not be constant. The consequence is that although species do not disappear, the individual members come and go. This is true of animate and inanimate objects.

The human as well as the animal species come under the law of matter and form. In both cases the body is the matter and the soul is the form. The term "soul" is here employed not in its religious connotation, but in the sense of "the vitality which is common to all living, sentient beings". When at death the body is decomposed into its elements, the soul likewise perishes because form cannot persist, except generically, apart from matter constituted into a body. Furthermore, the faculties of the soul are alike in man and the animal, except that in each they function in a distinctive manner.

Such a theory as this raises two vital questions, and in the treatment of these two problems Maimonides parts company with the Aristotelian School and elaborates an idea borrowed from the Arab metaphysicians. The two questions are : How does man differ from the animal ? In what sense is man immortal ? Maimonides' solution aims at answering both questions at once.

One of the soul's faculties is the rational. Man and the animal are endowed with it at birth, but only as a potentiality. It is a *tabula rasa* which is capable of use. If at death it remains in its original state, it must perish together with the other faculties of the soul. Should it, on the other hand, be changed from potentiality to actuality, it passes into real existence and thus becomes indestructible. We must see how Maimonides arrives at such a momentous conclusion.

It will simplify matters if we apply to the intellect the law of matter and form. Think of the intellect at birth, which is only a potentiality, as matter which is likewise only a potentiality until it is united to form. When the intellect passes into action by acquiring true ideas, it receives form and then becomes something real instead of being a mere capacity. This form can only be acquired by man, and in this respect he is differentiated from the animal. In fact unless he makes this acquisition, he is on the same level as the beast. It also follows that this " acquired intellect " is the true essence of the man, the quality which distinguishes him from his fellows.

Not all knowledge has this power of transmutation. Much of it only serves the purpose of training the intellect to function properly and comprehend true ideas. E.g., the study of Logic and Mathematics is not an end in itself ; it would not achieve the object of giving the intellect real existence. Such study is an essential prerequisite as an intellectual exercise for the purpose of putting the faculty into perfect working order.

In addition to this intellectual training another perfection is required. Body and soul (using this term in its psychological connotation) react one on the other. There cannot be a perfect soul in an imperfect body. Consequently there must be a strict discipline which eliminates everything that is injurious to the body and soul. As a practical guide to conduct, with this end in view, Maimonides recommends Aristotle's prescription of the Mean. Avoid all excess, and you keep away from what is harmful. He insists also on a strict dietetic regimen for the purpose of keeping the limbs and organs of the body, which are the instruments of the soul, in a healthy state.

True morality, in the fullest meaning of the word, is the very foundation of the Maimonidean system. If he is a rationalist in the supreme position he gives to intellect, he is a moralist in the emphasis he lays on physical and moral perfection, and, as we shall see, he is a religionist in the goal to which he directs his intellectualism.

Having prepared his intellect for its true function, man is then able to impress his rational soul with the " knowledge of God "—to comprehend Him so far as that is possible to the human being. Since in its action the intellect becomes identified with the ideas which are acquired, the rational faculty in its now real existence has obtained a form which partakes of the essence of God. That form is consequently indestructible. It cannot perish with the body; it survives death.

To help and inspire man in his effort to reach this goal, God revealed Himself in the Torah. This Revelation has a twofold purpose : first, to impart the knowledge of God and thus save man from erroneous ideas which would lead him astray ; and secondly, to perfect the social order as a means of aiding him in the search for the true goal. This is a point which Maimonides stresses. Man is a social being, and it is only in the life of a Society that he can hope to attain to a knowledge of God. Were he to dwell in solitude, apart from his fellowmen, his whole time and energy would be absorbed in keeping himself in physical existence. He would have to construct his house, provide material for his clothing, etc. What time would be left under these conditions for fulfilling the essential purpose of life ? Men must therefore join forces, form themselves into communities, submit to general laws which govern their corporate life, promote justice and order, avoid violence and all other disturbing factors. Residing in peace and security, they will find the leisure and the inclination to devote themselves to a moral and physical training, which will help them to undergo the mental preparation that leads to the supreme goal—the knowledge of God. In the acquisition of that knowledge, man has accomplished his aim in life. He has justified the endowment with which he had been equipped at birth, and has secured immortality.

Such in outline is Maimonides' conception of man and the Universe. That it will not stand the search-light of modern scientific knowledge is obvious, but also irrelevant. To perceive the grandeur of his achievement, his system must be judged from his own age, not ours. Viewed in the correct perspective, his teachings as a whole reveal a gigantic intellect and a noble soul. It is unquestionably true that " with Maimonides we reach the high water mark of medieval Jewish philosophy ".[32] Would much of the truth of this statement be lost if the qualifying adjective " Jewish " were omitted ?

IV : The Influence of Maimonides

The eminence of Maimonides does not rest upon his originality. In fact, his was not an original mind.[33] His gifts were rather in the direction of mastering vast fields of knowledge from various sources and reducing them to systematic order. Regarded purely as a metaphysician he ranks lower than Abraham ibn Daud from whom he largely borrowed when treating philosophical problems. Some of his successors, as, e.g., Levi ben Gerson and Ḥasdai Crescas, displayed superior gifts for speculative research and independent thought. What, then, gave him the unique position he held ?

Jewish scholars are agreed on the answer. Maimonides had established his reputation as a master of Rabbinic law before he wrote his philosophical treatise, the *Guide*. The appearance of this work, as a natural consequence, created an unusual stir. No scholar could afford to ignore it. There was eager curiosity to read what the first *savant* in Jewry had to say, even on the part of those who would ordinarily have taken no interest in a philosophical book.

It must also be remembered that Maimonides had anticipated parts of his *Guide* in the introductory sections of the *Yad* where he gave a popular outline of the accepted teachings on physical science, psychology and ethics, and had dealt with the last-named subject in the course of his Commentary on the Mishnah. He had thereby created an interest in philosophical study among the students of Rabbinic literature who might otherwise have held aloof from it. And as they looked to him as their master and guide in the intricacies of Jewish law, they naturally paid the utmost respect to his opinions in other fields of knowledge.

In that fact lay a danger which impressed some of his contemporaries strongly. His books might prove a guide to some perplexed minds ; but there was also the possibility that they would create perplexities and doubts in the minds of readers who previously had none. Some of his teachings, e.g., on Prophecy and Eschatology, might appear to him perfectly in accord with orthodox Judaism, but to others they seemed thoroughly heretical. The conservative mind which looked askance at philosophy and science as injurious to faith, grew alarmed at the new impetus that was being given to such studies by the writings of Maimonides.

During his lifetime his admirers were in the large majority, and the voice of criticism was checked by respect for the colossal knowledge and controversial prowess of the famous Rabbi. After his death, the storm burst with violence. Jewish scholars were riven into two camps. One had to be either a Maimonist or an anti-Maimonist ; but his supporters won in the end.34 Maimonides' reputation survived the contest and grew with succeeding generations. His summary of the Principles of Judaism was given an honoured place in the Prayer Book.35 His *Yad* became an indispensable compendium to every student of Talmudic law and remains such to this day.

INTRODUCTION

As for the *Guide* it has had a profound influence on many a Jewish thinker. Throughout the centuries that followed its author's death, it was the classical work on religious philosophy. What was thought of Maimonides by his admirers may be judged by the following extract from a medieval letter : " It is certain that if Joshua the son of Nun arose to forbid the Provençal Jews to study the works of Maimonides, he would scarcely succeed. For they have the firm intention to sacrifice their fortunes and even their lives in defence of the philosophical works of Maimonides ".[36] The *Guide* has been a formative influence in the intellectual life of many a Jewish thinker. A recent monograph has demonstrated that Spinoza owed much to this work.[37] The forerunners of Jewish emancipation, Solomon Maimon[38] and Moses Mendelssohn,[39] received their stimulus for philosophical study from it.

The impression it created was not even limited to the Jewish community. In its Latin translation[40] it influenced Albertus Magnus. It has been said by a competent authority, " Maimonides is the precursor of Thomas Aquinas, and the *Moreh Nebuchim* heralded and prepared the way for the *Summa Theologica* "[41]; for when Aquinas undertook to harmonise Aristotelian philosophy with the doctrines of the Church, he used Maimonides as his guide and model.[42] Maimonides has accordingly been a force in the moulding of religious and philosophical thought not only among his own people, but throughout the world of scholarship.

CHAPTER I

GOD THE CREATOR

§1. *The Existence of God.* The first Principle of the Jewish Faith is formulated by Maimonides in the following terms :

" The existence of the Creator (praised be He), i.e., that there is an existent Being invested with the highest perfection of existence. He is the cause of the existence of all existent things. In Him they exist and from Him emanates[1] their continued existence. If we could suppose the removal of His existence, then the existence of all things would entirely cease and there would not be left any independent existence whatsoever. But if on the other hand we could suppose the removal of all existent things but Him, His existence (blessed be He) would not cease to be, neither would it suffer any diminution. For He (exalted be He) is self-sufficient, and His existence needs the aid of no existence outside His. Whatsoever is outside Him, the Intelligences (i.e. the Angels) and the bodies of the Spheres,[2] and things below these, all of them need Him for their existence. This is the first cardinal doctrine of faith, which is indicated by the commandment, ' I am the Lord thy God ' (Exod. xx. 2) " (C.M., Introd. to *Ḥélek*).

With a similar declaration he opened his great work, the *Mishneh Torah* :

" The foundation of foundations and the pillar of the sciences is to know that there is a First Being and that He caused the existence of all beings; and all things that exist from heaven and earth and intervening space only exist from the reality of His existence. If it could be supposed that He is non-existent, nothing else could possibly exist; yet, if it could be supposed that all the things existing, except Himself, did not exist, He alone would still exist and would not cease because of their non-existence. For all things existing are dependent upon Him, but He (blessed be He) is not dependent upon them, not even any one of them. Therefore His reality is not like the reality of any one of them. That is the intention of the Prophet when he says, ' But the Lord God is the true3 God ' (Jer. x. 10)—He alone is reality and to none other is there a reality like His. Similarly declares the Torah,4 ' There is none else ' (Deut. iv. 39) —that is to say, there is no being, beside Himself, comparable to Him in reality.

" This Being is the God of the world, Lord of the whole earth. He controls the Universe with a power to which there is neither end nor limit, with a power unceasing; for the Universe revolves continuously, and it is impossible that it should revolve without one to cause it to revolve. It is He (blessed be He) Who is the cause of its revolution, without a hand and without a body.

" The recognition of this fact is a positive commandment5; as it is said, ' I am the Lord thy God '. Whoever brings upon his mind that there is another God besides Him transgresses a negative commandment, viz. ' Thou shalt have no other Gods before Me ' (Exod. xx. 3), and denies a cardinal doctrine of faith. This is, indeed, the great cardinal doctrine upon which all else depends " (*Yad, Yesodé ha-Torah* I, 1-6).

§2. *Proof of God's Existence.* That God exists is not merely a dogma of faith. Maimonides held that it was capable of rational demonstration. He bases a long and intricate argument on twenty-six Propositions with which he prefaced Part II of the *Guide*. These, " which are employed in the proof of the existence of God, or in the arguments demonstrating that God is neither corporeal nor a force connected with a material being, or that He is One, have been fully established and their correctness is beyond doubt. Aristotle and the Peripatetics who followed him have proved each of these Propositions ". Maimonides accepted twenty-five of them, but to one he demurred, " namely, the Proposition which affirms the Eternity of the Universe ".[6]

With the aid of these Propositions he establishes at one and the same time the proof of God's existence, unity and incorporeality, from the motion of the Sphere of the Universe.[7] His conclusion is :

" It may thus be considered as proved that the efficient cause of the motion of the Sphere, if that motion be eternal, is neither itself corporeal nor does it reside in a corporeal object ; it must move neither of its own accord nor accidentally ; it must be indivisible and unchangeable.[8] The Prime Motor of the Sphere is God, praised be His name !

" The hypothesis that there exist two Gods is inadmissible, because absolutely incorporeal beings cannot be counted, except as cause and effect.[9] The relation of time is not applicable to God, because motion cannot be predicated of Him.[10]

" The result of the above argument is consequently this: the Sphere cannot move *ad infinitum* of its own accord ; the Prime Motor is not corporeal, nor a force residing within a body ; it is One, unchangeable, and in its existence independent of time. Three of our postulates are thus proved by the principal philosophers " (*Guide* II, 1).

After detailing four proofs of God's Existence based on the Propositions, Maimonides offers the following argument as his own method of demonstration :

" The heavenly Spheres must either be transient, and in this case motion would likewise be temporary, or they must be eternal. If the Spheres are transient, then God is their Creator ; for if anything comes into existence after a period of non-existence, it is self-evident that an agent exists which has effected this result. It would be absurd to contend that the thing itself effected it. If, on the other hand, the heavenly Spheres be eternal, with a regular perpetual motion, the cause of this perpetual motion, according to the Propositions enumerated in the Introduction,[11] must be something that is neither a body, nor a force residing in a body, and that is God, praised be His name ! We have thus shown that whether we believe in the *creatio ex nihilo*, or in the Eternity of the Universe, we can prove by demonstrative arguments the existence of God, i.e., an absolute Being,[12] Whose existence cannot be attributed to any cause, or admit in itself any potentiality " (*Guide* II, 2).

§3. *God is the " cause " of every event in the world.* The Creator of the Universe is not only responsible for its origin, but is ultimately the cause of everything that exists and comes into being.

" It has been shown in the science of Physics that everything, except the Primal Cause, owes its origin to the following four causes :—the substance, the form, the *agens*,[13] the final cause. These are sometimes direct, sometimes indirect causes ; but each by itself is called a ' cause '. They (the philosophers) also believe—and I do not differ from their opinion— that God Himself is the *agens*, the form[14] and the end ; therefore they call God ' the Cause ', in order to express that He unites in Himself these three causes, viz., that He is the *agens*, the form and the final cause of the Universe. . . .

" Here I wish to show that God is the ' cause ' of every event that takes place in the world, just as He is the Creator[15] of the whole Universe as it now exists. It has already been explained in the science of Physics that a cause must again be sought for each of the four divisions of causes. When we have found for any existing thing those four causes which are in immediate connexion with it, we find for these again causes, and for these again other causes, and so on until we arrive at the first causes. E.g., a certain production has its *agens*, this *agens* again has its *agens*, and so on and on until at last we arrive at a first *agens*, which is the true *agens* throughout all the intervening links. If the letter *a* be moved by *b*, *b* by *c*, *c* by *d*, and *d* by *e*—and as the series does not extend to infinity, let us stop at *e*—there is no doubt that the *e* moves the letters *a*, *b*, *c* and *d*, and we say correctly that the *a* is moved by *e*. In that sense everything occurring in the Universe, although directly produced by certain nearer causes, is ascribed to the Creator. He is the *Agens*, and He is therefore the ultimate cause " (*Guide* I, 69).

§4. *God is the life of the Universe.* In the same Chapter of the *Guide* occurs this passage, amplifying the statement in the first Principle of Faith that all things exist in God :

" Every physical and transient form must be preceded by another such form, by which the substance has been fitted to receive the next form ; the previous form again has been preceded by another, and we arrive at length at that form which is necessary for the existence of all intermediate forms, which are the causes of the present form. That form to which the forms of all existing things are traced is God. . . .

" When we call God the ultimate form of the Universe, we do not use this term in the sense of form connected with substance, viz., as the form of that substance, as though God were the form of a material being. It is not in this sense that we use it, but in the following : Everything existing and endowed with a form is whatever it is through its form, and when that form is destroyed its whole existence terminates and is obliterated. The same is the case as regards the relation between God and all distant causes of existing beings. It is through the existence of God that all things exist, and it is He Who maintains their existence by that process which is called ' emanation '.[16]

" If God did not exist, suppose this were possible, the Universe would not exist, and there would be an end to the existence of the distant causes, the final effects, and the intermediate causes. Consequently God maintains the same relation to the world as the form has to a thing endowed with a form ; through the form it is what it is, and on it the reality and essence of the thing depends. In this sense we may say that God is the ultimate form, that He is the form of all forms ; that is to say, the existence and continuance of all forms in the last instance depend on Him, the forms are maintained by Him, in the same way as all things endowed with forms retain their existence through their forms. On that account

God is called, in the sacred language, ' the life of the Universe ' ".[17]

§5. *Emanation from God.* In the last-quoted passage, Maimonides refers to a " process which is called ' emanation ' ". It is an idea invented to explain how God, Who is incorporeal, can produce His desired effects in the Universe. The theory is thus explained :

" In Physics it has been shown that a body in acting upon another body must either directly be in contact with it, or indirectly through the medium of other bodies. E.g., a body that has been heated has been in contact with fire, or the air that surrounds the body has been heated by the fire and has communicated the heat to the body ; the immediate cause of the heat in this body is the corporeal substance of the heated air. The magnet attracts iron from a distance through a certain force communicated to the air round the iron. The magnet does therefore not act at all distances, just as fire does not act at every distance, but only as long as the air between the fire and the object is affected by the fire. When the air is no longer affected by the fire which is under a piece of wax, the latter does not melt. The same is the case with magnetism. When an object that has previously not been warm has now become warm, the cause of its heat must now have been created ; either some fire has been produced, or the distance of the fire from the object has been changed, and the altered relation between the fire and the object is the cause now created.

" In a similar manner we find the causes of all changes in the Universe to be changes in the combination of the elements that act upon each other when one body approaches another or separates from it. There are, however, changes which are not connected with the combination of the elements, but concern only the forms of the things. They require likewise an efficient cause; there must exist a force that produces the various forms. This cause is incorporeal, for that which produces form must itself be abstract form. . . .

" It is now clear that the action of bodies upon each other, according to their forms, prepares the substance for receiving the action of an incorporeal being, or Form. The existence of actions of purely incorporeal beings, in every case of change that does not originate in the mere combination of elements, is now firmly established. These actions do not depend on impact, or on a certain distance. They are termed ' influence ' (or ' emanation '), on account of their similarity to a water-spring.[18]   The latter sends forth water in all directions, has no peculiar side for receiving or spending its contents; it springs forth on all sides, and continually waters both neighbouring and distant places. In a similar manner incorporeal beings, in receiving power and imparting it to others, are not limited to a particular side, distance or time. They act continually; and whenever an object is sufficiently prepared, it receives the effect of that continuous action, called ' influence ' (or ' emanation ').

" God being incorporeal, and everything being the work of Him as the efficient cause, we say that the Universe has been created by the Divine influence, and that all changes in the Universe emanate from Him. In the same sense we say that He caused wisdom to emanate from Him and to come upon the Prophets.[19]   In all such cases we merely wish to express that an incorporeal Being, whose action we call ' influence ', has produced a certain effect. The term 'influence' has been considered applicable to the Creator on account of the similarity between His actions and those of a spring. There is no better way of describing the action of an incorporeal being than by this analogy ; and no term can be found that would accurately describe it. For it is as difficult to form an idea of that action as to form an idea of the incorporeal being itself. As we imagine only bodies or forces residing in bodies, so we only imagine actions possible when the agent is near, at a certain distance, and on a particular side.

" There are therefore persons who, on learning that God is incorporeal, or that He does not approach the object of His action, believe that He gives commands to Angels, and that the latter carry them out by approach or direct contact, as is the case when we produce something. These persons thus imagine also the Angels as bodies. Some of them, further, believe that God commands an action in words consisting, like ours, of letters and sounds, and that thereby, the action is done. All this is the work of the imagination, which is, in fact, identical with ' evil inclination ' " (*Guide* II, 12).

§6. *God not responsible for evil in the world.* Since Maimonides lays stress on God as the ultimate cause of all that exists, he could not escape the problem which is raised by the evil in the world. Is God in any way responsible for this evil ? His answer is clear and emphatic. Man is alone answerable for whatever is bad. Incidentally he insists that the good largely preponderates over the bad.

" Men frequently think that the evils in the world are more numerous than the good things ; many sayings and songs of the nations dwell on this idea.[20]

They say that a good thing is found only exceptionally, whilst evil things are numerous and lasting. Not only common people make this mistake, but even many who believe that they are wise. . . . The origin of the error is to be found in the circumstance that people judge the whole Universe by examining one single person. For an ignorant man believes that the whole Universe only exists for him ; as if nothing else required any consideration. If, therefore, anything happens to him contrary to his expectation, he at once concludes that the whole Universe is evil. If, however, he would take into consideration the whole Universe, form an idea of it, and comprehend what a small portion he is of the Universe, he will find the truth. . . .

" We hold that the Universe exists because the Creator wills it so ; that mankind is low in rank as compared with the uppermost portion of the Universe, viz., with the Spheres and the stars ; but, as regards the Angels, there cannot be any real comparison between man and Angels, although man is the highest of all beings on earth ; i.e., of all beings formed of the four elements.[21] Man's existence is nevertheless a great boon to him, and his distinction and perfection is a divine gift. The numerous evils to which individual persons are exposed are due to the defects existing in the persons themselves. We complain and seek relief from our own faults ; we suffer from the evils which we, by our own free will, inflict on ourselves and ascribe them to God, Who is far from being connected with them ! . . .

" The evils that befall men are of three kinds :— (i) The first kind of evil is that which is caused to man by the circumstance that he is subject to genesis and destruction, or that he possesses a body. It is on account of the body that some persons happen to have great deformities or paralysis of some of the organs. This evil may be part of the natural constitution of these persons, or may have developed subsequently in consequence of changes in the elements, e.g., through bad air, or thunderstorms, or landslips. We have already shown that, in accordance with the divine wisdom, genesis can only take place through destruction, and without the destruction of the individual members of the species, the species themselves would not exist permanently. Thus the true kindness, and beneficence and goodness of God is clear. He who thinks that he can have flesh and bones without being subject to any external influence, or any of the accidents of matter, unconsciously wishes to reconcile two opposites, viz., to be at the same time subject and not subject to change. If man were never subject to change, there could be no generation ; there would be one single being, but no individuals forming a species. . . .

" (ii) The second class of evils comprises such evils as people cause to each other, when, e.g., some of them use their strength against others. These evils are more numerous than those of the first kind ; their causes are numerous and known ; they likewise originate in ourselves, though the sufferer himself cannot avert them. . . .

" (iii) The third class of evils comprises those which every one causes to himself by his own action. This is the largest class, and is far more numerous than the second class. It is especially of these evils that all men complain—only few men are found that do not sin against themselves by this kind of evil. . . . This class of evil originates in man's vices, such as excessive desire for eating, drinking and love ;

indulgence in these things in undue measure, or in improper manner, or partaking of bad food. This course brings diseases and afflictions upon the body and soul alike. The sufferings of the body in consequence of these evils are well known ; those of the soul are twofold : First, such evils of the soul as are the necessary consequence of changes in the body, in so far as the soul is a force residing in the body ; it has therefore been said that the properties of the soul depend on the condition of the body.[22] Secondly, the soul, when accustomed to superfluous things, acquires a strong habit of desiring things which are neither necessary for the preservation of the individual nor for that of the species. This desire is without a limit, whilst things which are necessary are few in number and restricted within certain limits ; but what is superfluous is without end. E.g., you desire to have your vessels of silver, but golden vessels are still better ; others have even vessels of sapphire, or perhaps they can be made of emerald or rubies, or any other substance that could be suggested. Those who are ignorant and perverse in their thought are constantly in trouble and pain, because they cannot get as much of superfluous things as a certain other person possesses. They as a rule expose themselves to great dangers, e.g., by sea-voyage, or service of kings, and all this for the purpose of obtaining that which is superfluous and not necessary. When they thus meet with the consequences of the course which they adopt, they complain of the decrees and judgments of God. . . .
The error of the ignorant goes so far as to say that God's power is insufficient because He has given to this Universe the properties which they imagine cause these great evils, and which do not help all evil-disposed persons to obtain the evil which they seek,

and to bring their evil souls to the aim of their desires. . . .

" All the difficulties and troubles we meet in this respect are due to the desire for superfluous things ; when we seek unnecessary things, we have difficulty even in finding that which is indispensable. For the more we desire to have that which is superfluous, the more we meet with difficulties ; our strength and possessions are spent in unnecessary things, and are wanting when required for that which is necessary.

" Observe how Nature proves the correctness of this assertion. The more necessary a thing is for living beings, the more easily it is found and the cheaper it is ; the less necessary it is, the rarer and dearer it is. E.g., air, water and food are indispensable to man : air is most necessary, for if man is without air a short time he dies ; whilst he can be without water a day or two. Air is also undoubtedly found more easily and is cheaper than water. Water is more necessary than food ; for some people can be four or five days without food, provided they have water ; water also exists in every country in larger quantities than food and is also cheaper. The same proportion can be noticed in the different kinds of food ; that which is more necessary in a certain place exists there in larger quantities and is cheaper than that which is less necessary. No intelligent person, I think, considers musk, amber, rubies and emerald as very necessary for man except as medicines ; and they, as well as other like substances, can be replaced for this purpose by herbs and minerals. This shows the kindness of God to His creatures, even to us weak beings " (*Guide* III, 12).

Maimonides also attacks the problem from a

different point of view, by contending that evil is a negative, not positive, thing.

"Evils are evils only in relation to a certain thing,[23] and that which is evil in reference to a certain existing thing either includes the non-existence of that thing or the non-existence of some of its good conditions. The proposition has therefore been laid down in the most general terms, ' All evils are negations '. Thus for man death is an evil ; death is his non-existence. Illness, poverty and ignorance are evils for man ; all these are privations of properties. If you examine all single cases to which this general proposition applies, you will find that there is not one case in which the proposition is wrong except in the opinion of those who do not make any distinction between negative and positive properties, or between two opposites, or do not know the nature of things— who, e.g., do not know that health in general denotes a certain equilibrium and is a relative term. The absence of that relation is illness in general, and death is the absence of life in the case of any animal. The destruction of other things is likewise nothing but the absence of their form.[24]

After these propositions, it must be admitted as a fact that it cannot be said of God that He directly creates evil, or He has the direct intention to produce evil ; this is impossible. His works are all perfectly good. He only produces existence, and all existence is good ; whilst evils are of a negative character and cannot be acted upon. Evil can only be attributed to Him in the way we have mentioned. He creates evil only in so far as He produces the corporeal element such as it actually is ; it is always connected with negatives, and is on that account the source of all destruction and all evil. Those beings that do not possess this corporeal element are not subject to destruction or evil; consequently the true work of God is all good, since it is existence.

"The book which enlightened the darkness of the world says therefore, 'And God saw everything that He had made, and behold, it was very good' (Gen. i. 31). Even the existence of this corporeal element, low as it in reality is, because it is the source of death and all evils, is likewise good for the permanence of the Universe and the continuation of the order of things, so that one thing departs and the other succeeds" (*Guide* III, 10).

With regard to the "acts of God" which are a cause of suffering to the human race, he writes:

"His actions towards mankind also include great calamities, which overtake individuals and bring death to them, or affect whole families and even entire regions, spread death, destroy generation after generation, and spare nothing whatsoever. Hence there occur inundations, earthquakes, destructive storms, expeditions of one nation against the other for the sake of destroying it with the sword and blotting out its memory, and many other evils of the same kind. Whenever such evils are caused by us to any person, they originate in great anger, violent jealousy, or a desire for revenge. God is therefore called, because of these acts, 'jealous', 'revengeful', 'wrathful' and 'keeping anger' (Nahum i. 2); that is to say, He performs acts similar to those which, when performed by us, originate in certain psychical dispositions, in jealousy, desire for retaliation, revenge or anger; they are in accordance with the guilt of those who are to be punished, and not the result of any emotion, for He is above all defect! The same is the case with all divine acts; though resembling those acts which emanate from our passions and psychical dispositions, they are not due to anything superadded to His essence " (*Guide* I, 54).

§7. *All that God made serves a useful purpose.* Since God is perfect, His work must be perfect and all that He created must have its rightful place in His scheme of the Universe. Two passages may be quoted in which Maimonides gives expression to this view :

" I contend that no intelligent person can assume that any of the actions of God can be in vain, purposeless or unimportant. According to our view and the view of all that follow the Torah of Moses, all actions of God are ' exceedingly good '. Thus Scripture says, ' And God saw everything that He had made, and behold, it was very good ' (Gen. i. 31). And that which God made for a certain thing is necessary, or at least very useful for the existence of that thing. Thus food is necessary for the existence of living beings ; the possession of eyes is very useful to man during his life, although food only serves to sustain living beings a certain time, and the senses are only intended to procure to animals the advantages of sensation. The philosophers likewise assume that in Nature there is nothing in vain, so that everything that is not the product of human industry serves a certain purpose, which may be known or unknown to us. There are thinkers who assume that God does not create one thing for the sake of another,[25] that existing things are not to each other in the relation of cause and effect ; that they are all the direct result of the Will of God, and do not serve any purpose. According to this opinion we cannot ask why has He made this and not that ; for He does what pleases Him, without following a fixed system.

" Those who defend this theory must consider the actions of God as purposeless, and even as inferior to purposeless actions ; for when we perform purposeless actions, our attention is engaged by other things and we do not know what we are doing ; but God, according to these theorists, knows what He is doing, and knowingly does it for no purpose or use whatever. The absurdity of assuming that some of God's actions are trivial is apparent even at first sight, and no notice need be taken of the nonsensical idea that monkeys were created for our pastime. Such opinions originate only in man's ignorance of the nature of transient beings, and in his overlooking the principle that it was intended by the Creator to produce in its present form everything whose existence is possible ; a different form was not decreed by the divine wisdom, and the existence of objects of a different form is therefore impossible, because the existence of all things depends on the decree of God's wisdom. . . .

" Whatever God desires to do is necessarily done ; there is nothing that could prevent the realisation of His will. The object of His will is only that which is possible, and of the things possible only such as His wisdom decrees upon. When God desires to produce the best work, no obstacle or hindrance intervenes between Him and that work. This is the opinion held by all religious people and by the philosophers ; it is also our opinion. For although we believe that God created the Universe from nothing, most of our wise and learned men believe that the Creation was not the exclusive result of His will ; but His wisdom, which we are unable to comprehend, made the actual existence of the Universe necessary. The same unchangeable wisdom found it as necessary that non-existence should precede the existence of the Universe.

Our Sages frequently express this idea in the explanation of the words, ' He hath made everything beautiful in his time' (Eccles. iii. 11)[26], only in order to avoid that which is objectionable, viz., the opinion that God does things without any purpose whatever. . . . There is no necessity to believe otherwise ; philosophic speculation leads to the same result, viz., that in the whole of Nature there is nothing purposeless, trivial, or unnecessary, especially in the nature of the Spheres, which are in the best condition and order, in accordance with their superior substance " (*Guide* III, 25).

Maimonides developed the same theme, with greater detail, in another of his works :

" Know that the ancients carried out a thorough investigation, by means of the wisdom and thinking powers granted them, so that it was firmly established with them that every existing thing must of necessity have a purpose on account of which it exists, and nothing that exists does so in vain. After this general principle had been well founded by them, they began to classify all existing things in order to ascertain the purpose of each created species. With regard to everything that is serviceable, i.e., which has been made for a specific work, the purpose of its having been made is evident and research is unnecessary in connection therewith ; because a workman does not start on a piece of work unless its purpose is previously designed in his mind. E.g., a smith only makes a saw after he thinks out how it is possible to sever the wood-joints until the idea of a saw occurs to his mind ; then he commences to make it as an instrument for cutting wood. Hence we know that the design of the saw is for cutting down trees, the design of the axe for chopping wood, and the design of the needle for stitching garments together ; and so to all existing things there is a serviceable purpose.

" As for the things whose existence is due to God's work and Nature's wisdom—e.g., the various kinds of trees and herbs, metals and stones, the beasts—in some instances the purpose of their existence is hidden and nobody is cognisant of it unless it be ascertained through Prophecy or the power of knowing the future. It cannot, however, be ascertained through scientific investigation, because it is beyond the power of man to make such investigation until he understands and knows why Nature produced some ants with wings and others without wings, why it produced some worms with numerous legs and others with few, and what is the purpose of the worm and the ant. On the other hand, in the case of things greater than these, whose utility is more evident, men of wisdom discover the benefit derivable from them ; and the wiser the man, the greater his desire and the purer his motive to learn, the more perfect grows his knowledge. . . .

" In general it is necessary to know that all things in the sublunary world exist only for the sake of man ; likewise all species of animals—some of them for food, like sheep, oxen, etc., others for a use other than food, as the ass to bear what he is unable to carry in his hand, horses to travel a long distance in a short space of time. There are other species whose use we do not know, although they have a utility for man which is not understood. So also with trees and plants, some are for food, others to cure him of illnesses ; and similarly with herbs and other species. Wherever you find animals or plants which are not suitable for food and are useless according to your thinking, know that this is due to the weakness of our intellect ; and it is impossible for any herb or fruit or living creature, from elephant to worms, to be void of all utility for man. The proof of this is that in every generation there are discovered by us important uses for herbs and various kinds of fruits which were unknown to our predecessors. It is not in the power of a man's mind to comprehend the use of every plant of the earth ; but through experimentation by successive generations what is unknown becomes known.

" If, however, you were to ask, Why have deadly poisons been created, like the herb called belladonna or the blood-flower (*hæmanthus*), which are fatal to man and have no use, it is proper for you to know that these do serve a useful purpose ; because though death follows the eating of them, it does not when they are plastered on the body.   And when you understand that a great benefit accrues to man through vipers and snakes, how much more must this be so with things which are less injurious than these ! " (C.M., Introduction).

§8. *Is the Universe eternal or created ?* This question was a source of great trouble to Maimonides. The purpose of his *Guide* was to harmonise the statements of Scripture with Aristotelian philosophy. According to the traditional interpretation, the Bible teaches creation out of nothing, whereas Aristotle held that the Universe was eternal and uncreated. Reconciliation of the two conflicting doctrines was impossible. How, then, does Maimonides deal with the problem ? He first of all maintains that, on rational grounds, it cannot be solved definitely. " It is well-known to all clear and correct thinkers who do not wish to deceive themselves, that this question, viz., whether the Universe has been created or is eternal, cannot be answered with mathematical certainty ; here human intellect must pause. . . . The philosophers have for the last three thousand years been continually divided on that subject, as far as we can learn from their works and the record of their opinions " (*Guide* I, 71). Since reason cannot settle the question, there is nothing else to do but rely upon the declaration of Scripture.

He declares, however, " We do not reject the Eternity of the Universe because certain passages in Scripture confirm the Creation, for such passages are not more numerous than those in which God is represented as a corporeal being;[27] nor is it impossible or difficult to find for them a suitable interpretation " (*Guide* II, 25). He even maintains that had he accepted the Eternity of the Universe, " the Scriptural text might have been explained accordingly, and many expressions might have been found in the Bible and in other writings that would confirm and support this theory. But there is no necessity for this expedient, so long as the theory has not been proved. As there is no proof sufficient to convince us, this theory need not be taken into consideration ; we take the text of the Bible literally, and say that it teaches us a truth which we cannot prove " (*Ibid.*).

Hence he teaches dogmatically :

" Those who follow the Torah of Moses our Teacher hold that the whole Universe, i.e., everything except God, has been brought by Him into existence out of non-existence. In the beginning God alone existed and nothing else ; neither Angels nor Spheres, nor the things that are contained within the Spheres existed. He then produced from nothing all existing things such as they are,[28] by His will and desire. Even time itself is among the things created[29] ; for time depends on motion, i.e., on an accident[30] in things which move, and the things upon whose motion time depends are themselves created beings, which have passed from non-existence into existence. We say that God *existed* before the creation of the Universe, although the verb *existed* appears to imply the notion of time ; we also believe that He existed an infinite space of time before the Universe was created ; but in these cases we do not mean time in its true sense. We only use the term to signify something analogous or similar to time. For time is undoubtedly an accident, and, according to our opinion, one of the created accidents, like blackness and whiteness ; it is not a quality, but an accident connected with motion. . . .

" We consider time a thing created ; it comes into existence in the same manner as other accidents, and the substances which form the substratum for the accidents. For this reason, viz., because time belongs to the things created, it cannot be said that God produced the Universe *in the beginning.* Consider this well ; for he who does not understand it is unable to refute forcible objections raised against the theory of *Creatio ex nihilo.* If you admit the existence of time before the Creation, you will be compelled to accept the theory of the Eternity of the Universe. For time is an accident and requires a substratum.[31] You will therefore have to assume that something beside God existed before this Universe was created, an assumption which it is our duty to oppose.

" It is undoubtedly a fundamental principle of the Torah of our teacher Moses ; it is next in importance to the principle of God's Unity. Do not follow any other theory. Abraham, our father, was the first that taught it, after he had established it by philosophical research. He proclaimed, therefore, ' the name of the Lord the God of *eternity* '[32] (Gen. xxi. 33) ;

and he had previously expressed this theory in the words, ' The Possessor of heaven and earth ' (*ibid.* xiv. 22) " (*Guide* II, 13).

Since the statement " it cannot be said that God produced the Universe *in the beginning* " apparently contradicts the opening verse of the Bible, it is necessary to understand in which sense Maimonides uses this phrase. He explains it thus :

"There is a difference between *first* and beginning (or principle). The latter exists in the thing of which it is the beginning, or co-exists with it ; it need not precede it. E.g., the heart is the beginning of the living being ; the element is the beginning of that of which it is the basis. The term ' first ' is likewise applied to things of this kind, but is also employed in cases where precedence in time alone is to be expressed, and the thing which precedes is not the beginning (or the cause) of the thing that follows. E.g., we say A was the first inhabitant of this house, after him came B ; this does not imply that A is the cause of B inhabiting the house.

" In Hebrew, *tehillah* is used in the sense of ' first ' ; e.g., ' when God first (*tehillat*) spake to Hosea (Hos. i. 1) '. The beginning is expressed by *réshit*, derived from *rosh* ' head ', the principal part of the living being as regards position. The Universe has not been created out of an element that preceded it in time, since time itself formed part of the Creation. For this reason Scripture employs the term ' *beréshit* ' (in a principle,) in which the *bet* is a preposition denoting ' in '. The true explanation of the first verse of Genesis is as follows: ' In creating a principle[33] God created the beings above and the things below ' " (*Guide* II, 30).

Another reason which induced Maimonides to

accept the theory of Creation, as against Aristotle's doctrine of the Eternity of the Universe, was its pragmatic value, i.e., it provided a working hypothesis for the solution of other problems. He shows that clearly in the following passage :

" Accepting the Creation, we find that miracles are possible, that Revelation is possible, and that every difficulty in this question is removed. We might be asked, Why has God inspired a certain person and not another ? Why has He revealed the Torah to one particular nation, and at one particular time ? Why has He commanded this and forbidden that ? Why has He shown through a Prophet certain particular miracles ? What is the object of these laws ? And why has He not made the commandments and the prohibitions part of our nature, if it was His object that we should live in accordance with them ?

" We answer to all these questions : He willed it so ; or, His wisdom decided so. He created the world according to His will, at a certain time, in a certain form ; and as we do not understand why His will or His wisdom decided upon that particular form and upon that particular time, so we do not know why His will or wisdom determined any of the things mentioned in the preceding questions.

" But if we assume that the Universe has the present form as the result of fixed laws, there is occasion for the above questions ; and these could only be answered in an objectionable way, implying denial and rejection of the Biblical texts, the correctness of which no intelligent person doubts " (*Guide* II, 25).

§9. *Design in the Universe.* On the basis of the theory of Creation Maimonides is likewise able to argue that the Universe shows evidence of design. He declares that what Aristotle calls " laws of Nature " are in reality the will of God.

" According to Aristotle, and according to all that defend his theory, the Universe is inseparable from God ; He is the cause and the Universe the effect ; and this effect is a necessary one ; and as it cannot be explained why or how God exists in this particular manner, viz., being One and incorporeal, so it cannot be asked concerning the whole Universe why or how it exists in this particular way. For it is necessary that the whole, the cause as well as the effect, exist in this particular manner ; it is impossible for them not to exist, or to be different from what they actually are. This leads to the conclusion that the nature of everything remains constant, that nothing changes its nature in any way, and that such a change is impossible in any existing thing. It would also follow that the Universe is not the result of design, choice and desire ; for if this were the case, they would have been non-existing before the design had been conceived.

" We, however, hold that all things in the Universe are the result of design, and not merely of necessity ; He Who designed them may change them when He changes His design. But not every design is subject to change ; for there are things which are impossible, and their nature cannot be altered. . . .

" Everything is, according to Aristotle, the result of a law of Nature, and not the result of the design of a being that designs as it likes, or the determination of a being that determines as it pleases. He has not carried out the idea consistently, and it will never be done. He tries to find the cause why the Sphere moves from east and not from west ;34 why some Spheres move with greater velocity, others with less velocity, and he finds the cause of these differences in their different positions in reference to the uppermost Sphere. He further attempts to show why there are several Spheres for each of the seven planets, while there is only one Sphere for the large number of fixed stars. For all this he endeavours to state the reason, so as to show that the whole order is the necessary result of the laws of Nature.

"He has not attained his object. For as regards the things in the sublunary world, his explanations are in accordance with facts, and the relation between cause and effect is clearly shown. It can therefore be assumed that everything is the necessary result of the motions and influences of the Spheres. But when he treats of the properties of the Spheres, he does not clearly show the causal relation, nor does he explain the phenomena in that systematic way which the hypothesis of natural laws would demand. For let us consider the Spheres : in one case a Sphere with greater velocity is above a Sphere with less velocity,[35] in another case we notice the reverse ; in a third case there are two Spheres with equal velocities, one above the other.[36] There are, besides, other phenomena which speak strongly against the hypothesis that all is regulated by the laws of Nature. . . .

"According to our theory of the Creation, all this can easily be explained ; for we say that there is a being that determines the direction and the velocity of the motion of each Sphere ; but we do not know the reason why the wisdom of that being gave to each Sphere its peculiar property " (*Guide* II, 19).

§10. *Purpose of God's Creation.* That the Creator must have had a reason for calling the Universe into existence is certain. What was this reason ?

" Intelligent persons are much perplexed when they

inquire into the purpose of the Creation. I will now show how absurd this question is, according to each one of the different theories above-mentioned.37 An agent that acts with intention must have a certain ulterior object in that which he performs. This is evident, and no philosophical proof is required. It is likewise evident that that which is produced with intention has passed over from non-existence to existence. It is further evident, and generally agreed upon, that the being which has absolute existence, which has never been and never will be without existence, is not in need of an agent. The question, ' What is the purpose thereof ? ' cannot be asked about anything which is not the product of an agent ; therefore we cannot ask what is the purpose of the existence of God. He has not been created.

" According to these propositions it is clear that the purpose is sought for everything produced intentionally by an intelligent cause ; that is to say, a final cause must exist for everything that owes its existence to an intelligent being ; but for that which is without a beginning, a final cause need not be sought.

" After this explanation you will understand that there is no occasion to seek the final cause of the whole Universe, neither according to our theory of the Creation, nor according to the theory of Aristotle who assumes the Eternity of the Universe. For according to Aristotle, who holds that the Universe has not had a beginning, an ultimate final cause cannot be sought even for the various parts of the Universe. Thus it cannot be asked, according to his opinion, What is the final cause of the existence of the heavens ? Why are they limited by this measure or by that number ? Why is matter of this description ? What is the purpose of the existence of this species of animals or plants ? Aristotle considers all this as the result of a permanent order of things. Natural Philosophy investigates into the object of everything in Nature, but it does not treat of the ultimate final cause. . . .

" Now it is clear that man is the most perfect being formed of matter ; he is the last and most perfect of earthly beings, and in this respect it can truly be said that all earthly things exist for man, i.e., that the changes which things undergo serve to produce the most perfect being that can be produced. Aristotle, who assumes the Eternity of the Universe, need therefore not ask to what purpose does man exist, for the immediate purpose of each individual being is, according to his opinion, the perfection of its specific form. Every individual thing arrives at its perfection fully and completely when the actions that produce its form are complete. The ultimate purpose of the species is the perpetuation of this form by the repeated succession of genesis and destruction, so that there might always be a being capable of the greatest possible perfection. It seems therefore clear that, according to Aristotle who assumes the Eternity of the Universe, there is no occasion for the question what is the object of the existence of the Universe.[38]

" But of those who accept our theory that the whole Universe has been created from nothing, some hold that the inquiry after the purpose of the Creation is necessary, and assume that the Universe was only created for the sake of man's existence, that he might serve God. Everything that is done they believe is done for man's sake ; even the Spheres move only for his benefit, in order that his wants might be supplied.
. . . .

" On examining this opinion, as intelligent persons ought to examine all different opinions, we shall discover the errors it includes. Those who hold this view, viz., that the existence of man is the object of the whole Creation, may be asked whether God could have created man without those previous creations, or whether man could only have come into existence after the creation of all other things. If they answer in the affirmative, that man could have been created even if, e.g., the heavens did not exist, they will be asked what is the object of all these things, since they do not exist for their own sake, but for the sake of something that could exist without them? Even if the Universe existed for man's sake and man existed for the purpose of serving God, as has been mentioned, the question remains, What is the end of serving God? He does not become more perfect if all His creatures serve Him and comprehend Him as far as possible; nor would He lose anything if nothing existed beside Him.

" It might perhaps be replied that the service of God is not intended for God's perfection; it is intended for our own perfection—it is good for us, it makes us perfect. But then the question might be repeated, What is the object of our being perfect? We must in continuing the inquiry as to the purpose of the Creation at last arrive at the answer, It was the will of God, or His wisdom decreed it; and this is the correct answer. The wise men of Israel have, therefore, introduced in our prayers the following passage :— ' Thou hast distinguished man from the beginning, and chosen him to stand before Thee ; who can say unto Thee, What doest Thou? And if he be righteous, what does he give Thee? '[39] They have thus clearly stated that it was not a final cause that determined the existence of all things, but only His will.

" This being the case, we who believe in the Creation must admit that God could have created the Universe in a different manner as regard the causes and effects contained in it, and this would lead to the absurd conclusion that everything except man existed without any purpose, as the principal object, man, could have been brought into existence without the rest of the Creation. I consider, therefore, the following opinion as most correct according to the teaching of the Bible, and best in accordance with the results of philosophy, viz., that the Universe does not exist for man's sake, but that each being exists for its own sake, and not because of some other thing " (*Guide* III, 13).

§11. *Is the Universe Permanent ?* We have seen what importance Maimonides attaches to the belief that the Universe had a beginning and is not eternal. He also considers the question whether the world is permanent, and concludes that the matter has no bearing on one's religious faith. He leaves it an open question, although he personally believes in the permanence of the Universe.

" We have already stated that the belief in the Creation is a fundamental principle of our religion ; but we do not consider it a principle of our faith that the Universe will again be reduced to nothing. It is not contrary to the tenets of our religion to assume that the Universe will continue to exist for ever. It might be objected that everything produced is subject to destruction, as has been shown ; consequently the Universe, having had a beginning, must come to an end.

" This axiom cannot be applied, according to our views. We do not hold that the Universe came into existence, like all things in Nature, as the result of the laws of Nature. For whatever owes its existence to the action of physical laws is, according to the same laws, subject to destruction ; the same law which caused the existence of a thing after a period of non-existence is also the cause that the thing is not permanent ; since the previous non-existence proves that the nature of that thing does not necessitate its permanent existence. According to our theory, taught in Scripture, the existence or non-existence of things depends solely on the will of God and not on fixed laws, and, therefore, it does not follow that God must destroy the Universe after having created it from nothing. It depends on His will. He may, according to His desire or according to the decree of His wisdom, either destroy it or allow it to exist, and it is therefore possible that He will preserve the Universe for ever, and let it exist permanently as He Himself exists. . . .

" There remains only the question as to what the Prophets and our Sages say on this point, whether they affirm that the world will certainly come to an end or not. Most people amongst us believe that such statements have been made, and that the world will at one time be destroyed. I will show you that this is not the case ; and that, on the contrary, many passages in the Bible speak of the permanent existence of the Universe. Those passages which, in the literal sense, would indicate the destruction of the Universe, are undoubtedly to be understood in a figurative sense. If, however, those who follow the literal sense of the Scriptural texts reject our view, and assume that the ultimate certain destruction of the Universe is part of their faith, they are at liberty to do so. But we must tell them that the belief in the destruction is not necessarily implied in the belief in the Creation ; they believe it because they trust the writer who used a figurative expression, which they take literally. Their faith, however, does not suffer by it " (*Guide* II, 27).

§12. *God's Name.* In the view of the ancients, a name was not merely a convenient label to distinguish one person from another. It had significance and indicated some relationship to the nature or characteristic of the bearer. Consequently the " name " of God was a matter of considerable import to those who endeavoured to gain an understanding of His essence. Maimonides discusses the distinctive Name used of God in the Bible, viz., the Tetragrammaton or Name of four letters.

" It is well-known that all the names of God occurring in Scripture are derived from His actions,[40] except one, viz., the Tetragrammaton, which consists of the letters JHVH. This Name is applied exclusively to God, and is on that account called *Shém ha-mephorash*,[41] ' the proper Name '. It is the distinct and exclusive designation of the Divine Being ; whilst His other names are common nouns, and are derived from actions, to which some of our own are similar. . . .

" The derivation of the Name, consisting of JHVH, is not positively known, the word having no additional signification. This sacred Name, which, as you know, was not pronounced except in the Sanctuary by the appointed priests when they gave the sacerdotal blessing,[42] and by the High Priest on the Day of Atonement,[43] undoubtedly denotes something which is peculiar to God, and is not found in any other being. It is possible that in the Hebrew language, of which we have now but a slight knowledge, the Tetragrammaton, in the way it was pronounced, conveyed the meaning of ' absolute existence '. In short, the majesty of the Name and the great dread of uttering it, are connected with the fact that it denotes God Himself, without including in its meaning any names of the things created by Him. . . .

" It was not known to everyone how the Name was to be pronounced, what vowels were to be given to each consonant, and whether some of the letters capable of reduplication should receive a *dagesh*.[44] Wise men successively transmitted the pronunciation of the Name ; it occurred only once in seven years that the pronunciation was communicated to a distinguished disciple. I must, however, add that the statement, ' The wise men communicated the Tetragrammaton to their children and disciples once in seven years ',[45] does not only refer to the pronunciation but also to its meaning, because of which the Tetragrammaton was made a *nomen proprium* of God, and which includes certain metaphysical principles " (*Guide* I, 61f).

In addition to the distinctive Name used in the Scriptures, Rabbinical literature mentions, without specifying, divine appellations of a mystical character. Maimonides refers to these as follows :

" Our Sages knew in addition a name of God which consisted of twelve letters,[46] inferior in sanctity to the Tetragrammaton. I believe that this was not a single noun, but consisted of two or three words, the sum of their letters being twelve, and that these words were used by our Sages as a substitute for the Tetragrammaton whenever they met with it in the course of their reading the Scriptures, in the same manner as we at present substitute for it *Adonai* ' The Lord'. There is no doubt that this name also, consisting of twelve letters, was in this sense more distinctive than the name *Adonai* ; it was never withheld from any of the students ; whoever wished to learn it had the opportunity given to him without any reserve.

" Not so the Tetragrammaton ; those who knew it did not communicate it except to a son or a disciple, once in seven years. When, however, unprincipled men had become acquainted with that Name which consists of twelve letters and in consequence had become corrupt in faith—as is sometimes the case when persons with imperfect knowledge become aware that a thing is not such as they had imagined—the Sages concealed also that name, and only communicated it to the worthiest among the priests, that they should pronounce it when they blessed the people in the Temple; for the Tetragrammaton was then no longer uttered in the Sanctuary on account of the corruption of the people.[47] . . .

" There was also a name of forty-two letters[48] known among them. Every intelligent person knows that one word of forty-two letters is impossible. But it was a phrase of several words which had together forty-two letters. There is no doubt that the words had such a meaning as to convey a correct notion of the essence of God. This phrase of so many letters is called a name because, like other proper names, they represent one single object, and several words have been employed in order to explain more clearly the idea which the name represents; for an idea can more easily be comprehended if expressed in many words. . . .

" Many believe that the forty-two letters are merely to be pronounced mechanically; that by the knowledge of these, without any further interpretation, they can attain to these exalted ends, although it is stated that he who desires to obtain a knowledge of that name must be trained in the virtues and go through great preparations. On the contrary, it is evident that all this preparation aims at a knowledge of Metaphysics and includes ideas which constitute the ' secrets of the Torah ' " (*Guide* I, 62).

CHAPTER II

CONSTITUTION OF THE UNIVERSE

§1. *Threefold Division of the Universe.* Before proceeding with the Attributes of God as defined by Maimonides, an account must be given of his views on the structure of the Universe. The world, as he conceived it, consisted of three strata :

" The whole Creation is divided into three parts, viz., (i) the pure Intelligences ; (ii) the bodies of the Spheres endowed with permanent forms—(the forms of these bodies do not pass from one substratum to another, nor do their substrata undergo any change whatever) ; and (iii) the transient earthly beings, all of which consist of the same substance. Furthermore, we desire to show that the ruling power emanates from the Creator, and is received by the Intelligences according to their order ; from the Intelligences part of the good and the light bestowed upon them is communicated to the Spheres, and the latter, being in possession of the abundance obtained of the Intelligences, transmit forces and properties unto the beings of this transient world "[1] (*Guide* II, 11).

" All that the Holy One, blessed be He, created in His Universe is divisible into three classes. Some are creatures composed of matter and form, and are perpetually coming into existence and perishing ; e.g., the bodies of men, animals, plants and minerals. Others are creatures composed of matter and form, but do not change from body to body and from form to

65

form like the first class. Their form is fixed in their matter eternally and they are not liable to change like the others. They are the Spheres and the planets which are in them. Their matter is also unlike the matter of other things, and their form unlike other forms. Finally, there are creatures possessing form without any matter. Such are the Angels ; because the Angels are incorporeal, being merely forms distinguished one from another " (*Yad, Yesodé ha-Torah* II, 3).

§2. *The Intelligences or Angels.* The uppermost of the three strata is called by Maimonides " the Intelligences ", a term borrowed from Aristotle, which the Jewish philosopher identifies with the " Angels " mentioned in the Scriptures. He attaches considerable importance to these supreme creatures as the medium through which the divine influences pass to earth.

" The belief in the existence of Angels is connected with the belief in the existence of God ; and the belief in God and Angels leads to the belief in Prophecy and in the truth of the Torah. In order firmly to establish this creed, God commanded the Israelites to make over the Ark the form of two Angels.[2] The belief in the existence of Angels is thus inculcated into the minds of the people, and this belief is in importance next to the belief in God's existence ; it leads us to believe in Prophecy and in the Torah, and opposes idolatry. If there had only been one figure of a Cherub, the people would have been misled and would have mistaken it for God's image which was to be worshipped, in the fashion of the heathen ; or they might have assumed that the Angel represented by the figure was also a deity, and would then have adopted a dualism. By making two Cherubim and distinctly declaring ' the Lord is our God, the Lord is *One* ', Moses clearly proclaimed the theory of the existence of a number of Angels ; he left no room for the error of considering those figures as deities, since he declared that God is one, and that He is the Creator of the Angels who are more than one " (*Guide* III, 45).

" The Angels are likewise incorporeal ; they are Intelligences without matter, but they are nevertheless created beings, and God created them " (*Guide* I, 49).

All the Angels are not equal in degree. They fall into a series of classes, each class being dependent upon the one immediately superior to it.

" In what, then, are the angelic forms distinguishable one from another, since they are not bodies ? In that they are not equal in their status, but each one is lower in degree as compared with his fellow and exists through the power of the one next above him ; but all of them exist through the power and goodness of the Holy One, blessed be He. . . . Our statement ' lower in degree as compared with his fellow ' does not refer to degree of place, like a man who sits higher than his neighbour. It is used in the same sense as when it is said of two wise men, of whom one is greater in wisdom than the other, that the former is of a higher degree than the latter ; or when it is said of the cause that it is superior to the effect.

" The variety in the names of the Angels is in accordance with their varying degrees. Therefore they are called *Ḥayyot ha-Kodesh* (the holy creatures),[3] which are the highest of all ; *Ophannim* (wheels) ; *Erelim* (ambassadors ?)[4] ; *Ḥashmallim* (the shining ones ?)[5] ; *Seraphim* (the burning ones)[6] ; *Malachim* (messengers)[7] ; *Elohim* (the mighty ones)[8] ; *Bené*

Elohim (sons of the mighty)[9] ; *Cherubim* (those having the appearance of children)[10] and *Ishim* (men)[11].

" All these ten names by which the Angels are called have reference to their ten degrees ; and that degree, to which there is none superior than that of God, is the degree of the Intelligence designated *Ḥayyot*. . . . The tenth degree is that of the Intelligence which is called *Ishim*, these being the Angels who spoke with the Prophets and appeared to them in the prophetic vision. For this reason they are designated *Ishim* (men), because their degree is nearest to the degree of the knowledge of human beings " (*Yad, Yesodé ha-Torah* II, 5-7).

Maimónides derived the ten degrees of Angels not only from Scripture, but from philosophical literature.

" The later philosophers assumed ten Intelligences, because they counted the Spheres containing stars and the all-encompassing Sphere, although some of the Spheres included several distinct orbits. There are altogether nine Spheres, viz., the all-encompassing Sphere, that of the fixed stars, and those of the seven planets ; nine Intelligences correspond to the nine Spheres ; the tenth Intelligence is the Active Intellect. . . . As that which gives form to matter must itself be pure form,[12] so the source of intellect must itself be pure intellect, and this source is the Active Intellect "[13] (*Guide* II, 4).

It is through the medium of these Intelligences that God's Will operates in the Universe, an idea which is found both in Greek and Hebraic speculation.

" We have already stated above that the Angels are incorporeal. This agrees with the opinion of Aristotle. There is only this difference in the names employed—he uses the term ' Intelligences ' and we say ' Angels '. His theory is that the Intelligences

68

are intermediate beings between the Prime Cause and existing things, and that they effect the motion of the Spheres, on which motion the existence of all things depends. This is also the view we meet with in all parts of Scripture ; every act of God is described as being performed by Angels. But ' Angel ' means ' messenger ' ; hence every one that is entrusted with a certain mission is an Angel. Even the movements of the brute creation are sometimes due to the action of an Angel, when such movements serve the purpose of the Creator, Who endowed it with the purpose of performing that movement (*cf.* Dan. vi. 22). . . . The elements are also called Angels (*cf.* Ps. civ. 4). . . . It is also used of ideals perceived by Prophets in prophetic visions[14] and of man's animal powers.[15]

" When we assert that Scripture teaches that God rules this world through Angels, we mean Angels that are identical with the Intelligences. In some passages the plural is used of God, e.g., ' Let us make man in our image ' (Gen. i. 26) ; ' Go to, let us go down and there confound their language ' (*ibid.* xi. 7). Our Sages explain this in the following manner : God, as it were, does nothing without contemplating the host above.[16] I wonder at the expression ' contemplating ', which is the very expression used by Plato.[17] God, as it were, ' contemplates the world of ideals, and thus produces the existing beings '. In other passages our Sages expressed it more decidedly : ' God does nothing without consulting the host above '.[18] On the words, ' what they have already made ' (Eccles. ii. 12), the following remark is made in *Beréshit Rabba* and in *Midrash Kohélet* : ' It is not said " what He has made " but " what they have made " ; hence we infer that He, as it were, with His court, have agreed upon the form of each of the limbs of man before placing it in its position[19]; as it is said, " He hath made thee and established thee " (Deut. xxxii. 6) '. In *Beréshit Rabba*[20] it is also stated that whenever the term '*and the Lord*' occurred in Scripture, the Lord and His court is to be understood.

" These passages do not convey the idea that God spoke, thought, reflected, or that He consulted and employed the opinion of other beings, as ignorant persons have believed. How could the Creator be assisted by those whom He created! They only show that all parts of the Universe, even the limbs of animals in their actual form, are produced through Angels; for natural forces and Angels are identical. How bad and injurious is the blindness of ignorance! Say to a person who is believed to belong to the wise men of Israel that the Almighty sends His Angel to enter the womb of a woman and to form there the fœtus, he will be satisfied with the account; he will believe it, and even find in it a description of the greatness of God's might and wisdom; although he believes that the Angel consists of burning fire and is as big as a third part of the Universe, yet he considers it possible as a divine miracle. But tell him that God gave the seed a formative power which produces and shapes the limbs, and that this power is called ' Angel ', or that all forms are the result of the influence of the Active Intellect, and that the latter is the Angel, the Prince of the world, frequently mentioned by our Sages,[21] and he will turn away; because he cannot comprehend the true greatness and power of creating forces that act in a body without being perceived by our senses. Our Sages have already stated—for him who has understanding—that all forces that reside in a body are Angels, much more the forces that are active in the Universe " (*Guide* II, 6).

" Do not imagine that the Intelligences and the Spheres are like other forces which reside in bodies and act by the laws of Nature without being conscious of what they do. The Spheres and the Intelligences are conscious of their actions, and select by their own free will the objects of their influence, although not in the same manner as we exercise free will and rule over other things, which only concern temporary beings. . . . The difference is that what we do is the lowest stage of excellence, and that our influence and actions are preceded by non-action ; whilst the Intelligences and the Spheres always perform that which is good, they contain nothing except what is good and perfect, and they have continually been active from the beginning " (*ibid.* II, 7).

§3. *The Spheres.* The second stratum is called the Spheres. They are nine in number. They are to be thought of as hollow globes, one within the other after the manner of Chinese boxes, or, to use Maimonides' simile, the skins of an onion.

" The Sphere that is nearest to us is the Moon. The second above it is the Sphere in which is the planet called *Kochab* (Mercury). The third Sphere above this is that in which is *Nogah* (Venus). The fourth is that in which is *Ḥammah* (the Sun). The fifth is that in which is *Ma'adim* (Mars). The sixth is that in which is the planet *Tsédek* (Jupiter). The seventh is that in which is *Shabbetai* (Saturn). The eighth is that in which are all the other stars that are seen in the firmament. The ninth is the Sphere which revolves daily from East to West, and also encompasses and surrounds the whole. That you see all the stars as if they were entirely in one Sphere is due to the fact that the Spheres are pure and transparent like crystal and sapphire. Therefore the stars which are in the eighth Sphere are visible beneath the first Sphere.

"Each of the eight Spheres, in which are the planets, is divisible into many more Spheres, one above the other, like the skins of onions. Some of them are Spheres revolving from West to East, and others revolving from East to West, like the ninth Sphere which revolves from East to West. Between none of them is there a vacuum.

"All the Spheres are neither light nor heavy; they have neither a red, nor black, nor any other colour. That we see them tinged with a bluish colour is only an optical illusion due to the height of the atmosphere. Similarly they have neither flavour nor odour, because these accidents only exist in bodies which are beneath them.

"All these Spheres, which encompass the world, are circular like a globe, and the earth is suspended in the centre. Some of the planets, however, have small Spheres which are fixed in them and do not encompass the earth ; but a small Sphere which is non-encompassing is fixed in a greater which does encompass the earth.

"The number of all the Spheres which encompass the earth is eighteen, and the total of the small Spheres which do not encompass is eight. It is from the course of the stars, from knowing the rate of their daily and hourly revolutions, from their declension from the South to the North, or from the North to the South, and from their height above or proximity to the earth, that the number of all these Spheres, the form of their course and the direction of their revolutions may be ascertained—this being the science of the calculation of the cycles and planets (Astronomy), on which the wise men of Greece composed many books.

" As to the ninth Sphere which encompasses the whole, the wise men of old divided it into twelve parts, and to each part ascribed an appellation after the name of the figure perceived therein reflected by the stars which are beneath it. These are the signs of the Zodiac, the names of which are *Téleh* (Ram), *Shor* (Bull), *Te'omim* (Twins), *Sartan* (Crab), *Aryeh* (Lion), *Betulah* (Virgin), *Moznayim* (Scales), *Akrab* (Scorpion), *Késhet* (Bow), *Gedi* (Kid), *Deli* (Bucket), *Dagim* (Fishes).

" But in the ninth Sphere itself there is neither division nor any of those figures, not even a star. It is only by the junction of the constellations which are in the eighth Sphere that there appears in its large stars the form of these figures or something similar. These twelve figures only coincided with those parts at the time of the Flood, when these names were assigned to them ; but at this time they have moved somewhat, since all the stars in the eighth Sphere revolve in the same manner as the sun and moon, except that they revolve slowly. The part of a circle which the sun and moon traverse in a day, each of those stars traverses in about seventy years.

" Of all the visible planets, there are some among them which are small, so that the earth is larger than any of them ; but there are also among them great planets, each of which is many times larger than the earth. Now the earth is about forty times larger than the moon, and the sun about a hundred and seventy times larger than the earth ; therefore the moon is approximately a six thousand and eight hundredth part of the sun.[22] There is none among the planets larger than the sun, nor is there any planet smaller than *Kochab* (Mercury), which is in the second Sphere.

" All the planets and Spheres are entities possessed of soul, mind and understanding. Moreover they are endowed with life.[23] They exist and know the Creator of the Universe. Each of them, in proportion to its magnitude and degree, praises and glorifies its Creator, in the same manner that the Angels do. And just as they know the Holy One, blessed be He, so do they know themselves, and also know the Angels that are above them. The knowledge possessed by the planets and Spheres is inferior to the knowledge possessed by the Angels, but is superior to the knowledge possessed by human beings " (*Yad, Yesodé ha-Torah* III, 1-9).

What Maimonides intends in this last paragraph is elucidated in the following excerpt :

" The enunciation that the heavenly Sphere is endowed with a soul will appear reasonable to all who sufficiently reflect on it ; but at first thought they may find it unintelligible or even objectionable ; because they wrongly assume that when we ascribe a soul to the heavenly Spheres we mean something like the soul of man, or that of an ox or ass. We merely intend to say that the locomotion of the Sphere undoubtedly leads us to assume some inherent principle by which it moves ; and this principle is certainly a soul. For it would be absurd to assume that the principle of the circular motion of the Spheres was like that of the rectilinear motion of a stone downward or of fire upwards, for the cause of the latter motion is a natural property and not a soul ; a thing set in motion by a natural property moves only as long as it is away from the proper place of its element, but when it has again arrived there, it comes to rest ;

whilst the Sphere continues its circular motion in its own place.

It is, however, not because the Sphere has a soul, that it moves in this manner ; for animate beings move either by instinct or by reason. By ' instinct ' I mean the intention of an animal to approach something agreeable, or to retreat from something disagreeable ; e.g., to approach the water it seeks because of thirst, or to retreat from the sun because of its heat. . . . The heavenly Sphere does not move for the purpose of withdrawing from what is bad or approaching what is good. . . . The circular motion of the Sphere is consequently due to the action of some idea which produces this particular kind of motion ; but as ideas are only possible in intellectual beings, the heavenly Sphere is an intellectual being.[24]   But even a being that is endowed with the faculty of forming an idea, and possesses a soul with the faculty of moving, does not change its place on each occasion that it forms an idea ; for an idea alone does not produce motion, as has been explained in Aristotle's Metaphysics.[25] We can easily understand this when we consider how often we form ideas of certain things, yet do not move towards them though we are able to do so ; it is only when a desire arises for the thing imagined that we move in order to obtain it.

" We have thus shown that both the soul, the principle of motion and the intellect, the source of the ideas, would not produce motion without the existence of a desire for the object of which an idea has been formed. It follows that the heavenly Sphere must have a desire for the ideal which it has comprehended, and that ideal, for which it has a desire, is God, exalted be His name ! " (*Guide* II, 4).

§4. *The Sublunary Sphere.* The lowest stratum is the earth inhabited by the human race. Both the terrestrial Sphere and all it contains are formed out of four elements—fire, air, water and earth—which are qualities attached to one all-pervading substance.

" God created beneath the lunar Sphere a matter which is unlike the matter of the Spheres. He also created four forms for this matter which are unlike the forms of the Spheres, and each form is fixed in a part of this matter. The first form is that of fire ; it was united to a part of this matter and there resulted from both of them the body of fire. The second form is that of air ; it was united to a part of the matter and there resulted from both of them the body of air. The third form is that of water ; it was united to a part of it and there resulted from both of them the body of water. The fourth form is that of earth ; it was united to a part of it and there resulted from both of them the body of earth. Consequently there are beneath the firmament four different bodies, one above the other, and each one encompasses that which is beneath it on all its sides, like a wheel. The first body, which is nearest the lunar Sphere, is the body of fire ; beneath it is the body of air ; beneath that is the body of water ; and beneath that is the body of earth. There is between them no space which is void and entirely without matter.

" These four bodies are not entities possessed of soul. They have no understanding or perception, but are like inanimate bodies. . . .

" These four bodies, viz., fire, air, water and earth, are the elements of all the created things which are under the firmament. Whatever exists, whether it be man, cattle, bird, insect, fish, plant, mineral, gems, pearls or other stones used for building, mountains, lumps of clay—the matter of them all is composed of these four elements. Consequently all the bodies which are under the firmament, these four elements excepted, are composed of matter and form, and their matter is composed of these four elements. Each of the four elements, however, is composed of nothing but matter and form alone.

" The nature of fire and air is that their movement is from below, i.e., from the centre of the earth upward towards the firmament. The nature of water and earth, on the other hand, is to move from under the firmament downward as far as the centre, the centre of the earth being the nethermost point of all. Their motion is not dependent upon their consciousness or volition, but only upon a property and characteristic which had been implanted in them. The nature of fire is hot and dry ; it is the lightest of all the elements. Air is hot and moist. Water is cold and moist. Earth is dry and cold ; it is the heaviest of them all. Since water is lighter than earth, it is as a consequence found on top of the earth. Air, being lighter than water, consequently floats on the surface of the water. Fire is lighter than air.

" Because these are the elements of all bodies under the firmament, every body—whether it be that of man, cattle, beast, bird, fish, plant, mineral or stone —will be found to have its matter composed of fire, air, water and earth. All these four are intermingled ; and at the time that they are mingled together, each one of them becomes altered to such an extent that the compound of the four is found to have no resemblance to any one of them when by itself, and in the mixture there is not even a single particle of fire by itself, water by itself, earth by itself, or air by itself—they are all changed and converted into one body.

" In every body composed of the four elements will be found together cold, warmth, moisture and dryness. Yet some of them are bodies in which the element of fire predominates, as for instance those which possess animal life, and therefore warmth is most conspicuous in them. Others are bodies in which the element of earth predominates, as stones ; consequently dryness is most conspicuous in them. Others, again, are bodies in which the element of water predominates, and therefore moisture will be most conspicuous in them. In like manner one body will be found to be warmer than another warm body, or one dry body with greater dryness than another dry body. There will likewise be found bodies in which cold alone is perceptible, and bodies in which moisture alone is perceptible ; or bodies in which cold and dryness are perceptible together and in an equal degree, or cold and moisture together and in an equal degree, or warmth and dryness together and in an equal degree or warmth and moisture together and in an equal degree. In proportion to the quantity of the element which is in the basis of the mixture will the effect of that element and its nature be perceived in the component body.

" Everything that is compounded of these four elements must ultimately be dissolved. Some dissolve after a few days, others after many years. It is impossible for a thing that has been compounded of them not to be again decomposed into them ; it is not even possible for gold or the ruby not to become decomposed and reduced again to its elements, part of it returning to fire, part to water, part to air, and part to earth. . . .

" Whatever is destroyed is not reduced to the four elements immediately on its destruction ; but when destroyed, it first becomes another thing, and that other thing becomes still another. Finally, however, things must be reduced to their elements, and consequently all things pass through a complete circle of change.

" These four elements interchange constantly, daily and hourly, but part of them only and not their entire mass. For instance, the part of the earth nearest to water changes, crumbles to pieces and becomes water ; likewise the part of water nearest to air changes, vapourises and becomes air. Similarly with air, that part of it which is nearest to fire changes, whirls about and becomes fire. So also with fire, that part of it which is nearest to air changes, whirls about, condenses and becomes air. Again, that part of air which is nearest to water changes, condenses and becomes water ; and finally, that part of water which is nearest to earth changes, condenses and becomes earth.

" This change takes place very gradually and over a long space of time. Nor is it the entire element that is changed, so that the whole of the water should ever become air, or the whole of the air fire ; for it is impossible that one of the four elements should cease to exist. Part only of the fire is changed to air, and part only of the air is changed to fire. It is the same with each element and the others, an interchange being found to occur between all four of them, and they for ever pass through a complete circle of change.

" This change arises from the revolution of the Sphere. It is through this revolution that the four elements intermingle, and there result from them all other substances—as men, living creatures, plants, stones, minerals. But it is God Who imparts to each substance the form which is suitable to it through the

medium of the Angels of the tenth degree, viz., the
Intelligences called *Ishim* (men) " (*Yad, Yesodé
ha-Torah* III, 10-IV, 6).

§5. *The Universe a united whole.* Complex though the
structure of the world be, yet it forms a harmonious
whole. It is a single entity. Maimonides illustrates
this truth by drawing an analogy between the Universe
and the human body.

" Know that this Universe, in its entirety, is
nothing else but one individual being ; that is to say,
the outermost heavenly Sphere, together with all
included therein, is as regards individuality beyond
all question a single being. The variety of its
substances—I mean the substances of that Sphere
and all its component parts—is like the variety of the
substances of a human being ; just as, e.g., *A* is one
individual, consisting of various solid substances,
such as flesh, bones, sinews, of various humours[26] and
of various spiritual elements.[27] In like manner this
Sphere in its totality is composed of the celestial orbs,
the four elements and their combinations ; there is
no vacuum whatever therein, but the whole space is
filled up with matter. Its centre is occupied by the
earth, earth is surrounded by water, air encompasses
the water, fire envelopes the air, and this again is
enveloped by the fifth substance (quintessence). . . .

" As the human body consists both of principal
organs and of other members which depend on them
and cannot exist without the control of those organs,
so does the Universe consist both of principal parts,
viz., the quintessence, which encompasses the four
elements and of other parts which are subordinated
and require a leader, viz., the four elements and the
things composed of them.

" Again the principal part of the human body, viz., the heart, is in constant motion, and is the source of every motion noticed in the body ; it rules over the other members, and communicates to them through its own pulsations the force required for their functions. The outermost Sphere by its motion rules in a similar way over all other parts of the Universe, and supplies all things with their special properties. Every motion in the Universe has thus its origin in the motion of that Sphere ; and the soul of every animated being derives its origin from the soul of that same Sphere.

. . .

" When for one instant the beating of the heart is interrupted, man dies, and all his motions and powers come to an end. In a like manner would the whole Universe perish, and everything therein cease to exist, if the Spheres were to come to a standstill.

" The living being as such is one through the action of its heart, although some parts of the body are devoid of motion and sensation, as e.g., the bones, the cartilage and similar parts. The same is the case with the entire Universe ; although it includes many beings without motion and without life, it is a single being living through the motion of the Sphere, which may be compared to the heart of an animated being. You must therefore consider the entire globe as one individual being which is endowed with life, motion and a soul. This mode of considering the Universe is indispensable, that is to say, it is very useful for demonstrating the Unity of God[28] ; it also helps to elucidate the principle that He Who is One has created only *one* being. . . .

" There also exists in the Universe a certain force which controls the whole, which sets in motion the chief and principal parts, and gives them the motive power for governing the rest. Without that force, the existence of this Sphere, with its principal and secondary parts, would be impossible. It is the source of the existence of the Universe in all its parts. That force is God, blessed be His name ! " (*Guide* I, 72).

Chapter III

ATTRIBUTES OF GOD

MAIMONIDES devotes a long section of his *Guide*[1] to the subject of the divine attributes, because several important theological and philosophical problems depend for their solution upon the true understanding of God's essence. An incorrect comprehension of the qualities possessed by God and of His nature must react upon one's whole religious mentality. Before dealing with the principal attributes ascribed to God, it is necessary to grasp the interpretation which Maimonides gives to the term.

§1. *Why attributes are ascribed to God.* If the Deity is to be anything more than an abstraction of thought, it is inevitable that we should think and speak of Him "in the language of the children of men".[2] From this fact springs the danger of misapprehending God, because we view Him through a distorting medium. The terminology applied to finite beings is misleading when used of the Infinite. The difficulty cannot be completely obviated ; its worst effects can only be guarded against by careful reasoning.

"There is a great difference between bringing to view the existence of a thing and demonstrating its true essence. We can lead others to notice the existence of an object by pointing to its accidents, actions, or even most remote relations to other objects.

E.g., if you wish to describe the king of a country to one of his subjects who does not know him, you can give a description and an account of his existence in many ways. You will either say to him, the tall man with a fair complexion and grey hair is the king, thus describing him by his accidents ; or you will say, the king is the person round whom are seen a great multitude of men on horse and on foot, and soldiers with drawn swords, over whose head banners are waving, and before whom trumpets are sounded ; or it is the person living in the palace in a particular region of a certain country ; or it is the person who ordered the building of that wall or the construction of that bridge ; or by some other similar acts and things relating to him. . . .

" The same is the case with the information concerning the Creator given to the ordinary classes of men in all prophetical books and in the Torah. For it was found necessary to teach all of them that God exists, and that He is in every respect the most perfect Being, that is to say, He exists not only in the sense in which the earth and the heavens exist, but He exists and possesses life, wisdom, power, activity, and all other properties which our belief in His existence must include. That God exists was therefore shown to ordinary men by means of similes taken from physical bodies ; that He is living by a simile taken from motion, because ordinary men consider only the body as fully, truly and undoubtedly existing ; that which is connected with a body but is itself not a body, although believed to exist, has a lower degree of existence on account of its dependence on the body for existence. . . .

" The perception by the senses, especially by hearing and seeing, is best known to us ; we have no

84

idea or notion of any other mode of communication between the soul of one person and that of another than by means of speaking, i.e., by the sound produced by lips, tongue and the other organs of speech. When, therefore, we are to be informed that God has *a knowledge* of things, and that communication is made by Him to the Prophets who convey it to us, they represent Him to us as seeing and hearing, i.e., as perceiving and knowing those things which can be seen . and heard. They represent Him to us as speaking, i.e., that communications from Him reach the Prophets ; that is to be understood by the term " Prophecy ", as will be fully explained.3 God is described as working, because we do not know any other mode of producing a thing except by direct touch. He is said to have a soul in the sense that He is living, because all living beings are generally supposed to have a soul. . . .

" Again, since we perform all these actions only by means of corporeal organs, we figuratively ascribe to God the organs of locomotion, as feet and their soles4 ; organs of hearing, seeing and smelling as ear, eye and nose ; organs and substance of speech as mouth, tongue and sound ; organs for the performance of work as hand, its fingers, its palm and the arm. In short, these organs of the body are figuratively ascribed to God, Who is above all imperfection, to express that He performs certain acts ; and these acts are figuratively ascribed to Him to express that He possesses certain perfections different from those acts themselves. E.g., we say that He has eyes, ears, hands, a mouth, a tongue, to express that He sees, hears, acts and speaks ; but seeing and hearing are attributed to Him to indicate simply that He perceives. . . . Action and speech are likewise figuratively applied to God, to express that a certain influence has emanated from Him.

" The physical organs which are attributed to God in the writings of the Prophets are either organs of locomotion, indicating life ;- organs of sensation, indicating perception ; organs of touch, indicating action ; or organs of speech, indicating the divine inspiration of the Prophets. The object of all these indications is to establish in our minds the notion of the existence of a living being, the Maker of everything, Who also possesses a knowledge of the things which He has made " (*Guide* I, 46).

§2. *There is no similarity between God's attributes and man's.* A point which Maimonides emphasises throughout is that a quality ascribed to God has no affinity with the same quality as used of the human being. The term is the same, because we cannot invent intelligible expressions which could be reserved exclusively for the Deity. The identity of term does not imply identity of quality.

" Similarity is based on a certain relation between two things ; if between two things no relation can be found, there can be no similarity between them, and there is no relation between two things that have no similarity to each other. E.g., we do not say this heat is similar to that colour, or this voice is similar to that sweetness. This is self-evident. Since the existence of a relation between God and man, or between Him and other beings, has been denied, similarity must likewise be denied. . . .

" Thus those who believe in the presence of essential attributes in God, viz., Existence, Life, Power, Wisdom and Will, should know that these attributes, when applied to God, have not the same meaning as when applied to us, and that the difference does not only consist in magnitude, or in the degree of perfection, stability and durability. It cannot be said, as they practically believe, that His existence is only more stable, His life more permanent, His power greater, His wisdom more perfect, and His will more general than ours, and that the same definition applies to both. This is in no way admissible, for the expression ' more than ' is used in comparing two things as regards a certain attribute predicated of both of them in exactly the same sense, and consequently implies similarity between God and His creatures " (*Guide* I, 56).

" In the same way as all people must be informed, and even children must be trained in the belief that God is One, and that none besides Him is to be worshipped, so must all be taught by simple authority that God is incorporeal ; that there is no similarity in any way whatsoever between Him and His creatures; that His existence is not like the existence of His creatures, His life not like that of any living being, His wisdom not like the wisdom of the wisest of men ; and that the difference between Him and His creatures is not merely quantitative, but absolute as between two individuals of two different classes. I mean to say that all must understand that our wisdom and His, or our power and His, do not differ quantitatively or qualitatively, or in a similar manner ; for two things, of which the one is strong and the other weak, are necessarily similar, belong to the same class, and can be included in one definition. . . . Anything predicated of God is totally different from our attributes ; no definition can comprehend both ; therefore His existence and that of any other being totally differ from each other, and the term existence is applied to both homonymously "5 (*Guide* I, 35).

TEACHINGS OF MAIMONIDES

§3. *An attribute is an accident; therefore God has no attributes apart from His essence.* Not only can no comparison be made between God's qualities and man's, but He does not possess attributes in the same sense that the human being possesses them.

" It is a self-evident truth that the attribute is not inherent in the object to which it is ascribed, but it is superadded to its essence, and is consequently an *accident.*[6] If the attribute denoted the essence of the object, it would be either mere tautology, as if, e.g., one would say ' man is man ', or the explanation of a name, as, e.g., ' man is a speaking animal ' ; for the words '-speaking animal ' include the true essence of man, and there is no third element besides life and speech in the definition of man. When he, therefore, is described by the attributes of life and speech, these are nothing but an explanation of the name ' man ', that is to say, that the thing which is called man consists of life and speech.

" It will now be clear that the attribute must be one of two things, either the essence of the object described—in that case it is a mere explanation of a name, and on that account we might admit the attribute in reference to God, but we reject it from another cause, as will be shown[7]—or the attribute is something different from the object described, some extraneous superadded element. In that case the attribute would be an accident, and he who merely rejects the appellation ' accidents ' in reference to the attributes of God does not thereby alter their character; for everything superadded to the essence of an object joins it without forming part of its essential properties and that constitutes an accident " (*Guide* I, 51).

" It is known that existence is an accident appertaining to all things, and therefore an element

88

superadded to their essence. This must evidently be the case as regards everything the existence of which is due to some cause ; its existence is an element superadded to its essence. But as regards a being whose existence is not due to any cause—God alone is that being, for His existence, as we have said, is absolute—existence and essence are perfectly identical. He is not a substance to which existence is joined as an accident, as an additional element. His existence is always absolute, and has never been a new element or an accident in Him. Consequently God exists without possessing the attribute of existence. Similarly He lives without possessing the attribute of life ; knows without possessing the attribute of knowledge ; is omnipotent without possessing the attribute of omnipotence ; is wise without possessing the attribute of wisdom. All this reduces itself to one and the same entity ; there is no plurality in Him " (*Guide* I, 57).

§4. *God only describable by negative attributes.* For the reason that human language is misleading when applied to God, one approximates most nearly to the truth by speaking of Him in negative terms. It is preferable to say what He is not than attempt to describe what He is.

" Know that the negative attributes of God are the true attributes. They do not include any incorrect notions or any deficiency whatever in reference to God ; while positive attributes imply polytheism[8] and are inadequate. It is now necessary to explain how negative expressions can in a certain sense be employed as attributes, and how they are distinguished from positive attributes. Then I shall show that we cannot describe the Creator by any means except by negative attributes.

" An attribute does not exclusively belong to the one object to which it is related ; while qualifying one thing, it can also be employed to qualify other things, and is in that case not peculiar to that one thing. E.g., if you see an object from a distance, and on enquiring what it is, are told that it is a living being, you have certainly learnt an attribute of the object seen, and although that attribute does not exclusively belong to the object perceived, it expresses that the object is not a plant or a mineral.   Again, if a man is in a certain house, and you know that something is in the house but not exactly what, you ask what is in that house and you are told, not a plant nor a mineral. You have thereby obtained some special knowledge of the thing ; you have learnt that it is a living being although you do not yet know what kind of a living being it is.   The negative attributes have this in common with the positive, that they necessarily circumscribe the object to some extent, although such circumscription consists only in the exclusion of what otherwise would not be excluded.   In the following point, however, the negative attributes are dis-tinguished from the positive.   The positive attributes although not peculiar to one thing, describe a portion of what we desire to know, either some part of its essence or some of its accidents ; the negative attributes, on the other hand, do not, as regards the essence of the thing which we desire to know, in any way tell us what it is, except it be indirectly, as has been shown in the instance given by us.

" After this introduction, I would observe that— as has already been shown—God's existence is absolute, that it includes no composition, and that we comprehend only the fact that He exists, not His essence.9 Consequently it is a false assumption to hold that He has any positive attribute ; for He does not possess existence in addition to His essence. It therefore cannot be said that the one may be described as an attribute of the other ; much less has He in addition to His existence a compound essence, consisting of two constituent elements to which the attribute could refer ; still less has He accidents which could be described by an attribute. Hence it is clear that He has no positive attribute whatever " (*Guide* I, 58).

" He is not a magnitude that any quality resulting from quantity as such could be possessed by Him ; He is not affected by external influences, and therefore does not possess any quality resulting from emotion. He is not subject to physical conditions, and therefore does not possess strength or similar qualities; He is not an animate being, that He should have a certain disposition of the soul or acquire certain properties, as meekness, modesty, etc., or be in a state to which animate beings as such are subject, as, e.g., in that of health or illness. Hence it follows that no attribute coming under the head of quality, in its widest sense, can be predicated of God. Consequently, these three classes of attributes, describing the essence of a thing, or part of the essence, or a quality of it, are clearly inadmissible in reference to God, for they imply composition, which is out of question as regards the Creator. We say, with regard to this latter point, that He is absolutely One " (*Guide* I, 52).

The view which Maimonides held of the divine attributes led him to the paradoxical conclusion that the greater our knowledge of God, the less are we able to affirm of Him.

" The following question might perhaps be asked : Since there is no possibility of obtaining a knowledge of the true essence of God, and since it has also been proved that the only thing that man can apprehend of Him is the fact that He exists, and that all positive attributes are inadmissible, as has been shown ; what is the difference among those who have obtained a knowledge of God ?   Must not the knowledge obtained by our teacher Moses and by Solomon be the same as that obtained by any one of the lowest class of philosophers, since there can be no addition to this knowledge ?   But, on the other hand, it is generally accepted among theologians and also among philosophers that there can be a great difference between two persons as regards the knowledge of God obtained by them.

" Know that this is really the case, that those who have obtained a knowledge of God differ greatly from each other, for in the same way as by each additional attribute an object is more specified and is brought nearer to the true apprehension of the observer, so by each additional negative attribute you advance toward the knowledge of God, and you are nearer to it than he who does not negative, in reference to God, those qualities which you are convinced by proof must be negatived.   There may thus be a man who after having earnestly devoted many years to the pursuit of one science and to the true understanding of its principles, till he is fully convinced of its truths, has obtained as the sole result of this study the conviction that a certain quality must be negatived in reference to God, and the capacity of demonstrating that it is impossible to apply it to Him. . . .

" It will now be clear to you that every time you establish by proof the negation of a thing in reference to God, you become more perfect ; while with every additional positive assertion you follow your imagination and recede from the true knowledge of God " (*Guide* I, 59).

§5. *The Unity of God.* Having expounded Maimonides' general view of God's attributes, we may proceed to deal with specific qualities. First in importance is the Unity of God. Maimonides places it second in his enumeration of the Scriptural commandments.

" The second ordinance is the commandment which He commanded us—to believe firmly in the Unity, i.e., we should believe that the Maker of existence and its First Cause is One ; according to His declaration, ' Hear, O Israel, the Lord is our God, the Lord is One ' (Deut. vi. 4). In many passages of Rabbinic literature you will find such statements as, ' On condition that you proclaim the Unity of My name ', ' On condition that you proclaim My Unity ', etc. By such a phrase they intend that He in fact redeemed us from bondage and performed for us the benefits and kindnesses which He did, on the condition that we believe in the Unity ; and we are indeed under this obligation. The Rabbis often speak of ' the commandment concerning the Unity '. They further designate this commandment ' the sovereignty of Heaven ' ; they use the expression ' for the purpose of receiving upon oneself the yoke of the kingdom of Heaven '— meaning the acknowledgment of the Unity[10] and the belief therein " (*Mitswot*, Command. II).

The Unity of God is likewise the second of the Principles of Faith which he formulated, and he states it in the following terms :

" This implies that this Cause of all is one ; not one of a genus or of a species, and not as one human being who is a compound divisible into many unities ;

not a unity like the ordinary material body which is one in number but takes on endless divisions and parts. But He, the exalted One, is a unity in the sense that there is no unity like His in any way. This is the second cardinal doctrine of Faith which is indicated by the assertion, ' Hear, O Israel, the Lord is our God, the Lord is One ' " (C.M., Introduction to *Hélek*).

" God is one ; He is not two or more than two, but one. The oneness of any of the single things existent in the Universe is unlike His Unity. He is not one as a species, since this includes numerous individuals ; nor one as a body, since this is divisible into parts and sections ; but a Unity which is unique in the world.

" If there were several deities, they would necessarily be corporeal; because things that can be numbered, which are alike in their essence, are distinguishable one from another only by the accidents which occur in bodily forms. If, then, the Creator were corporeal, He would have limitations, because it is impossible for a body to be without a limit ; and everyone whose body has a limit must likewise be limited in power.

" As for our God, blessed be His name, since His power is without limit and never ceases, seeing that the Sphere revolves continuously, His power must be other than physical strength. And since He is not a body, the accidents of bodies cannot occur to Him, so that He should be divided and distinguished from any other being. Consequently it is impossible that He should be other than One " (*Yad, Yesodé ha-Torah* I, 7).

Maimonides advances several proofs for God's Unity. One which is based on his philosophical

Propositions is too intricate to quote ; but the following are more easily understood.

" If there were two Gods, they would necessarily have one element in common by virtue of which they were Gods, and another element by which they were distinguished from each other and existed as two Gods. The distinguishing element would either be in both different from the property common to both —in that case both of them would consist of different elements and neither of them would be the First Cause, or have absolutely independent existence. But their existence would depend on certain causes[11]—or the distinguishing element would only in one of them be different from the element common to both : then that being could not have absolute independence.

" *Another proof of the Unity of God.* It has been demonstrated by proof that the whole existing world is one organic body, all parts of which are connected together[12]; also, that the influences of the Spheres above pervade the earthly substance and prepare it for its forms. Hence it is impossible to assume that one deity be engaged in forming one part and another deity in forming another part of that organic body, of which all parts are closely connected together. A duality could only be imagined in this way, either that at one time the one deity is active, the other at another time, or that both act simultaneously, nothing being done except by both together. The first alternative is certainly absurd for many reasons ; if at the time the one deity be active the other *could* also be active, there is no reason why the one deity should then act and the other not ; if, on the other hand, it be impossible for the one deity to act when the other is at work, there must be some other cause besides these deities which at a certain time enables the one to act and disables the other. Such difference would not be caused by time, since time is without change, and the object of the action likewise remains one and the same organic whole. Besides, if two deities existed in this way, both would be subject to the relations of time, since their actions would depend on time[13]; they would also in the moment of acting pass from potentiality to actuality and require an agent for such transition; their essence would besides include possibility of existence.[14]

" It is equally absurd to assume that both together produce everything in existence, and that neither of them does anything alone; for when a number of forces must be united for a certain result, none of these forces acts of its own accord, and none is by itself the immediate cause of that result, but their union is the immediate cause. It has, furthermore, been proved that the action of the absolute cannot be due to an external cause.[15] The union is also an act which presupposes a cause effecting that union, and if that cause be one, it is undoubtedly God; but if it also consists of a number of separate forces, a cause is required for the combination of these forces, as in the first case. Finally, one simple being must be arrived at that is the cause of the existence of the Universe which is one whole. It would make no difference whether we assumed that the First Cause had produced the Universe by *creatio ex nihilo*, or whether the Universe co-existed with the First Cause. It is thus clear how we can prove the Unity of God from the fact that this Universe is one whole " (*Guide* II, 1).

§6. *The Incorporeality of God.* Inseparably connected with the doctrine of God's Unity is that of His

Incorporeality. Maimonides usually couples them together in his philosophical discussions. He makes it the third of his Principles of Faith.

" The removal of materiality from God. This signifies that this Unity is not a body nor the power of a body, nor can the accidents of bodies overtake Him, as, e.g., motion and rest, whether in the essential or accidental sense. . . . Wherever in the Scriptures God is spoken of with the attributes of material bodies, like motion, standing, sitting, speaking and such like, all these are figures of speech, as the Sages said, ' The Torah speaks in the language of men ' " (C.M., Introduction to *Ḥélek*).

" Behold it is explicitly taught in the Torah and the Prophets that the Holy One, blessed be He, is not corporeal ; as it is said, ' The Lord He is God in heaven above and upon the earth beneath ' (Deut. iv. 39). But a body cannot be in two places at the same time ! It is further said, ' Ye saw no manner of form ' (*ibid.*, 15) ; and it is also stated, ' To whom then will ye liken Me that I should be equal ? ' (Isa. xl. 25). Were He a body, He would be like other bodies.

" If it be so that He is incorporeal, what of the Scriptural phrases : ' under His feet ' (Exod. xxiv. 10), ' written with the finger of God ' (*ibid.* xxxi. 18), ' the hand of the Lord ' (*ibid.* ix. 3), ' the eyes of the Lord ' (Deut. xi. 12), ' the ears of the Lord ' (Numb. xi. 18), and other expressions like these ? All these terms are used in accordance with the mental capacity of human beings who can only comprehend corporeal beings. The Torah therefore speaks in human language, and all these are merely metaphorical expressions, the same as ' If I whet My glittering sword ' (Deut. xxxii. 41). Has He, then, a sword, or does He slay with a sword ! It is only a simile ; and in like manner all the expressions quoted above are metaphorical.

" A proof of this is that one Prophet declares that he saw the Holy One, blessed be He, ' His garment white as snow ' (Dan. vii. 9), whereas another saw Him 'with crimsoned garments' (Isa. lxiii. 1). Moses, our teacher, himself saw Him by the Red Sea like a warrior waging battle (Exod. xv. 3), and upon Sinai like the leader of a congregation wrapped in the *Tallit*[16] —proving that He had neither likeness nor form, but all this was only in prophetic imagery and vision " (*Yad, Yesodé ha-Torah*, I, 8f).

As with the Unity of God, Maimonides proves His incorporeality with the aid of the philosophical Propositions. Another argument offered by him is :

" Every corporeal object is composed of matter and form[17] ; every compound of these two elements requires an agent for effecting their combination. Besides, it is evident that a body is divisible and has dimensions ; a body is thus undoubtedly subject to accidents. Consequently nothing corporeal can be a unity, either because everything corporeal is divisible or because it is a compound ; that is to say, it can logically be analysed into two elements ; because a body can only be said to be a certain body when the distinguishing element is added to the corporeal substratum, and must therefore include two elements ; but it has been proved that the Absolute admits of no dualism whatever " (*Guide* II, 1).

§7. *God is timeless and spaceless.* The fourth of the Principles of Faith is called by Maimonides " The Priority of God ", which he defines as follows : " This means that the Unity Whom we have described is first in the absolute sense. No existent thing outside

Him is primary in relation to Him" (C.M., Introd. to *Hélek*). Treating this idea from the philosophical standpoint, he insists that time has no meaning with reference to God.

" When we say God is the First, to express that He has not been created, the term ' First ' is decidedly inaccurate, for it can in its true sense only be applied to a being that is subject to the relation of time ; the latter, however, is an accident to motion which again is connected with a body. Besides the attribute ' first ' is a relative term, being in regard to time the same as the terms ' long ' and ' short ' are in regard to a line. Both expressions, ' first ' and ' created ', are equally inadmissible in reference to any being to which the attribute of time is not applicable, just as we do not say ' crooked ' or ' straight ' in reference to taste, ' salted ' or ' insipid ' in reference to the voice.

" These subjects are not unknown to those who have accustomed themselves to seek a true understanding of the things, and to establish their properties in accordance with the abstract notions which the mind has formed of them, and who are not misled by the inaccuracy of the words employed. All attributes, such as ' the first ', ' the last ', occurring in the Scriptures in reference to God, are as metaphorical as the expressions ' ear ' and ' eye '. They simply signify that God is not subject to any change or innovation whatever ; they do not imply that God can be described by time, or that there is any comparison between Him and any other being as regards time, and that He is called on that account ' the first ' and ' the last ' " (*Guide* I, 57).

" It is quite clear that there is no relation between God and time or space. For time is an accident connected with motion, in so far as the latter includes the relation of anteriority and posteriority, and is expressed by number,[18] as is explained in books devoted to this subject; and since motion is one of the conditions to which only material bodies are subject, and God is immaterial, there can be no relation between Him and time. Similarly there is no relation between Him and space "[19] (*Guide* I, 52).

§8. *God and the impossible.* Although Maimonides firmly held the doctrine of divine omnipotence, he yet maintains that there are things impossible for God to do.

" That which is impossible has a permanent and constant property which is not the result of some agent and cannot in any way change, and consequently we do not ascribe to God the power of doing what is impossible. No thinking man denies the truth of this maxim ; none ignore it but such as have no idea of Logic. There is, however, a difference of opinion among philosophers with reference to the existence of any particular thing. Some of them consider its existence to be impossible and hold that God cannot produce the thing in question, whilst others think that it is possible, and that God can create it if He pleases to do so. E.g., all philosophers consider that it is impossible for one substratum to have at the same moment two opposite properties, or for the elementary components of a thing, substance and accident, to interchange, so that the substance becomes accident and the accident becomes substance, or for a material substance to be without accident. Likewise it is impossible that God should produce a being like Himself, or annihilate, corporify or change Himself. The power of God is not assumed to extend to any of these impossibilities. . . .

" There are things which are impossible, whose existence cannot be admitted, and whose creation is excluded from the power of God ; and the assumption that God does not change their nature does not imply weakness in God or a limit to His power. Consequently things impossible remain impossible, and do not depend on the action of an agent " (*Guide* III, 15).

We may here insert Maimonides' explanation of miracles. It is based on a Rabbinic theory. The difficulty they raise is that a change in the laws of Nature seems to imply a change in the will of God and would be an imputation against His perfect knowledge. If He foresaw the special circumstances which required the performance of the miracle, why did He not provide in advance means for meeting that ccntingency ? The reply which Maimonides makes is that God did make that provision. The miracle was ordained at the time of Creation and thus comes within the laws of Nature.

" Our Sages said very strange things as regards miracles—they are found in *Beréshit Rabba* and in *Midrash Kohélet*[20]—viz., that the miracles are to some extent also natural ; for they say, when God created the Universe with its present physical properties, He made it part of these properties that they should produce certain miracles at certain times, and the sign of a Prophet consisted in the fact that God told him to declare when a certain thing will take place, but the thing itself was effected according to the fixed laws of Nature. If this is really the meaning of the passage referred to, it testifies to the greatness of the author, and shows that he held it to be impossible that there should be a change in the laws of Nature or a change in the will of God as regards the physical properties of things after they have once been established " (*Guide* II, 29).

§9. *God's Knowledge*. Maimonides' view on this attribute is that it is incomprehensible to the human mind, because " knowledge " as ascribed to God has no similarity with the knowledge possessed by man. God's knowledge is identical with His essence. " He is His knowledge, and His Knowledge is He ", is his final conclusion   (C.M., *Eight Chapters* VIII).

" The Holy One, blessed be He, perceives His essence and knows it just as it is. But He does not know with a knowledge which is distinct from Himself in the manner that we know. We and our knowledge are not one ; but with the Creator, blessed be He, He, His knowledge and His life are one from every point of view and in every mode of Unity. If He were a living being with life, and cognisant with a knowledge, distinct from Himself, there would be several deities, viz., He, His life and His knowledge.[21] This, however, is not so ; but He is one from every point of view and in every mode of Unity.

" Hence you may say that He is the knower, the known and knowledge itself all in one. Such an idea as this the mouth has not the power of expressing, nor the ear of grasping, nor the human mind of perfectly comprehending. . . . He does not perceive creatures and know them by means of the creatures, as we know them ; but He knows them by means of Himself, so that from that fact that He knows Himself, He knows everything, because everything is dependent for its existence upon Him " (*Yad, Yesodé ha-Torah* II, 10).

The statement that God is " the knower, the known and knowledge itself all in one " is demonstrated in the *Guide :*

" There is no doubt that he who has not studied any works on mental philosophy, who has not comprehended the nature of the mind, who has no knowledge of its essence, and considers it in no other way than he would consider the nature of whiteness and of blackness, will find this subject extremely difficult, and to him our principle that the *intellectus*, the *intelligens* and the *intelligibile*[22] are in God one and the same thing, will appear as unintelligible as if we said that the whiteness, the whitening substance and the material which is whitened are one and the same thing. And, indeed, many ignorant people refute at once our principle by using such comparisons. Even amongst those who imagine that they are wise, many find this subject difficult and are of opinion that it is impossible for the mind to grasp the truth of this proposition, although it is a demonstrated truth, as has been shown by Metaphysicians. . . .

" All intellect is identical with its action[23] ; the intellect in action is not a thing different from its action, for the true nature and essence of the intellect is comprehension, and you must not think that the intellect in action is a thing existing by itself, separate from comprehension, and that comprehension is a different thing connected with it ; for the essence of the intellect is comprehension. In assuming an intellect in action you assume the comprehension of the thing comprehended. . . .

" Now it has been proved that God is an intellect which always is in action and that there is in Him at no time a mere potentiality, that He does comprehend at one time and is without comprehension at another time, but He comprehends constantly ; consequently He and the things comprehended are one and the same thing, that is to say, His essence[24] ; and the act of comprehending because of which it is said that He comprehends, is the intellect itself, which is likewise

His essence ; God is therefore always the *intellectus*, the *intelligens* and the *intelligibile*.

" We have thus shown that the identity of the intellect, the *intelligens* and the *intelligibile*, is not only a fact as regards the Creator, but as regards all intellect when in action.²⁵ There is, however, this difference, that from time to time our intellect passes over from mere potentiality to reality, and that the pure intellect, i.e., the active intellect, finds sometimes obstacles, though not in itself but accidentally in some external cause. . . . God alone, and none besides Him, is an intellect constantly in action, and there is, neither in Himself nor in anything beside Him, any obstacle whereby His comprehension would be hindered. Therefore He always includes the *intelligens*, the *intellectus* and the *intelligibile*, and His essence is at the same time the *intelligens*, the *intelligibile* and the *intellectus*, as is necessarily the case with all intellect in action " (*Guide* I, 68).

If it be true that God's knowledge is identical with His essence, it must be absolute. It cannot change and it cannot increase ; it remains constant.

" It is generally agreed upon that God cannot at a certain time acquire knowledge which He did not possess previously ; it is further impossible that His knowledge should include any plurality, even according to those who admit the Divine attributes. As these things have been fully proved, we, who assert the teaching of the Torah, believe that God's knowledge of many things does not imply any plurality ; His knowledge does not change like ours when the objects of His knowledge change.

" Similarly we say that the various events are known to Him before they take place ; He constantly knows them, and therefore no fresh knowledge is acquired by Him. E.g., He knows that a certain person is non-existent at present, will come to existence at a certain time, will continue to exist for some time and will then cease to exist. When this person, in accordance with God's foreknowledge concerning him, comes into existence, God's knowledge is not increased ; it contains nothing that it did not contain before, but something has taken place that was known previously exactly as it has taken place. This theory implies that God's knowledge extends to things not in existence and includes also the infinite. We nevertheless accept it, and contend that we may attribute to God the knowledge of a thing which does not yet exist, but the existence of which God foresees and is able to effect. But that which never exists cannot be an object of His knowledge ; just as our knowledge does not comprise things which we consider as non-existing " (*Guide* III, 20).

" Our knowledge is acquired and increased in proportion to the things known by us. This is not the case with God. His knowledge of things is not derived from the things themselves ; if this were the case, there would be change and plurality in His knowledge ; on the contrary, the things are in accordance with His eternal knowledge, which has established their actual properties and made part of them purely spiritual, another part material and constant as regards its individual members, a third part material and changeable as regards the individual beings according to eternal and constant laws. Plurality, acquisition and change in His knowledge is therefore impossible. He fully knows His unchangeable essence, and has thus a knowledge of all that results from any of His acts.

" It we were to try to understand in what manner this is done, it would be the same as if we tried to be the same as God and to make our knowledge identical with His knowledge.[26]   Those who seek the truth and admit what is true must believe that nothing is hidden from God; that everything is revealed to His knowledge which is identical with His essence ; that this kind of knowledge cannot be comprehended by us ; for if we knew its method, we would possess that intellect by which such knowledge could be acquired.   Such intellect does not exist except in God, and is at the same time His essence " (*Guide* III, 21).

The problem of God's knowledge and man's free will is discussed in Chapter VIII, §6.

CHAPTER IV

THE WORSHIP OF GOD

§1. *God alone to be worshipped.* The fifth Principle of Faith declares :

" That it is He (be He exalted !) Who must be worshipped, aggrandised, and made known by His greatness and the obedience shown to Him. This must not be done to any existing beings lower than He—not to the Angels nor the Spheres nor the elements, or the things which are compounded from them. For these are all fashioned in accordance with the works they are intended to perform. They have no judgment or free will, but only a love for Him (be He exalted !). Let us adopt no mediators to enable ourselves to draw near unto God, but let the thoughts be directed to Him, and turned away from whatsoever is below Him. This fifth principle is a prohibition of idolatry. The greater part of the Torah is taken up with the prohibition of idol-worship " (C.M., Introd. to *Ḥélek*).

§2. *Prayer.* Since God is worshipped mainly through prayer, we first give Maimonides' teachings on this subject.

" We are told to offer up prayers to God, in order to establish firmly the true principle that God takes notice of our ways, that He can make them successful if we worship Him or disastrous if we disobey Him, that success and failure are not the result of chance or accident. . . . For the belief of the people that their troubles are mere accidents[1] causes them to continue in their evil principles and their wrong actions, and prevents them from abandoning their evil ways. . . . For this reason God commanded us to pray to Him, to entreat Him, and to cry before Him in time of trouble " (*Guide* III, 36).

This is the lowest form of prayer, viz., petition ; the higher form, viz., communion, is indicated in the following passage :

" We must bear in mind that all such religious acts as reading the Torah, praying, and the performance of other precepts, serve exclusively as the means of causing us to occupy and fill our mind with the precepts of God and free it from worldly business ; for we are thus, as it were, in communication with God and undisturbed by any other thing. If we, however, pray with the motion of our lips and our face toward the wall,[2] but at the same time think of our business ; if we read the Torah with our tongue whilst our heart is occupied with the building of our house, and we do not think of what we are reading ; if we perform the commandments only with our limbs, we are like those who are engaged in digging in the ground or hewing wood in the forest, without reflecting on the nature of those acts, or by Whom they are commanded, or what is their object. We must not imagine that in this way we attain the highest perfection ; on the contrary, we are then like those in reference to whom Scripture says, ' Thou art near in their mouth, and far from their reins ' (Jer. xii. 2). . . .

" Turn your thoughts away from everything while you read the *Shema'* or during the *Tefillah*,[3] and do not content yourself with being devout when you read the first verse of the *Shema'* or the first paragraph of the

Tefillah.4 When you have successfully practised this for many years, try in reading the Torah or listening to it,5 to have all your heart and all your thought occupied with understanding what you read or hear. After some time when you have mastered this, accustom yourself to have your mind free from all other thoughts when you read any portion of the other books of the Prophets, or when you say any blessing, and to have your attention directed exclusively to the perception and the understanding of what you utter. When you have succeeded in properly performing these acts of divine service, and you have your thought, during their performance, entirely abstracted from worldly affairs, take then care that your thought be not disturbed by thinking of your wants or of superfluous things. In short, think of worldly matters when you eat, drink, bathe, talk with your wife and little children, or when you converse with other people. These times, which are frequent and long, I think, must suffice to you for reflecting on everything that is necessary as regards business, household and health. But when you are engaged in the performance of religious duties, have your mind exclusively directed to what you are doing.

" When you are alone by yourself, when you are awake on your couch, be careful to meditate in such precious moments on nothing but the intellectual worship of God, viz., to approach Him and to minister before Him in the true manner which I have described to you—not in hollow emotions. This I consider as the highest perfection wise men can attain by the above training " (*Guide* III, 51).

In a remarkable passage in his *Pirké ha-Hatslaḥah*, " Chapters of Bliss ",6 Maimonides describes the effects of ecstatic prayer.

"He who prays should turn to God, standing on his feet, feeling delight in his heart and expressing it with his lips, his hands outstretched, his organs of speech intent on utterance, and the rest of his bodily organs shaking and trembling. He will not cease throughout his prayer to issue pleasant sounds, concentrating and preparing himself, supplicating, bending the knee, prostrating himself, weeping, because he is in the presence of the great and awesome King. There comes upon him a sense of sinking and shuddering until he finds himself in the world of Intelligences.7 The soul of the honourable man is humbled and it frees him from the senses, so that he is as though withdrawn from them and with his imaginative faculty he beholds and hears things in which there is no doubt. Inasmuch as the future and the past are in the same degree with respect to those things, since they (the future and past) exist together in matters elucidated to the Intelligences, he looks upon future events as though he were gazing at past events, and those which he recounts are true".

The text that follows is in a doubtful state, but the general sense is : He reaches that stage where he is above the effects of war, famine, and pestilence, even death and life. Whatever he lacks is supplied to him. He distinguishes between friend and foe ; nothing which he needs is withheld from him, and he is in the category of "the living, perfect, intelligent". He is then made conscious of his deficiencies until he is filled with remorse and weeps bitterly (*Responsa* II, 32c).

§3. *Love and fear of God.* Two emotions are aroused by the worship of the Most High, which are usually denoted as love and fear.

" God declares in plain words that it is the object
of all religious acts to produce in man fear of God
and obedience to His word—the state of mind which
it is our duty to seek. Comp. ' If thou wilt not observe
to do all the words of this law that are written in this
book, that thou mayest fear this glorious and fearful
Name, the Lord thy God ' (Deut. xxviii. 58). Consider
how clearly it is stated here that the only object and
aim of ' all the words of this law ' is to make men
fear ' the glorious and fearful Name '. That this end
is attained by certain acts we learn likewise from the
phrase employed in this verse : ' If thou wilt not
observe *to do* . . . that thou mayest fear '. For
this phrase clearly shows that fear of God is inculcated
into our hearts when we act in accordance with the
positive and the negative precepts. But the truths
which the Torah teaches us—the knowledge of God's
Existence and Unity—create in us love of God. You
know how frequently the Torah exhorts us to love
God. Comp. ' And thou shalt love the Lord thy God
with all thine heart, and with all thy soul, and with
all thy might ' (*ibid*. vi. 5). The two objects, love
and fear of God, are acquired by two different means.
The love is the result of the truths taught in the Torah,
including the true knowledge of the Existence of God ;
whilst fear of God is produced by the practices
prescribed in the Torah " (*Guide* III, 52).

" This glorious and fearful God commands us to
love Him and to fear Him ; for it is said : ' And thou
shalt love the Lord thy God ', and it is also said, ' Thou
shalt fear the Lord thy God ' (*ibid*. 13). Which is the
way to love and fear Him ? At the time when one
reflects on His works and His wonderful and stupendous
creations, and from them perceives His wisdom which
is incomparable and unbounded, he immediately loves,

praises, glorifies, and yearns with an ardent longing to know the great God. As David said, ' My soul thirsteth for God, for the living God ' (Ps. xlii. 3). And when one reflects upon these very things, he immediately starts back, is struck with fear and terror, and is conscious that he is a creature insignificant, lowly and immature, standing with only a slight and scanty knowledge ; as David said, ' When I consider Thy heavens, the work of Thy fingers . . . what is man that Thou art mindful of him ? ' (Ps. viii. 4f) " (*Yad, Yesodé ha-Torah* II, 1f).

" He commanded us to love Him (exalted be He), in that we should reflect and meditate upon His ordinances, decrees and deeds until we comprehend Him and delight with extreme pleasure in the comprehension of Him. That is the love prescribed for us. . . . The Rabbis declared that this commandment also includes the idea that we should invite all mankind to His worship and to belief in Him.[8] Exactly as, when you love a person, you proclaim his praises and eulogise him and invite other people to be friendly with him, so—by way of simile—when you love God truly in accordance with the comprehension of His essence which has been attained by you, you will undoubtedly invite the careless and ignorant to know the truth which you know. . . .

" He commanded us to believe firmly in the fear of Him (exalted be He), and the dread of Him, and not be like those confident people who rest in security. On the contrary, we should stand in awe of the imposition of His punishment at all times " (*Mitswot*, Command. IIIf).

Although both these emotions are aroused in man, the feeling of love should predominate as the motive for the worship of God.

" Let not a man say, I will fulfil the commandments of the Torah, occupy myself with its wisdom, for the purpose of obtaining all the blessings which are written therein, or for the purpose of meriting the life of the world to come ; and I will refrain from the transgressions against which the Torah utters a warning for the purpose of escaping the curses which are written therein, or for the purpose of not being cut off from the life of the world to come. It is not becoming to serve God in this manner ; for He who serves God thus performs the service from fear, which is not the standard of the Prophets or the wise. Indeed, none serve the Lord in this manner except ignorant men, or women and children who are taught to serve Him from fear, until their mind is developed and they serve Him from love.

" He who serves God from love occupies himself with the Torah and the commandments and walks in the paths of wisdom, not for the sake of any worldly advantage, nor from fear of calamity, nor for the purpose of acquiring good fortune ; but he practises truth because it is truth, and the good which is its consequence follows in due course. This standard is exceedingly lofty and not every wise man can attain it. This is the standard which the patriarch Abraham reached, whom the Holy One, blessed be He, called His ' friend ' (Isa. xli. 8), because he had served Him only from love. This is the standard which the Holy One, blessed be He, ordained for us through Moses ; as it is said, ' And thou shalt love the Lord thy God '. For when a man loves the Lord with that love which is due to Him, he will as a matter of course fulfil all the commandments from love.

" What is the love which is due to Him ? It is that one shall love the Lord with a love so great and ardent until his soul is bound up in the love of the Lord, and consequently he ever grows in it. He is like a love-sick man whose mind is never free from his love for a certain woman and grows in it whether sitting or rising, both when eating and drinking—greater even than this must be the love of God in the heart of His lovers who continually grow more fervent, as He commanded us, ' with all thy heart and with all thy soul '. That is what Solomon intended when he said metaphorically, ' For I am lovesick ' (Cant. ii. 5). The whole of the Song of Songs is an allegory on this theme " (*Yad, Teshubah* X, 1-3).

§4. *Different degrees in worship of God.* Since the worship of God depends upon the " knowledge " of God and men inevitably differ in their capacity for attaining this knowledge, it must follow that there are different degrees in the worship of Him. Maimonides explains this by means of a parable :

" A king is in his palace, and all his subjects are partly in the country and partly abroad. Of the former, some have their backs turned towards the king's palace and their faces in another direction ; and some are desirous and zealous to go to the palace, seeking ' to inquire in his temple ' and to minister before him, but have not yet seen even the face of the wall of the house. Of those that desire to go to the palace, some reach it and go round about in search of the entrance gate ; others have passed through the gate and walk about in the ante-chamber ; and others have succeeded in entering into the inner part of the palace and being in the same room with the king in the royal palace. But even the latter do not immediately on entering the palace see the king or speak to him ; for, after having entered the inner part of the palace, another effort is required before they can stand before the king—at a distance or close by—hear his words, or speak to him.

" I will now explain the simile which I have made. The people who are abroad are all those that have no religion, neither one based on speculation nor one received by tradition. Such are the extreme Turks that wander about in the North,9 the Kushites10 who live in the South, and those in our country who are like these. I consider these as irrational beings and not as human beings ; they are below mankind but above monkeys, since they have the form and shape of man and a mental faculty above that of the monkey.

" Those who are in the country, but have their backs turned towards the king's palace, are those who possess religion, belief and thought, but happen to hold false doctrines, which they either adopted in consequence of great mistakes made in their own speculations or received from others who misled them. Because of these doctrines they recede more and more from the royal palace the more they seem to proceed. These are worse than the first class, and under certain circumstances it may become necessary to slay them and to extirpate their doctrines, in order that others should not be misled.11

" Those who desire to arrive at the palace and to enter it, but have never yet seen it, are the mass of religious people ; the multitude that observe the divine commandments but are ignorant. Those who arrive at the palace but go round about it are those who devote themselves exclusively to the study of the practical law ; they believe traditionally in true principles of faith and learn the practical worship of God, but are not trained in philosophical treatment of the principles of the Torah, and do not endeavour to establish the truth of their faith by proof. Those who undertake to investigate the principles of religion have come into the ante-chamber ; and there is no doubt that these can also be divided into different grades. But those who have succeeded in finding a proof for everything that can be proved, who have a true knowledge of God so far as a true knowledge can be attained, and are near the truth wherever an approach to the truth is possible, they have reached the goal and are in the palace in which the king lives " (*Guide* III, 51)

Like Hillel who affirmed that " the ignorant man cannot be pious ",[12] Maimonides despised those men whose religion consisted in a blind, unquestioning performance of ritual without any rational basis to support it. In his *Ethical Will* which he addressed to his son, he warns him against intercourse with the Jews of certain districts, " because they are greater fools, in my estimation, than all other men, although they are extremely orthodox ; but God being my witness, I regard them as no better than the Karaites[13] who deny the Oral Law, since all their occupation with the Torah, Scriptures and Talmud is brainless " (*Responsa* II, 40b).

§5. *Judaism and other Religions.* Maimonides naturally believed that of all religions Judaism was the only Faith revealed by God, and it alone was in every respect true. He declared :

" The desire of the other religions is to make their falsehoods resemble the Faith instituted by God ; but the divine work cannot be like the handiwork of man except to a child who has no knowledge of either. The difference between our religion and the other religions, to which it is sought to liken them, is none other than like the difference between the living, sentient man and the image carved by the workman from wood, or moulded from such metals as silver or gold, or sculptured from a block of marble or other stone and shaped into human form. The fool who knows neither the divine wisdom nor human work, on beholding that image resembling a man in all his visible exterior and like to him in build and appearance, thinks that it was made in exactly the same way as the human being is made, since he is ignorant of the internality of both ; but the wise man, who possesses that knowledge, is aware that inside the image there is no functioning organ " (*Iggéret Téman, Responsa* II, 2a).

For all his exclusive attachment to Judaism, Maimonides adopted a remarkably tolerant attitude towards other religions. Although he, of course, regarded Jesus and Mohammed as false prophets, mainly on the ground that their teachings often militated against the unchangeable ordinances of the Torah, he yet refers to their activities as being, under God's wisdom, "nothing else than a means for preparing the way for the king Messiah" (*Yad, Melachim* XI, 4).[14] In other words, the two daughter-religions, were the means of spreading the knowledge of Israel's God and thereby hastened the advent of His Kingdom.

In answer to a correspondent he wrote : " It is permissible to teach Christians the commandments and the doctrine of reward and punishment, for a considerable number of them may recant. They acknowledge that our Torah was given to us from heaven by our teacher Moses (peace be upon him !), and it is regarded in its entirety by them as Holy Writ, although they at times interpret it wrongly " (*Responsa* I, 14b).

Of the Mohammedans he wrote : " They are in no way idolaters, and idol-worship has long passed from their mouth and heart. They ascribe Unity to God as is proper, a Unity without defect. . . . And if anyone should say that the temple which they praise is a house of idolatry and idol-worship[15] is stored there which their fathers used to worship ; what if they do prostrate themselves before it to-day, so long as their heart is directed to heaven ! " (*Responsa* I, 34d.)

Towards the sect of Karaites, who practised the ordinances of the Pentateuch but refused to acknowledge the authority of the Oral Law as expounded by the Rabbis, he likewise assumed a liberal attitude. Although most of his contemporaries regarded them with bitter hostility, he declared : " These Karaites, who reside here in No-Ammon, Egypt, Damascus, and other places of Arabia and elsewhere, deserve to be treated with respect, and we should associate with them and conduct ourselves towards them with humility, truth and peace, so long as they, on their side, conduct themselves towards us properly, cease to slander the Rabbis of our time, and especially withhold their gibes at the words of the sainted Rabbis of the Mishnah and Talmud, in whose teachings and customs, established for us by their command and by the command of Moses, derived from God, we walk. On those conditions, it is proper for us to respect them, inquire after their welfare even in their own homes, circumcise their children even on the Sabbath,[16] bury their dead and mourn with them in their bereavements " (*Responsa* I, 35c).

In reply to a proselyte who inquired whether, when reciting the Hebrew liturgy in private or with the Congregation, it was right for him to utter such phrases as " Our God and God of *our fathers* ",[17] " Who hast sanctified *us* with Thy commandments and commanded *us* ", " Who brought *us* out of the land of Egypt ", etc., he wrote :

" It is your duty to say them all as prescribed and do not change a single word. Exactly as the man born an Israelite prays, so do you likewise whether you pray in private or whether you conduct a service in public. The root of the matter is that our father Abraham it was who taught all peoples and informed them of the true religion and the Unity of God, spurned idolatry and overthrew its worship, brought many children beneath the wings of the *Shechinah* and instructed them, and exhorted his sons and the members of his household to observe the way of the Lord. Therefore every one who becomes a convert until the end of all generations, and every one who acknowledges the Unity of God as it is written in the Torah, is a disciple of our father Abraham and a member of his household. . . . Consequently Abraham is the father of his seed, the pure ones who walk in his ways, and the father of his disciples, viz., proselytes. For that reason you have the right to say, ' Our God and God of *our fathers* ', because the patriarch Abraham is your father. . . . Let not your descent be lightly esteemed in your eyes. If we trace our genealogical tree to Abraham, Isaac and Jacob, you may trace yours to the Creator of the Universe " (*Responsa* I, 34a, b).[18]

In agreement with Rabbinical teaching he maintained : " You must know that the Merciful One demands the heart,[19] and the criterion is the intention of the heart. Therefore the teachers of truth, our Rabbis, declared, ' The pious of the gentiles have a portion in the world to come ',[20] if they have attained what is due from them to attain relative to a knowledge of the Creator, and corrected their soul with the virtues. And there is no doubt about the matter that whoever corrects his soul with purity of morals and purity of knowledge in the faith of the Creator will assuredly be of the children of the world to come. On that account our Rabbis stated, ' Even the gentile who occupies himself with the Torah of Moses is equal to the High Priest ' "[21] (*Responsa* II, 23d *et seq.*).

§6. *Idolatry.* The point which is most strongly emphasised in the fifth Principle of Faith is that there must be no intermediary between God and man. To interpose any object of worship is idolatry. Maimonides very acutely points out that the idol-worshipper does not necessarily believe that the image of wood and stone is actually a deity with power to respond to prayer, but the image is the intermediary whose task it is to act on behalf of the Creator. This is an interpretation confirmed by modern anthropological science.

" You must know that idolaters when worshipping idols do not believe that there is no God besides them ; and no idolater ever did assume that any image made of metal, stone or wood has created the heavens and the earth, and still governs them. Idolatry is founded on the idea that a particular form represents the agent between God and His creatures " (*Guide* I, 36).

Maimonides attempts to trace how idolatry came into the world and corrupted the religious faith of mankind.

" In the days of Enosh,[22] the sons of men made a grievous error. Even the counsel of the wise men of that generation was perverted, and Enosh himself was also one of those who erred. Their error was this :

They said, Since God created these planets and Spheres to control the Universe, set them in the heights and invested them with glory, and they are servants which minister before Him, they must be worthy of being praised and glorified, and having homage paid to them. This must be the will of God, blessed be He, that we should exalt and glorify whatever He has exalted and made glorious ; just as a king desires that those who attend on him should be honoured since that is honour paid to the king himself.

" When this idea entered their mind, they began to build temples to the planets, offer sacrifices to them, praise them, glorify them with words, and bow down to them, for the purpose—according to their evil thought—of obtaining the favour of the Creator. This was the fundamental principle of idolatry, and so the worshippers who understood its principle used to declare. They did not assert that there was no God except that planet. . . .

" Later, as time passed, false prophets arose among the sons of men, who said that God had commanded them saying, Worship such and such a planet, or all the planets ; offer sacrifices and drink-offerings to it in such and such a manner, build a temple for it, and make an image of it ; so that all the people, women and children and all the other inhabitants of the earth may bow down to it.

" The false prophet displayed to them an image which he had invented in his own heart, saying to them that this was the image of such and such a planet, which had been revealed to him in his prophecy. In this manner they began to make images in temples, under trees, on the tops of mountains and on hills, to assemble together and bow down to them, declaring to all the people that this image had the power of doing good and harm, and it was proper to worship and fear it.

" Their priests used to say to them, By this service you will multiply and prosper ; do such and such and avoid doing such and such. Then other deceivers began to arise and declare that the planet itself, or some Sphere or Angel, spoke to them, saying, Worship me in such and such a manner—describing the mode of its worship—do so and so, avoid doing so and so. This thing spread throughout the world, viz., the worship of images with rites differing one from the other, the offering of sacrifices and prostrating oneself. After a time, the glorious and revered Name was forgotten from the mouth and mind of all mortals and they knew Him not. As the result of this, all the people of the earth, the women and children, knew only the image of wood and stone, and the temple built of stone, to which they were trained from their infancy to bow down and worship and swear by its name.

" Even the wise men among them, e.g., their priests, imagined that there was no other God except the planets and Spheres, for whose sake and in whose likeness those images had been made. But as for the Rock of the Universe, there was no man who perceived or knew Him, apart from a few individuals in the world, as, e.g., Enoch, Methuselah, Noah, Shem, and Eber. In this manner the world went on revolving until the pillar of the world was born, viz., Abraham our father " (*Yad, Akum* I, 1f).

§7. *Superstition a form of idolatry.* Consistent with the teaching that the destinies of man are decreed by God alone, Maimonides denied the existence of influences other than those controlled by the Creator

which can affect the life of the human being. This
denial cuts at the root of superstition, against which
he has strong things to say in his writings. Despite
the fact that even in the literature of the Rabbis
frequent reference is made to " evil spirits ", he refuses
to regard them as real entities. Thus the phrase *ruaḥ
ra'ah* is explained by him to mean in one place
" melancholia " (C.M., *Shabbat*, II, 5), and in another
" Any injury which befalls a man not through the
action of his fellow, whatever the cause be " (C.M.,
Erubin IV, 1).

Although, according to his theory, the Spheres are
a channel through which the will of the Creator passes
to earth, he sternly denounces astrology as a delusion
and a falsehood.[22a] He considers it as coming within
the category of idolatry.

" Witchcraft is intimately connected with astrology;
those that practise it assign each plant, animal or
mineral to a certain star, and believe that the above
processes of witchcraft[23] are different forms of worship
offered to that star, which is pleased with that act,
word, or offering of incense, and fulfils their wishes "
(*Guide* III, 37).

" Thou mayest not believe the absurd ideas of
astrologers, who falsely assert that the constellation
at the time of one's birth determines whether one is
to be virtuous or vicious, the individual being thus
necessarily compelled to follow out a certain line of
conduct " (C.M., *Eight Chapters* VIII).

" I know that nearly all men are led greatly astray
in matters of this kind and think there is some reality
in them ; but it is not so. There are even good and
pious men of our own Faith who think there is reality
in these practices, but they are only forbidden by the
Torah. They do not understand that these things are

hollow frauds, and we are commanded by the Torah not to practise them in the same way as it warns us against falsehood " (C.M., *Abod. Zar.* IV, 7).

" Remove this belief in astrology from your heart, cleanse your mind of it, and wash your intellect as people remove filth from soiled garments by washing ; because there is nothing real in all these things. No sound scholars, even those who do not believe the Torah, hold them as true ; how much less, then, those who accept the Torah " (*Iggéret Téman, Responsa* II, 5b).

" Know, my masters, that the whole subject of astrology, whereby people say so and so will happen or not happen, and the constellation at a man's birth determines that he should be such and such, and this will befall him and not that—all these things are not science at all but folly ; and I have irrefutable proofs with which to destroy their very foundations. Never has one of the philosophers of Greece, who were true philosophers, occupied himself with this subject or written about it in his books. None made the mistake of calling it a science with the exception of the Chaldeans, Egyptians and Canaanites, to whom it was a religion in those days ; but the wise men of Greece, and they were philosophers, who composed books on the sciences and studied all wisdom, endeavoured with convincing proofs to destroy all their theories, root and branch. Also the wise men of Persia believed that the astrology of the Chaldeans, Egyptians and Canaanites was false. . . . Nobody adheres to it except a simpleton who believes anything or the person who wishes to deceive others " (*Responsa* II, 25b).

As with astrology, so with enchantment and omens. They are not only forbidden by the Torah, but they are meaningless and senseless.

"We may not practise divination as do the heathens ; as it is said, 'Ye shall not practise divination' (Lev. xix. 26). What is divination? As, e.g., when a person says, Because a piece of my bread dropped from my mouth, or my stick dropped from my hand, I will not go to-day to a certain place, for if I were to go, my business would not be transacted ; or, because a fox crossed on my right side, I shall not go outside the door of my house to-day, for if I were to go out a deceiver will meet me. Similarly those who listen to the chirping of birds and say that so and so will happen or not happen, such and such is advisable to do and something else is not ; or others who say, Kill this cock which crowed like a raven, or kill this hen which crowed like a cock. So also the man who makes omens for himself, saying, If such and such a thing happen to me, I will do a certain thing, and if it should not happen to me, I will not do it—like Eleazar, the servant of Abraham (Gen. xxiv.). All divinations such as these are prohibited. . . .

"All these practices are falsehood and deception, with which idolaters of old used to mislead the ignorant masses to be guided by them. It is unfit for Israelites, who are of a higher mental calibre, to be led away by these vanities, or bring it upon their minds that there is the slightest use in them. Whoever believe in such like things and imagine in their heart that they are truth and wisdom, but only forbidden by the Torah, are nothing but fools and weak-minded, or are of the class of women and children whose intellect is imperfect. But men of wisdom and enlightened minds know with irrefutable evidence that all these things, prohibited by the Torah, are not matters of wisdom, but inanities by which the weak-minded are led astray, and for the sake of which they abandon all ways of truth. . . .

Therefore the Torah, in warning us against all these vanities, declares, ' Thou shalt be whole-hearted with the Lord thy God ' (Deut. xviii. 13) " (*Yad, Akum* XI, 4, 16).

" He prohibited us against divination, i.e., that one should agitate the faculty of conjecture by a mode of excitation ; because all who possess such a faculty are they who announce what will take place before it happens. This is in fact true of them when their faculty of conjecture is strong, and in most cases it does hit upon the truth and what is correct.[24] In this manner they perceive what is yet to be ; and they strive for superiority in this just as all individual persons strive for superiority, one against the other, in the various other faculties of the soul. And it is inevitable that these possessors of the faculty of conjecture, by the procedure which they adopt,[25] agitate their faculty and display its functioning.

" Some of them strike violent blows with a rod upon the ground, give vent to extraordinary cries, make their mind void of thought, and remain silent with downcast eyes for a long time until a kind of epileptic condition overtakes them ; then they announce what will take place. I actually witnessed this on one occasion in the extreme part of North Africa. Others throw small stones into a leather tablecloth and stare at them a long while ; then they make an announcement. This was a well-known practice in every place I passed through. Others, again, throw a long leather strap to the ground, gaze at it, and make an announcement. The purpose of all this was to agitate the faculty which is in them, not that the act itself accomplishes anything or gives any indication.

" On this point the masses are in error, because,

when some of these announcements are verified with them, they think that it is these acts which give the indication as to what will happen. They are then induced to proceed still further in their error until they imagine that some of these acts are the cause of the event happening ; just as the astrologers affirm that the decrees of the stars are in the same category, meaning, they are a kind of faculty-excitation, and therefore individuals are not equal in the correctness of the announcements they make although they are equal in the science of the laws.

" Whoever performs any of these acts or anything similar which falls in the same class is called a ' diviner ' ; and He declared, ' There shall not be found among you one that useth divination " (Deut. xviii. 10). . . .

" He prohibited us against the practice of astrology, i.e., that we should say, This day is lucky for such and such a task and we propose to do it ; or this day is unlucky to do such and such a task and we will defer it. This is what the Torah refers to in the statement, ' There shall not be found among you a soothsayer ' (ibid.) " (Mitswot, Prohib. XXXI.f).

In similar manner he denounces charms and amulets, especially those in which the divine Name is used.

" You must beware of sharing the error of those who write amulets. Whatever you hear from them or read in their works, especially in reference to the names which they form by combination, is utterly senseless ; they call these combinations shémot (' names ') and believe that their pronunciation demands sanctification and purification, and that by using them they are enabled to work miracles. Rational persons ought not to listen to such men, nor in any way believe their assertions " (Guide I, 61).

" They who write inside the *Mezuzah*[26] the names of Angels or the names of saints, or a Scriptural verse, or sections of the liturgy, are in the class of those who have no share in the world to come. Not enough for these fools that they set at nought the divine commands, but they treat a great precept, viz., the proclamation of God's Unity and the duty to love and serve Him, as though it were an amulet for their own profit, thinking in their folly that this is a thing that will gain them advantage in the matter of the vain things of the world " (*Yad, Tefillin* V, 4).

And, finally, all superstitious use of the text of the Bible is sternly decried.

" Whoever whispers a charm over a wound by quoting a verse from Scripture, and likewise whoever reads a Scriptural verse over an infant that it be not terrified, or places a scroll of the Torah or phylacteries on a child so that it should sleep—not only are such persons in the category of diviners and soothsayers, but they are also to be included in the class of those who deny the Torah ; because they use the words of Torah for the healing of the body, whereas they were only intended for the healing of souls " (*Yad, Akum* XI, 12).

CHAPTER V

PROPHECY

§1. *Prophecy a natural gift.* Maimonides' teachings
on Prophecy will probably come as a surprise to the
reader who meets with them for the first time. They
were not original with him, but had previously been
advanced by Abraham ibn Daud. The first intention
of Maimonides was to write a separate treatise on
Prophecy. In his Introduction to *Ḥélek* he mentions
" the book on Prophecy which I have begun " (see
also *Eight Chapters* I), but he abandoned the plan
and incorporated his material in Part II of the *Guide*
(Chaps. XXXII-XLVIII).

In brief, Maimonides maintained that Prophecy
was not in essence an endowment bestowed by God
upon a few selected individuals, but a degree of mental
and moral perfection to which all may aspire. Man
by his own will and effort created the potential gift
of Prophecy which God converted into an actuality.
He embodies his opinions in his sixth Principle of
Faith :

" Prophecy. This implies that it should be known
that among this human species there exist persons of
very intellectual natures and possessing much perfection. Their souls were pre-disposed for receiving
the form of the intellect. Then this human intellect
joins itself with the Active Intellect, and an exalted
emanation is shed upon them.[1] These are the

Prophets. This is Prophecy and this is its meaning "
(C.M., Introd. to *Ḥélek*).

§2. *Three views of Prophecy.* Maimonides enumerates
three opinions on the subject.

" (i) Among those who believe in Prophecy, and
even among our co-religionists, there are some ignorant
people who think as follows : God selects any person
He pleases, inspires him with the spirit of Prophecy,
and entrusts him with a mission. It makes no
difference whether that person be wise or stupid, old
or young ; provided he be, to some extent, morally
good.[2] For these people have not yet gone so far as
to maintain that God might also inspire a wicked
person with His spirit. They admit that this is
impossible, unless God has previously caused him to
improve his ways.

" (ii) The philosophers[3] hold that Prophecy is a
certain faculty of man in a state of perfection, which
can only be obtained by study. Although the faculty
is common to the whole race, yet it is not fully
developed in each individual, either on account of the
individual's defective constitution, or on account of
some other external cause. This is the case with every
faculty common to a class. It is only brought to a
state of perfection in some individuals, and not in all ;
but it is impossible that it should not be perfect in
some individual of the class[4] ; and if the perfection is
of such a nature that it can only be produced by an
agent, such an agent must exist. Accordingly, it is
impossible that an ignorant person should be a
Prophet ; or that a person being no Prophet in the
evening should, unexpectedly on the following morning,
find himself a Prophet, as if Prophecy were a thing
that could be found unintentionally. But if a person,

perfect in his intellectual and moral faculties, and also perfect, as far as possible, in his imaginative faculty, prepares himself in the manner which will be described, he must become a Prophet ; for Prophecy is a natural faculty of man. It is impossible that a man who has the capacity for Prophecy should prepare himself for it without attaining it, just as it is impossible that a person with a healthy constitution should be fed well and yet not properly assimilate his food.

" (iii) The third view is that which is taught in Scripture, and which forms one of the principles of our religion. It coincides with the opinion of the philosophers in all points except one. For we believe that, even if one has the capacity for Prophecy and has duly prepared himself, it may yet happen that he does not actually prophesy. It is in that case the will of God that withholds from him the use of the faculty. According to my opinion, this fact is as exceptional as any other miracle and acts in the same way. For the laws of Nature demand that everyone should be a Prophet who has a proper physical constitution, and has been duly prepared as regards education and training. . . .

" There are, however, numerous passages in Scripture as well as in the writings of our Sages, which support the principle that it depends chiefly on the will of God who is to prophesy, and at what time, and that He only selects the best and the wisest. We hold that fools and ignorant people are unfit for this distinction. It is as impossible for any one of these to prophesy as it is for an ass or a frog ; for Prophecy is impossible without study and training ; when these have created the possibility, then it depends on the will of God whether the possibility is to be turned into reality " (Guide II, 32).

§3. *The Psychology of Prophecy.* The Greek philosophers classified the activities of the soul under five heads, one of them being imagination.[6] According to Maimonides, Prophecy receives its stimulus from the imaginative faculty.

" Prophecy is, in truth and reality, an emanation sent forth by the Divine Being through the medium of the Active Intellect, in the first instance to man's rational faculty, and then to his imaginative faculty. It is the highest degree and greatest perfection man can attain ; it consists in the most perfect development of the imaginative faculty. Prophecy is a faculty that cannot in any way be found in a person, or acquired by man, through a culture of his mental and moral faculties ; for even if these latter were as good and perfect as possible, they would be of no avail, unless they were combined with the highest natural excellence of the imaginative faculty.

" You know that the full development of any faculty of the body, such as the imagination, depends on the condition of the organ by means of which the faculty acts. This must be the best possible as regards its temperament and its size, and also as regards the purity of its substance. Any defect in this respect cannot in any way be supplied or remedied by training. For when any organ is defective in its temperament, proper training can in the best restore a healthy condition to some extent, but cannot make such an organ perfect. But if the organ is defective as regards size, position, or as regards the substance and the matter of which the organ is formed, there is no remedy.

" Part of the functions of the imaginative faculty is to retain impressions by the senses, to combine them, and chiefly to form images. The principal and

highest function is performed when the senses are at
rest and pause in their action, for then it receives to
some extent, divine inspiration in the measure as it is
predisposed for this influence. This is the nature
of those dreams which prove true, and also of Prophecy,
the difference being one of quantity, not of quality.
Thus our Sages say that dream is the sixtieth part of
Prophecy7 ; and no such comparison could be made
between two things of different kinds, for we cannot
say the perfection of man is so many times the perfection of a horse.

" In *Beréshit Rabba* the following saying of our
Sages occurs : ' Dream is the *nobélet* (the unripe fruit)
of Prophecy '.8 This is an excellent comparison, for
the unripe fruit (*nobélet*) is really the fruit to some
extent, only it has fallen from the tree before it was
fully developed and ripe. In a similar manner the
action of the imaginative faculty during sleep is the
same as at the time when it receives a Prophecy, only
in the first case it is not fully developed, and has not
yet reached its highest degree. But why need I
quote the words of the Sages when I can refer to the
following passage of Scripture : ' If there be among
you a prophet, I, the Lord, do make Myself known
unto him in a vision, I do speak with him in a dream '
(Num. xii. 6). Here the Lord tells us what the real
essence of Prophecy is, that it is a perfection acquired
in a dream or in a vision ; the imaginative faculty
acquires such an efficiency in its action that it sees the
thing as if it comes from without, and perceives it as
if through the medium of bodily senses " (*Guide* II, 36).

Since the Prophet is possessed of the highest degree
of intellectual perfection and speaks under the direct
influence of the divine Spirit, his utterances as a
Prophet are unchallengeable when once his claim to

the dignity is admitted. Therefore Prophecy must be the supreme source of human knowledge.

" You must know that there is a degree of knowledge higher than the degree of the philosophers, and that is Prophecy. Prophecy belongs to a separate world where proof and debate do not apply ; for when it is once made clear that it is a prophetic utterance, there is no room left for proof. Consequently you find that men never demand proof of a Prophet except concerning the Prophecy itself—whether it is a Prophecy or not ; and that is what is called a sign. But they do not seek a proof beyond the Prophecy, because the Prophecy is superior to the proof and not *vice versa.* . . . To debate a prophetic utterance on the basis of philosophy, which is of a lower degree, can lead to no clear decision, since it cannot attain its heights. It is like one who proposes to collect all the waters of the world into a single small flask " (*Responsa* II, 23c).

" The true Prophets undoubtedly conceive ideas that result from premisses which human reason could not comprehend by itself ; thus they tell things which men could not tell by reason and ordinary imagination alone ; for the action of the Prophets' mental capacities is influenced by the same agent that causes the perfection of the imaginative faculty, and that enables the Prophet thereby to foretell a future event with such clearness as if it was a thing already perceived with the senses, and only through them conveyed to his imagination. This agent perfects the Prophet's mind, and influences it in such a manner that he conceives ideas which are confirmed by reality, and are so clear to him as if he deduced them by means of syllogisms " (*Guide* II, 38).

Being thus endowed, the Prophets must necessarily

be the supreme authorities on questions of religious beliefs, and reliance should be placed on their teaching.

" Just as a blind man is saved from stumbling when he depends on a seeing man by walking behind him, because he knows that he lacks the sight which would indicate the right way to him ; just as the invalid who is ignorant of medical science is saved when he obeys the advice of the doctor who prescribes for him, since he himself does not know which things kill and which cure, and therefore listens to all that the physician tells him ; so it is proper for the multitude to place full reliance in the Prophets, the men possessed of real eyes, and be content when these teach that a certain doctrine is true and another false " (*Iggéret Téman, Responsa* II, 5d).

But on matters which come within the domain of reason, the Prophet speaks with no exceptional authority and his opinion may be rejected if proved unsound.

" In the matter of opinion the Prophet is like the rest of men. If a Prophet expresses an opinion and a non-Prophet likewise expresses an opinion, and should the former declare, ' The Holy One, blessed be He, has informed me that my view is correct ', do not believe him. If a thousand Prophets, all of the status of Elijah and Elisha, were to entertain an opinion and a thousand and one Sages held the opposite, we must abide by the majority and reject the view of the thousand distinguished Prophets " (C.M., Introduction).

§4. *Qualifications of a Prophet.* The Prophet must be perfect in every respect. Even his physical constitution must be such as to make a perfect instrument for the activities of his soul.

" The substance of the brain must from the very beginning be in the most perfect condition as regards purity of matter, composition of its different parts, size and position ; no part of his body must suffer from ill-health ; he must in addition have studied and acquired wisdom, so that his rational faculty passes from a state of potentiality to that of actuality ; his intellect must be as developed and perfect as human intellect can be ; his passions pure and equally balanced ; all his desires must aim at obtaining a knowledge of the hidden laws and causes that are in force in the Universe ; his thoughts must be engaged in lofty matters ; his attention directed to the knowledge of God, the consideration of His works, and of that which he must believe in this respect. There must be an absence of the lower desires and appetites, of the seeking after pleasure in eating, drinking and cohabitation ; and, in short, every pleasure connected with the sense of touch. . . .

" It is further necessary to suppress every thought or desire for unreal power and dominion9 ; that is to say, for victory, increase of followers, acquisition of honour, and service from the people without any ulterior object. . . . A man who satisfies these conditions, whilst his fully developed imagination is in action, influenced by the Active Intellect according to his mental training—such a person will undoubtedly perceive nothing but things very extraordinary and divine, and see nothing but God and His Angels. His knowledge will only include that which is real knowledge, and his thought will only be directed to such general principles as would tend to improve the social relations between man and man "10 (*Guide* II, 36).

" There are some who direct all their mind toward

the attainment of perfection in Metaphysics, devote themselves entirely to God, exclude from their thought every other thing, and employ all their intellectual faculties in the study of the Universe, in order to derive therefrom a proof for the existence of God, and to learn in every possible way how God rules all things[11] ; they form the class of those who have entered the palace, viz., the class of Prophets " (*Guide* III 51).

" No Prophet received the gift of Prophecy unless he possessed all the mental virtues and a great majority of the most important moral ones.[12] . . . It is not an indispensable requirement that a Prophet should possess all the moral virtues, and be entirely free from every defect, for we find that Scripture testifies in reference to Solomon, who was a Prophet, that ' the Lord appeared to Solomon in Gibeon ' (1 Kings iii. 5), although we know that he had the moral defect of lust, which is plainly evident from the fact that he took so many wives, a vice springing from the disposition of passion which resided in his soul. . . . Thou must not be surprised to learn, however, that a few moral imperfections lessen the degree of prophetic inspiration ; in fact, we find that some moral vices cause Prophecy to be entirely withdrawn. Thus, for instance, wrath may do this, as our Rabbis say, ' If a Prophet becomes enraged, the spirit of Prophecy departs from him '[13] . . . Grief and anxiety may also cause a cessation of Prophecy, as in the case of the patriarch Jacob who, during the days when he mourned for Joseph, was deprived of the Holy Spirit, until he received the news that his son lived, whereupon Scripture says, ' The spirit of Jacob, their father, revived ' (Gen. xlv. 27), which the *Targum*[14] renders, ' And the spirit of Prophecy descended upon their father, Jacob '. The Sages, moreover, say

' The spirit of Prophecy rests not upon the idle, nor upon the sad, but upon the joyous[15] ' " (C.M., *Eight Chapters*, VII).

§5. *Degrees of Prophecy.* Not all Prophets are on the same plane of equality, because the term " Prophecy " does not denote always exactly the same thing. Maimonides enumerates no fewer than eleven degrees, and he utters the warning note :

" Not all the degrees of Prophecy which I will enumerate qualify a person for the office of a Prophet. The first and second degrees are only steps leading to Prophecy, and a person possessing either of these two degrees does not belong to the class of Prophets whose merits we have been discussing. When such a person is occasionally called Prophet, the term is used in a wider sense, and is applied to him because he is almost a Prophet. . . . It is possible for a Prophet to prophesy at one time in the form of one of the degrees which I am about to enumerate, and at another time in another form. In the same manner, as the Prophet does not prophesy continuously, but is inspired at one time and not at another, so he may at one time prophesy in the form of a higher degree, and at another time in that of a lower degree ; it may happen that the highest degree is reached by a Prophet only once in his lifetime, and afterwards remains inaccessible to him, or that a Prophet remains below the highest degree until he entirely loses the faculty ; for ordinary Prophets[16] must cease to prophesy a shorter or longer period before their death " (*Guide* II, 45).

There follows in the Chapter an enumeration of the eleven degrees of which a summary is here given :

(i) " The first degree of Prophecy consists in the divine assistance which is given to a person, and induces and encourages him to do something good and grand, e.g., to deliver a congregation of good men from the hands of evil-doers ; to save one noble person, or to bring happiness to a large number of people ; he finds in himself the cause that moves and urges him to this deed. This degree of divine influence is called ' the spirit of the Lord ' ; and of the person who is under that influence we say that the spirit of the Lord came upon him, clothed him, or rested upon him, or the Lord was with him,[17] and the like ".

In this class the " judges of Israel and noble chiefs " are to be included. " This faculty was always possessed by Moses from the time he had attained the age of manhood ; it moved him to slay the Egyptian, and to prevent evil from the two men that quarrelled. It was so strong that, after he had fled from Egypt out of fear and arrived in Midian, a trembling stranger, he could not restrain himself from interfering when he saw wrong being done ".[18] When David was anointed by Samuel, he was likewise filled with this spirit.[19]

(ii) " The second degree is this : A person feels as if something came upon him, and as if he had received a new power that encourages him to speak. He treats of science, or composes hymns, exhorts his fellow-men, discusses political and theological problems. All this he does while awake, and in the full possession of his senses. Such a person is said to speak by the Holy Spirit. David composed the Psalms, and Solomon the Book of Proverbs, Ecclesiastes and the Song of Solomon by this Spirit ; and Daniel, Job, Chronicles and the rest of the Hagiographa were written in this Holy Spirit ; therefore they are called *Ketubim* (writings, or written), i.e., written by men inspired by the Holy Spirit. Our Sages mention this expressly concerning the Book of Esther.[20] . . .

"We must especially point out that David, Solomon and Daniel belonged to this class, and not to the class of Isaiah, Jeremiah, Nathan the Prophet, Ahijah the Shilonite,[21] and those like them. . . . There is no doubt that this is one degree below that form of Prophecy to which the words, ' I do speak with him in a dream ' are applied. For this reason the nation desired to place the Book of Daniel among the Hagiographa and not among the Prophets.[22] I have, therefore, pointed out to you, that the Prophecy revealed to Daniel and Solomon, although they saw an Angel in the dream, was not considered by them as a perfect Prophecy, but as a dream containing correct information. They belonged to the class of men that spoke, inspired by the *ruaḥ ha-kodesh*, ' the Holy Spirit '. Also in the order of the holy writings, no distinction is made between the Books of Proverbs, Ecclesiastes, Daniel, Psalms, Ruth and Esther ; they are all written by divine inspiration. The authors of these Books are called Prophets in the more general sense of the term."

(iii) " The third class is the lowest class of actual Prophets, i.e., of those who introduce their speech by the phrase, ' And the word of the Lord came unto me ', or a similar phrase. The Prophet sees an allegory in a dream—under those conditions which we have mentioned when speaking of real Prophecy —and in the prophetic dream itself the allegory is interpreted. Such are most of the allegories of Zechariah."

(iv) " The Prophet hears in a prophetic dream something clearly and distinctly, but does not see the speaker. This was the case with Samuel in the beginning of his prophetic mission."

(v) " A person addresses the Prophet in a dream,

as was the case in some of the prophecies of Ezekiel ."
Cf. Ezek. xl. 4.

(vi) " An Angel speaks to him in a dream ; this
applies to most of the Prophets." *Cf.* Gen. xxxi. 11.

(vii) " In a prophetic dream it appears to the
Prophet as if God spoke to him." *Cf.* Isa. vi. 1, 8,
1 Kings xxii. 19.

(viii) " Something presents itself to the Prophet
in a prophetic vision ; he sees allegorical figures, such
as were seen by Abraham in the vision ' between the
pieces ' (Gen. xv. 9f) ; for it was in a vision by day-
time, as is distinctly stated."

(ix) " The Prophet hears words in a prophetic
vision." *Cf. ibid.* 4.

(x) " The Prophet sees a man that speaks to him
in a prophetic vision." (*Cf. ibid.* xviii. 1 ; Josh. v. 13.)

(xi) " He sees an Angel that speaks to him in the
vision, as was the case when Abraham was addressed
by an Angel at the sacrifice of Isaac (Gen. xxii. 15).
This I hold to be—if we except Moses—the highest
degree a Prophet can attain according to Scripture,
provided he has, as reason demands, his rational
faculties fully developed. But it appears to me
improbable that a Prophet should be able to perceive
in a prophetic vision God speaking to him ; the action
of the imaginative faculty does not go so far, and
therefore we do not notice this in the case of the
ordinary Prophets. Scripture says expressly, ' I do
make Myself known unto Him in a *vision*, I do speak
with him in a *dream* ' ; the speaking is here connected
with *dream*, the influence and the action of the intellect
is connected with *vision*.

" When I, therefore, met with statements in
Scripture that a Prophet heard words spoken to him
and that this took place in a vision, it occurred to me

that the case in which God appears to address the Prophet seems to be the only difference between a vision and a dream, according to the literal sense of the Scriptural text. But it is possible to explain the passages in which a Prophet is reported to have heard in the course of a vision words spoken to him, in the following manner : at first he had a vision but subsequently fell into a deep sleep, and the vision was changed into a dream. Thus we explained the words, ' A deep sleep fell upon Abram ' (Gen. xv. 12) ; and our Sages remark thereon, ' This was a deep sleep of Prophecy.'[23] According to this explanation, it is only in a dream that the Prophet can hear words addressed to him ; it makes no difference in what manner words are spoken. Scripture supports this theory, ' I do speak with him in a dream '. But in a prophetic vision only allegories are perceived, or rational truths are obtained, that lead to some knowledge in science, such as can be arrived at by reasoning. This is the meaning of the words, ' I do make Myself known unto him in a vision '. According to this second explanation, the degrees of Prophecy are reduced to eight, the highest of them being the prophetic vision, including all kinds of vision, even the case in which a man appears to address the Prophet ".

In a striking and picturesque passage—one of the very rare specimens of fine writing in his compositions —Maimonides thus describes the difference between men with respect to the illumination which constitutes Prophecy :

" At times the truth shines so brilliantly that we perceive it as clear as day. Our nature and habit then draw a veil over our perception, and we return to a darkness almost as dense as before. We are like those who, though beholding frequent flashes of lightning, still find themselves in the thickest darkness of the night. On some the lightning flashes in rapid succession, and they seem to be in continuous light, and their night is as clear as the day. This was the degree of prophetic excellence attained by Moses, the greatest of Prophets, to whom God said, ' But as for thee, stand thou here by Me ' (Deut. v. 31; Heb. 28), and of whom it is written ' the skin of his face shone ' (Exod. xxxiv. 29). Some perceive the prophetic flash at long intervals ; this is the degree of most Prophets. By others only once during the whole night is a flash of lightning perceived. This is the case with those of whom we are informed, ' They prophesied, and they did so no more ' (Num. xi. 25). There are some to whom the flashes of lightning appear with varying intervals ; others are in the condition of men whose darkness is illumined not by lightning, but by some kind of crystal or similar stone, or other substances that possess the property of shining during the night ; and to them even this small amount of light is not continuous, but now it shines and now it vanishes, as if it were ' the flame of the rotating sword ' " (*Guide*, Introduction).

§6. *Test of a true Prophet.* The criterion of a true Prophet is not his ability to work miracles, but to foretell the future in detail. The verification of his statements is the guarantee of his genuine call.

" Any Prophet that may rise up for us and declare that the Lord had sent him need not perform a sign, like one of the signs of Moses our teacher, or like the signs of Elijah and Elisha which involved a change in the course of Nature[24] ; but his sign should be the announcement of events which are to happen in the world and the verification of his words. Therefore if a man who is worthy of Prophecy come with a mission from God, and if he come not to add or diminish but to serve the Lord with the commandments of the Torah, we should not say to him, ' Divide the sea for us ', or ' Revive a dead body ', or so on ; ' then we shall believe you '. What we should say to him is, ' If you are a prophet, foretell events that are to happen ', and he tells them. We then wait to see whether his words will come to pass or not ; should even the least part of what he foretold fail, it is certain that he is a false prophet. If all his words come to pass, he must be regarded by us as faithful[25] ; but we must examine him several times, and if all his prediction prove to be correct, then he is a true Prophet.

" But do not the soothsayers and diviners foretell that which is to happen ![26] What difference, then, is there between the Prophet and them ? With sooth-sayers, diviners and such men, part of their words is fulfilled and part is not. . . . It is also possible that none of their words should be fulfilled at all, but they are entirely erroneous. . . . In the case of the Prophet, however, all his words are fulfilled. . . . When, therefore, a Prophet rises up for us, it is only to inform us of things which are to happen in the world, such as plenty or famine, war or peace, etc. He may even inform us of things concerning an individual, just as Saul, when he sustained a loss, went to a Prophet that he might inform him of the place where the lost thing was to be found.[27] It is things like this that a Prophet is to declare, and not by any means to establish a new religion,[28] or add or abrogate any commandment.

" With regard to threats of punishment which the

Prophet utters, as, e.g., if he were to predict that
such and such a person will die, or that in such and such
a year there will be a famine or war, etc. ; and if it
happen that his words do not come to pass, this is not
necessarily a refutation of his Prophecy, and we must
not say, ' Behold, he has spoken and it has not come
to pass ! ' Because the Holy One, blessed be He, is
slow to anger and of great kindness and relents concerning threatened calamity. It is therefore possible
that the sinners had repented and had been forgiven,
like the people of Nineveh (Jonah iii. 10) ; or it may
be that He allowed them a respite, as with Hezekiah
(2 Kings xx. 5). If, however, the Prophet assured
them of something good, saying that such and such
will happen, but the good did not come to pass, then
it is certain that he is a false prophet ; because every
good thing which God decrees, though it be conditional,
He never retracts.29 . . . Hence we learn that the
prophet can only be tested by the good which he
foretells. . . .

" If a Prophet receives the testimony of another
Prophet that he is a true Prophet, he is thereby
confirmed as such, and it is unnecessary to submit him
to examination ; for behold, Moses our teacher
testified on behalf of Joshua and all Israel believed in
him, even before he produced a sign. Such is the rule
for future generations, viz., when a Prophet has become
known for his Prophecy and his words have been
repeatedly believed in ; or when a Prophet testified
for him and he has been walking in the ways of
Prophecy—it is then unlawful to doubt or suspect
whether his Prophecy is untrue. It is further unlawful
to test him more than is necessary, so that we must
not be constantly proving him ; but when it has once
become known that this man is a Prophet, they are

to believe and know that the Lord is among them, and they must not doubt or suspect him " (*Yad, Yesodé ha-Torah*, X ; C.M., Introduction).

§7. *Moses the greatest of the Prophets.* Maimonides attached such importance to the uniqueness of Moses' status as a Prophet, that he formulated it into a Principle of Faith. He was doubtless led to do this because of the rival claim of each of the daughter-religions that it had produced a prophet greater than he. The seventh Principle, accordingly, declares :

" The Prophecy of Moses our teacher. This implies that we must believe that he was the father of all the Prophets before him, and those who came after him were all beneath him in rank. He was chosen by God from the whole human kind. He comprehended more of God than any man in the past or future ever comprehended or will comprehend. And we must believe that he reached a state of exaltedness beyond the sphere of humanity, so that he attained to the angelic rank and became included in the order of the Angels. There was no veil which he did not pierce. No material hindrance stood in his way, and no defect whether small or great mingled itself with him. The imaginative and sensual powers of his perceptive faculty were stripped from him. His desiderative power was stilled and he remained pure intellect only. It is in this significance that it is remarked of him that he discoursed with God without any angelic intermediary. . . .

" The Prophecy of Moses differs from that of all other Prophets in four respects :—

" (i) Whosoever the Prophet, God spake not with him but by an intermediary. But Moses had no intermediary, as it is said, ' Mouth to mouth did I speak with him ' (Num. xii. 8).

" (ii) Every other Prophet received his inspiration only when in a state of sleep . . . or in the day when deep sleep has fallen upon the Prophet and his condition is that in which there is a removal of his sense-perceptions, and his mind is a blank like a sleep. . . . But to Moses the word came in the day-time when ' he was standing between the two Cherubim ' (see Exod. xxv. 22 ; Num. xii. 6-8).

" (iii) When the inspiration comes to the Prophet, although it is in a vision and by means of an Angel, his strength becomes enfeebled, his physique becomes deranged. And very great terror falls upon him, so that he is almost broken through it. . . . But not so with Moses. The word came unto him and no confusion in any way overtook him, as we are told in the verse, ' And the Lord spake unto Moses face unto face as a man 'speaketh unto his neighbour ' (Exod. xxxiii. 11). This means that just as no man feels disquieted when his neighbour talks with him, so he (peace to him !) had no fright at the discourse of God, although it was face to face ; this being the case by reason of the strong bond uniting him with the intellect, as we have described.

" (iv) To all the Prophets the inspiration came not at their own choice but by the will of God. The Prophet at times waits a number of years without an inspiration reaching him. And it is sometimes asked of the Prophet that he should communicate a message he has received, but the Prophet waits some days or months before doing so, or does not make it known at all. We have seen cases where the Prophet prepares himself by enlivening his soul and purifying his spirit, as did Elisha in the incident when he declared, ' But now bring me a minstrel ! ' (2 Kings iii. 15), and then the inspiration came to him. He does not necessarily receive the inspiration at the time that he is ready for it. But Moses our teacher was able to say at whatsoever time he wished, ' Stand, and I shall hear what God shall command concerning you ' (Num. ix. 8). It is again said, ' Speak unto Aaron thy brother that he come not at all times into the sanctuary ' (Lev. xvi. 2) ; with reference to which verse the Talmud remarks that the prohibition, ' that he come not at all times ', applies only to Aaron. But Moses may enter the sanctuary at all times "³⁰ (C.M., Introd. to *Ḥélek*).

A phrase used in the above extract needs elucidation, viz., " There was no veil which he did not pierce ". The term *ḥijab*, " veil " or " barrier ", through which man contemplates the Deity, was borrowed by Maimonides from Mohammedan theology. The Koran, e.g., states, " It is not fit for man that God should speak with him but by vision or from behind a veil " (Sura XLII). Man's defects throw up barriers or veils which separate between him and God ; consequently the elimination of vices causes the removal of the partitions and brings about the approximation of man to God. Moses being superior in moral and intellectual attainments to the other Prophets, what intervened between him and God was thinner, and therefore his vision was more distinct.

" Many passages are found in the Midrash, the Haggadah, and also the Talmud, which state that some of the Prophets beheld God from behind many barriers, and some from behind only a few, according to the proximity of the Prophet to Him and the degree of his prophetic power. Consequently, the Rabbis said that Moses, our teacher, saw God from behind a single, clear, that is transparent, partition. As they express it, ' He (Moses) looked through a translucent *specularia*'.[31] *Specularia* is the name of a mirror made of some transparent body like crystal or glass. . . .

" When Moses, our teacher, discovered that there remained no partition between himself and God which he had not removed, and when he had attained perfection by acquiring every possible moral and mental virtue, he sought to comprehend God in His true reality, since there seemed no longer to be any hindrance thereto. He, therefore, implored of God, ' Show me, I beseech Thee, Thy glory ' (Exod. xxxiii. 18). But God informed him that this was impossible, as his intellect, since he was a human being, was still influenced by matter. So, God's answer was, ' For no man can see[32] Me and live ' (*ibid.* 20). Thus, there remained between Moses and his comprehension of the true essence of God only one transparent obstruction, which was his human intellect still resident in matter.[33]

" God, however, was gracious in imparting to him, after his request, more knowledge of the divine than he had previously possessed, informing him that the goal he sought was impossible of attainment, because he was yet a human being. . . . It is impossible for mortal man to attain this high degree of comprehension, though Moses (peace be upon him) almost, but not quite, reached it " (C.M., *Eight Chapters* VII).

How is this unique claim made on behalf of Moses established ? Maimonides answers the question in this way :

" The Israelites did not believe Moses, our teacher, in consequence of the signs which he performed ; for he whose belief rests on signs must still have a suspicion in his mind of the possibility that the sign might have been performed by magic or wizardry. All the signs which Moses performed in the wilderness he did through necessity and not to adduce evidence of his Prophecy. When it was necessary to drown the Egyptians, he divided the sea and plunged them into it. When we had need for food, he brought us down manna. When they were thirsty, he split the rock for them. When the band led by Korah denied him, the earth swallowed them up. And so it was with all the other signs.

"On what ground, then, did they believe in him? It was in consequence of their presence at Mount Sinai ; when our own eyes, and not another's, beheld, and when our own ears, and not another's, heard, the fire and the thunderings and the lightnings, whilst he approached the thick darkness and the Voice spake unto him in our own hearing, ' Moses, Moses ! go and say unto them thus '. . . . But how do we know that their presence at Mount Sinai alone was evidence of his Prophecy that it was true beyond all suspicion ? Because it is said, ' Lo, I come unto thee in a thick cloud, that the people may hear when I speak with thee, and may also believe thee for ever ' (Exod. xix. 9). It is to be inferred that previous to this, they did not believe him with a perfect and lasting faith, but with a belief which was still open to doubt and suspicion.

" Consequently the very men to whom he was sent are the witnesses to the truth of his Prophecy, and it was unnecessary to perform any other sign for them, since both they and he were witnesses in the matter. Just as two witnesses who together saw an incident mutually testify, each to the other, that they speak the truth, and neither of them need give proof to the other, so with regard to Moses, our teacher, after their presence at Mount Sinai, all the Israelites became his witnesses and there was no need for him to perform any sign for them. . . .

" It follows that if a Prophet were to arise and perform great signs and wonders, but sought to refute the Prophecy of Moses, our teacher, we are not to listen to him, and we are to know with certainty that those signs had been performed by magic and wizardry, because the Prophecy of Moses, our teacher, was not established by signs, so that we could compare the signs of one with those of the other. But with our own eyes we saw and with our own ears we heard, just as Moses himself heard. . . . Therefore the Torah said that even if the sign or the wonder came to pass, you shall still not hearken unto the words of that prophet (*cf.* Deut. xiii. 3f). For lo, this man came to you with a sign or wonder to refute what you saw with your eyes ; and since we only believe a sign in consequence of the commandment which Moses has ordained for us, how can we receive the sign of a man who comes to refute the Prophecy of Moses, our teacher, which we saw and heard ! " (*Yad, Yesodé ha-Torah* VIII).

Chapter VI

THE TORAH

§1. *The Torah a Revelation from God*. The verbal inspiration of the Torah is the very foundation of Maimonides' whole system of thought. In every letter it is the work of God. He was led to stress this doctrine probably because the Mohammedans made a similar claim for the Koran. They declared that it was eternal and uncreated. It existed everlastingly in writing upon a vast table which was located by God's throne, and a transcript was brought from heaven to earth by the angel Gabriel.[1] The prophet did not compose a single word of it. The form in which Maimonides enunciated his eighth Principle of Faith was no doubt determined by the claim which was made on behalf of the Koran:

" That the Torah has been revealed from heaven. This implies our belief that the whole of this Torah found in our hands this day is the Torah that was handed down by Moses and that it is all of divine origin. By this I mean that the whole of the Torah came unto him from before God in a manner which is metaphorically called ' speaking ', but the real nature of that communication is unknown to everybody except to Moses (peace to him !) to whom it came. In handing down the Torah, Moses was like a scribe writing from dictation the whole of it, its chronicles, its narratives and its precepts. It is in this sense that he is termed ' lawgiver '.[1a]

152

"And there is no difference between verses like 'and the sons of Ham were Cush and Mizraim, Phut and Canaan' (Gen. x. 6), or 'And his wife's name was Mehetabel, the daughter of Matred' (*ibid.* xxxvi. 39), or 'And Timna was concubine' (*ibid.* 12), and verses like 'I am the Lord thy God' (Exod. xx. 2), and 'Hear, O Israel' (Deut. vi. 4). They are all equally of divine origin and all belong to 'The Torah of God which is perfect, pure, holy and true'.[2] In the opinion of the Rabbis, Manasseh was the most renegade and the greatest of all infidels, because he thought that in the Torah there was a kernel and a husk,[3] and that these histories and anecdotes have no value and emanate from Moses. This is the significance of the expression 'The Torah does not come from heaven',[4] which, say the Rabbis, is the remark of one who believes that all the Torah is of divine origin save a certain verse which (says he) was not spoken by God but by Moses himself. And of such a one the verse says 'He hath despised the word of the Lord' (Num. xv. 31). May God be exalted far above and beyond the speech of the infidels! For truly in every letter of the Torah there reside wise maxims and admirable truths for him to whom God has given understanding. You cannot grasp the uttermost bounds of its wisdom. 'The measure thereof is longer than the earth, and broader than the sea' (Job xi. 9). Man has but to follow in the footsteps of the anointed one of the God of Jacob, who prayed 'Open Thou mine eyes that I may behold wondrous things out of Thy Torah' (Ps. cxix. 18).

"The interpretation of traditional law is in like manner of divine origin. And that which we know to-day of the nature of *Succah, Lulab, Shofar,* Fringes and Phylacteries[5] is essentially the same as that which God commanded Moses, and which the latter told us. In the success of his mission Moses realised the mission of a ' trusted servant of God ' (*cf.* Num. xii. 7) " (C.M., Introd. to *Ḥélek*).

Such is the sanctity of the Torah that Maimonides informed a correspondent that the script used in the Synagogue Scrolls should not be employed for secular purposes.

" It is right for you to know that this script which is called *ketab ashuri*[6]—inasmuch as the Torah was given in it and the tables of the Covenant were written in it—should properly only be used for the Scriptures. From the olden days Jews have been scrupulous in this matter, and their writings, scholarly compositions and secular documents were written in the *ketab 'ibri*[7]. You therefore find engraven upon the holy shekel secular phrases written in the *ketab 'ibri* ; but we never find a single letter of the *ketab ashuri* on any Israelite antiquity which has been discovered, neither on a coin nor on stone, but they are all in the *ketab 'ibri*. For this reason the Sephardim[8] have altered their script and so changed the letters of the alphabet until they appear as an entirely different writing, in order to permit of their use for secular matters " (*Responsa* I, 3b, c).

§2. *Aim of the Torah.* What is the purpose of the divine Revelation ? What does it aim at effecting in the life of the human being ? This is Maimonides' reply :

" The general object of the Torah is twofold : the well-being of the soul and the well-being of the body. The well-being of the soul is promoted by correct opinions communicated to the people according to their capacity. Some of these opinions are therefore imparted in a plain form, others allegorically ; because certain opinions are in their plain form too strong for the capacity of the common people. The well-being of the body is established by a proper management of the relations in which we live one to another. This we can attain in two ways : first by removing all violence from our midst ; that is to say, that we do not do every one as he pleases, desires, and is able to do ; but every one of us does that which contributes towards the common welfare. Secondly, by teaching every one of us such good morals as must produce a good social state. . . .

" The latter object is required first ; it is also treated in the Torah most carefully and most minutely, because the well-being of the soul can only be obtained after that of the body has been secured. For it has already been found that man has a double perfection : the first perfection is that of the body, and the second perfection is that of the soul. The first consists in the most healthy condition of his material relations, and this is only possible when man has all his wants supplied as they arise ; if he has his food and other things for his body, e.g., shelter, bath and the like. But one man alone cannot procure all this ; it is impossible for a single man to obtain this comfort ; it is only possible in society, since man, as is well-known, is by nature social.9

" The second perfection of man consists in his becoming an actually intelligent being ; i.e., he knows about the things in existence all that a person perfectly developed is capable of knowing. This second perfection certainly does not include any action or good conduct, but only knowledge, which is arrived at by speculation or established by research. . . .

" The true Torah, which as we said is one, and beside which there is no other Torah, viz., the Torah of our teacher Moses, has for its purpose to give us the twofold perfection. It aims first at the establishment of good mutual relations among men by removing injustice and creating the noblest feelings. In this way the people in every land are enabled to stay and continue in one condition, and every one can acquire his first perfection. Secondly, it seeks to train us in faith, and to impart correct and true opinions when the intellect is sufficiently developed " (*Guide* III, 27).

" It is also the object of the perfect Torah to make man reject, despise and reduce his desires as much as is in his power. He should only give way to them when absolutely necessary. It is well known that it is intemperance in eating, drinking and sexual intercourse that people mostly rave and indulge in ; and these very things counteract the ulterior perfection of man,[10] impede at the same time the development of his first perfection,[11] and generally disturb the social order of the country and the economy of the family. For by following entirely the guidance of lust, in the manner of fools, man loses his intellectual energy, injures his body, and perishes before his natural time ; sighs and cares multiply ; there is an increase of envy, hatred and warfare for the purpose of taking what another possesses. The cause of all this is the circumstance that the ignorant considers physical enjoyment as an object to be sought for its own sake. God in His wisdom has therefore given us such commandments as would counteract that object, and prevent us altogether from directing our attention to it and has debarred us from everything that leads only to excessive desire and lust. This is an important thing included in the objects of our Torah " (*Guide* III, 33).

" The ordinances of the Torah are not an infliction on the world, but a medium of mercy, kindness and peace in the world " (*Yad, Shabbat* II, 3).

" Every narrative in the Torah serves a certain purpose in connection with religious teaching. It either helps to establish a principle of faith, or to regulate our actions, and to prevent wrong and injustice among men " (*Guide* III, 50).

§3. *Permanence of the Torah.* Confronted as Judaism was by the claim of Christianity and Mohammedanism that each had brought a new dispensation to man which superseded the Revelation at Sinai, it was inevitable that Maimonides should make the immutability of the Torah a Principle of Faith. His ninth Principle is on

" The abrogation of the Torah. This implies that this Torah of Moses will not be abrogated and that no other Torah will come from God. Nothing is to be added to it nor taken away from it, neither in the written nor oral law, as it is said, ' Thou shalt not add thereto nor diminish from it ' (Deut. xiii. 1) " (C.M., Introd. to *Ḥélek*).

" It is a clear and explicitly stated feature of the Torah that it is an ordinance to endure for all eternity, and it does not admit of any alteration, diminution or addition. . . . Hence we learn that no Prophet has permission to introduce any innovation at any future time. Should, therefore, a man arise, either from among the nations or from among Israel, and perform any sign or wonder and declare that the Lord has sent him to add any commandment or to abrogate any commandment or to explain any of the commandments otherwise than we have heard from Moses; or should he declare that the commandments which have been ordained for the Israelites are not for all time and for all generations, but were only temporary enactments; behold this man is a false prophet, for he indeed comes to refute the Prophecy of Moses.[12] The penalty to which he is liable is death by strangulation,[13] because he presumed to speak in the name of the Lord that which He had not commanded him. For He, blessed be His Name, had commanded Moses that this ordinance should be for us and our children ' for ever ', and God is not a man that He should lie " (*Yad, Yesodé ha-Torah* IX, 1).

Maimonides, on the other hand, allows the possibility of temporary abrogation, or the adaptation of a law, should circumstances demand it, provided that this is sanctioned by competent authority.

" When a Prophet's status has been confirmed in the manner we have established, and he has made a reputation like Samuel or Elijah or others, he has the power to do with the Torah what no other being is able to do. What I mean is, when he commands to abrogate temporarily one of the positive commandments or permits something which is forbidden by a negative commandment, it is obligatory upon us to hearken to his word and obey his order ; and whoever disregards him is liable to death ' at the hand of Heaven '. The exception is a command to practise idolatry. That is what the Rabbis declare, ' In whatever a Prophet tells you to do involving a transgression of the words of the Torah obey him, except in the matter of idolatry '.[14] There is, however, a proviso, viz., that the Prophet's order shall not be permanent, that he shall not say that the Holy One, blessed be He, commanded to abrogate this ordinance for ever, but that He commands so for a special reason and for the needs of the moment " (C.M., Introduction).

" God knew that the judgments of the Torah will always require an extension in some cases and curtailment in others, according to the variety of places, events and circumstances. He therefore cautioned against such increase and diminution, and commanded, ' Thou shalt not add thereto nor diminish from it ' ; for constant changes would tend to disturb the whole system of the Torah, and would lead people to believe that the Torah is not of Divine origin. But permission is at the same time given to the wise men, i.e., the great court (Synhedrion) of every generation to make fences round the judgments of the Torah for their protection, and to introduce bye-laws (fences) in order to ensure the keeping of the Torah. Such fences once erected remain in force for ever. The Mishnah therefore teaches : ' And make a fence round the Torah '.[15]

" In the same manner they have the power temporarily to dispense with some religious act prescribed in the Torah, or to allow that which is forbidden, if exceptional circumstances and events require it ; but none of the laws can be abrogated permanently. By this method the Torah will remain perpetually the same, and will yet admit at all times and under all circumstances such temporary modifications as are indispensable. If every scholar had the power to make such modifications, the multitude of disputes and differences of opinion would have produced an injurious effect. Therefore it was commanded that of the Sages only the great Synhedrion and none else, should have this power ; and whoever would oppose their decision should be killed.[16] For if any critic were allowed to dispute the decision of the Synhedrion, the object of this Torah would not be attained ; it would be useless " (*Guide* III, 41).

§4. *Study of the Torah.* Judaism attaches great importance not only to the practice of the Torah, but also to its study. The fulfilment of its ordinances should be intelligent, not mechanical. A point like this would naturally make a strong appeal to a man of the type of Maimonides, and he often refers to it in his writings.

" Every Israelite is under the obligation to study the Torah, whether he be poor or rich, whether in good or bad health, whether young or in extreme age when his powers are on the wane, even if he be a poor man who is supported by charity and begs from door to door. Even the father of a family is under the obligation to fix a time for study of the Torah day and night ; as it is said, ' Thou shalt meditate therein day and night ' (Josh. i. 8).

" Some of the eminent Sages of Israel were hewers of wood, others were drawers of water, and others even blind ; still they devoted themselves to the study of the Torah day and night. They belong to the class who handed down the tradition from man to man, direct from the mouth of Moses our teacher.

" Up to what time has a man the duty to study the Torah ? Until the day of his death ; as it is said, ' Lest they depart from thy heart all the days of thy life ' (Deut. iv. 9). All the time that he is not occupying himself with study, he is liable to forget. He must divide the time of his study into three parts : a third for study of the written law, a third for the oral law, and a third for reflection and consideration of what follows from the premisses—to draw inferences and make comparisons, and understand the hermeneutical rules by which the Torah is expounded,[17] until he knows the principle of these rules, and how he is to conclude what is lawful and what unlawful and such like matters based on tradition " (Yad, Talmud Torah I, 8-11).

" Among all the commandments there is none which is of equal importance with that of studying the

Torah ; this equals in importance all the commandments put together,[18] because study leads to practice.
Hence study in every case takes precedence over
practice " (*ibid.* III, 3).

§5. *Interpretation of the Torah.* Maimonides insists
that when a Scriptural passage is quoted to support
an argument, great care must be exercised that it is
not given a meaning which it could not bear in its
context. His canon of exegesis is thoroughly sound :
    " Know that it is not permitted anyone to take
one word from a passage, the whole of which is closely
connected, to use as an argument and a support ; but
it is proper for him to study the context. That is to
say, he should first study the word on which he intends
to rely from the beginning of the phrase—how it fits
in there—to the end of the phrase ; then he will know
the intention of the speaker of the passage and he can
extract proof from it. It is improper, however, to
extract proof from a word which is torn from what
precedes and follows " (*Iggéret Téman, Responsa* II, 4b).
    As for the obscure and difficult passages which are
to be found in the Scriptures, he gives his son this
advice :
    " Whenever you find a deep verse and an obscure
passage in the Torah or in the Prophets, or in the books
of the Sages which you do not understand and whose
hidden meaning you cannot perceive, and it appears
as if it contradicted the fundamental doctrines of the
Torah or is apparently nonsense, be not moved from
your faith and let not your mind be confused. Remain
firm in your conviction and ascribe the deficiency to
yourself. Set it aside, and do not contaminate your
whole faith for lack of understanding of some profound
subject " (*Ethical Will, Responsa* II, 38 b, c).

The full meaning of the Scriptures is not to be read on the surface. One has to penetrate to the depths to understand clearly what is taught. The literal interpretation is consequently often superficial, and one must resort to an allegorical exposition to grasp the import of a passage.

" We read in Midrash *Shir ha-Shirim Rabba*,[19] ' To what were the words of the Torah to be compared before the time of Solomon ? To a well the waters of which are at a great depth, and though cool and fresh, yet no man could drink of them. A clever man joined cord to cord, and rope to rope, and drew up and drank. So Solomon went from figure to figure, and from subject to subject, till he obtained the true sense of the Torah '. So far go the words of our Sages. I do not believe that any intelligent man thinks that ' the words of the Torah ', mentioned here as requiring the application of figures in order to be understood, can refer to the rules for building tabernacles, for preparing the *Lulab*,[20] or for the four kinds of trustees.[21] What is really meant is the apprehension of profound and difficult subjects, concerning which our Sages said, ' If a man loses in his house a *séla*'[22] or a pearl, he can find it by lighting a taper worth only one *issar*. Thus the parables in themselves are of no great value, but through them the words of the holy Torah are rendered intelligible '.

" These likewise are the words of our Sages ; consider well their statement, that the deeper sense of the words of the holy Torah are pearls, and the literal acceptation of a figure is of no value in itself. They compare the hidden meaning included in the literal sense of the simile to a pearl lost in a dark room which is full of furniture. It is certain that the pearl is in the room, but the man can neither see it nor know where it lies. It is just as if the pearl were no longer in his possession, for, as has been stated, it affords him no benefit whatever until he kindles a light. The same is the case with the comprehension of that which the simile represents " (*Guide*, Introduction).

In his search for " the deeper sense " of the Scriptures, Maimonides occasionally displays a boldness which shocked many of his contemporaries. He even dared to suggest that the opening chapter of the Bible was not to be understood literally.

" The account given in Scripture of the Creation is not, as is generally believed, intended to be in all its parts literal. For if this were the case, wise men would not have kept its explanation secret,[23] and our Sages would not have employed figurative speech in treating of the Creation in order to hide its true meaning, nor would they have objected to discuss it in the presence of the common people. The literal meaning of the words might lead us to conceive corrupt ideas and to form false opinions about God, or even entirely to abandon and reject the principles of our Faith. It is therefore right to abstain and refrain from examining this subject superficially and unscientifically. We must blame the practice of some ignorant preachers and expounders of the Bible, who think that wisdom consists in knowing the explanation of words, and that greater perfection is attained by employing more words and longer speech. It is, however, right that we should examine the Scriptural texts by the intellect, after having acquired a knowledge of demonstrative science, and of the true hidden meaning of Prophecies " (*Guide* II, 29).

Several supernatural incidents recorded in the Bible are explained by Maimonides as having occurred not actually but in a vision.

163

" When it is said in reference to Jacob, ' And there wrestled a man with him ' (Gen. xxxii. 25), this took place in a prophetic vision, since it is expressly stated in the end (v. 31) that it was an Angel. . . .

" That which happened to Balaam on the way, and the speaking of the ass, took place in a prophetic vision, since further on, in the same account, an Angel of God is introduced as speaking to Balaam.

" I also think that what Joshua perceived when ' he lifted up his eyes and looked, and behold there stood a man over against him ' (Josh. v. 13) was a prophetic vision, since it is stated afterwards (v. 14) that it was ' the captain of the host of the Lord ' " (*Guide* II, 42).

Referring to the book of Job, he writes : " According to both theories, viz., the theory that Job did exist and the theory that he did not exist, the introduction to the book is certainly a fiction ; I mean the portion which relates to the words of the adversary, the words of God to the former, and the handing of Job to him " (*Guide* III, 22).

§ 6. *Specimens of allegorical interpretation.* In Maimonides' writings we meet with allegorical interpretations of Biblical passages after a style with which Philo has familiarised us. The following are specimens :

" How wonderfully wise is the simile of King Solomon, in which he compares matter to a faithless wife[24] ; for matter is never found without form, and is therefore always like such a wife who is never without a husband, never single ; and yet, though being wedded, constantly seeks another man in the place of her husband ; she entices and attracts him in every possible manner till he obtains from her what her husband has obtained. The same is the case with matter. Whatever form it has, it is disposed to receive another form ; it never leaves off moving and casting off the form which it has in order to receive another. . . .

" As regards the portion beginning, ' A woman of valour who can find ? '²⁵ it is clear what is meant by the figurative expression ' a woman of valour '. When man possesses a good sound body that does not over-power him nor disturb the equilibrium in him, he possesses a divine gift. In short, a good constitution facilitates the rule of the soul over the body, but it is not impossible to conquer a bad constitution by training " (*Guide* III, 8).

On Proverbs vii. 6-26 he comments : " The general principle expounded in all these verses is to abstain from excessive indulgence in bodily pleasures. The author compares the body, which is the source of all sensual pleasures, to a married woman who at the same time is a harlot. . . . All obstacles which prevent man from attaining his highest aim in life, all the deficiencies in the character of man, all his evil propensities, are to be traced to the body alone. The predominant idea running throughout the figure is, that man shall not be entirely guided by his animal or material nature ; for the material substance of man is identical with that of the brute creation " (*Guide*, Introduction).

More remarkable still are the following : " Know, my son Abraham, (the blessed God be merciful to you) that the Tabernacle and its furniture are symbolic of the body of an honourable man. It first mentions the Ark which is doubtless the heart, since that too is the first organ in the body. In the Ark were likewise the tables of the covenant which correspond to the human intellect. When it is stated ' the cherubim shall spread out their wings on high ' (Exod. xxv. 20), the symbol is here sound condition. The table of shew-bread alludes to the liver, the candelabrum to the gall. The altar of burnt-offering, of which it is said ' Fire shall be kept burning upon the altar continually, it shall not go out' (Lev. vi. 6), has a symbolic reference to man's natural heat. The altar of incense is the emanation from God to man " (*Ethical Will, Responsa* II, 39d).

" The seven-branched candelabrum is a symbol of the five senses and the powers of the soul, all functioning in the service of Him Who is blessed " (*Pirké ha-Hatslahah, Responsa* II, 32b).

" Know, my son, that the kings of the house of David are emblematic of one aspect of the human intellect, viz., when it is said of them, ' He did that which was right in the eyes of the Lord '—it is the intellect engaged with the divine emanation. The reverse is that which is devoted to physical lusts ; and when it is mentioned that a heathen king came to fight against them, it doubtless refers to the *Yétser ha-ra* (the evil propensity in man). Know, further, my son, (may the blessed God preserve you) that Samaria is a symbol of the debased and accursed matter over which only wicked kings have dominion—they are the lusts " (*Ethical Will, Responsa* II, 39c).

In the same passage he treats several Biblical narratives in an emblematic manner for the purpose of deriving moral truths. E.g., he makes Pharaoh represent the *Yétser ha-ra,* Israel the truth, Moses the divine intellect, Egypt the body and Goshen the heart. Truth, residing in the heart, is enslaved by evil desire in the body, and is released by the intervention of the divine intellect.

The story of Saul and David is similarly treated. David is truth and Saul the evil impulse. The latter

pursued truth to a place called Secu (1 Sam. xix. 22)
which denotes the heart.   But truth (David) had gone
to Ramah ('a high place ', i.e., the brain) to be with
Samuel (v. 22), the emblem of the divine intellect.
Finding himself powerless against his intended victims,
Saul ' stripped off his clothes ' (v. 24), i.e., the evil
impulse divested itself of its base lusts.

§7. *The Commandments of the Torah.*   Study must
lead to practice.   The Torah does not only offer food
for the mind and soul, but it presents man with a
complete guide of life.   Its ordinances are numerous,
but they were not intended by God to be a yoke
pressing heavily upon the human being.   Maimonides
contends that the reverse is true.   The Torah in fact
lightened the load which mankind was carrying at the
time of the Revelation.

  " I maintain that the Torah which was revealed to
Moses our teacher, and which is called by his name,
aims at facilitating the service and lessening the
burden ;   and if a person complains that certain
precepts cause him pain and great trouble, he cannot
have thought of the habits and doctrines that were
general in those days.   Let him consider the difference
between a man burning his own son in serving his god,
and our burning a pigeon to the service of our God.
Scripture relates, ' For even their sons and their
daughters do they burn in the fire to their gods ' (Deut.
xii. 31).   This was the way in which the heathen worshipped their gods, and instead of such a sacrifice we
have the burning of a pigeon or a handful of flour in
our worship " (*Guide* III, 47).

  The commandments were intended to be a source
of happiness to man, and it is in that spirit alone that
the ordinances of the Torah can be properly fulfilled.

"The joy with which a man rejoices in the performance of the commandments and in the love of God Who ordained them is a great service. Whoever withholds himself from this joy deserves punishment ; as it is said, 'Because thou didst not serve the Lord thy God with joyfulness and with gladness of heart . . . therefore shalt thou serve thy enemy' (Deut. xxviii. 47f). The person who makes his mind haughty and thinks himself too proud in these circumstances is a sinner and a fool. Against this fault does Solomon utter a warning in the words, 'Glorify not thyself in the presence of the King' (Prov. xxv. 6). But the person who lowers his dignity and abases himself in these circumstances is the truly great and honourable, serving God from a motive of love. Similarly said David, king of Israel, 'I will be yet more vile than this, and will be base in mine own sight' (1 Sam. vi. 22) ; for true greatness and honour is but to rejoice before the Lord" (*Yad, Lulab* VIII, 15).

"When a man performs any of the commandments from no other motive than love of God and His service, he thereby publicly sanctifies His Name" (*Ma'amar Kiddush ha-Shém, Responsa* II, 14b).

§8. *Reasons of the Commandments.* An important section of the *Guide* is concerned with the reasons underlying specific ordinances of the Torah. Maimonides held firmly that, with rare exceptions, the motive of the enactment could be discovered by research. His method is particularly interesting because he anticipated the modern study of comparative religion. He maintains the theory that many Biblical ordinances have a relationship with the practices of idolatry and were intended to wean mankind from heathenish rites ; consequently it is necessary to study idolatrous systems to gain an insight into the Pentateuchal legislation. In one of his letters he states : " I also read deeply subjects connected with idolatry, until I imagine that there is not a single book on this theme in Arabic, translated from other languages, which I have not read and fathomed to its depths. From these books there has become clear to me the reason of all the commandments, although all men think that they are without reason and merely the decrees of Scripture " (*Responsa* II, 25b).

Elsewhere he insists : " Although all the statutes of the Torah are divine decrees, it is proper to reflect upon them and assign a reason wherever it is possible " (*Yad, Temurah* IV, 13). Another reference to the same subject is : " It is proper for a man to reflect upon the laws of the holy Torah and understand their purpose to the utmost of his ability. But in those instances where he cannot find a reason and cannot understand the cause, let them not be light in his eyes, nor let him presume ' to break through to go up to the Lord lest He break forth upon him ' (*cf.* Exod. xix. 21f); nor should his thoughts in connection with them be the same as with secular subjects. See how strict the Torah is on the matter of *Me'ilah*.[26] If wood and stones and dust and ashes—since the name of the Lord of the Universe had been called over them only in words —become holy things, and whoever employs them for secular purposes commits a ' transgression ' and even if he had done so in error he must undergo expiation ; how much more so must a man not spurn the commandments which God has ordained because he does not understand their reason, and invent explanations concerning God which are incorrect, applying to them his ideas on secular subjects " (*Yad, Me'ilah* VIII, 8).

" As Theologians are divided on the question

whether the actions of God are the result of His wisdom, or only of His will without being intended for any purpose whatever, so they are also divided as regards the object of the commandments which God gave us. Some of them hold that the commandments have no object at all, and are only dictated by the will of God.²⁷ Others are of opinion that all commandments and prohibitions are dictated by His wisdom and serve a certain aim ; consequently there is a reason for each one of the precepts ; they are enjoined because they are useful. All of us, the common people as well as the scholars, believe that there is a reason for every precept, although there are commandments the reason of which is unknown to us, and in which the ways of God's wisdom are incomprehensible. . . .

" There are commandments which are called *ḥukkim* ' ordinances ', like the prohibition of wearing garments of wool and linen, boiling meat and milk together, and the sending of the goat into the wilderness on the Day of Atonement.²⁸ Our Sages use in reference to them phrases like the following : ' These are things which I have fully ordained for you, and you dare not criticise them ' ; ' Your evil inclination is turned against them ' ; and 'Non-Jews find them strange '.²⁹ But our Sages generally do not think that such precepts have no cause whatever and serve no purpose ; for this would lead us to assume that God's actions are purposeless. On the contrary, they hold that even these ordinances have a cause, and are certainly intended for some use, although it is not known to us, owing either to the deficiency of our knowledge or the weakness of our intellect.

" Consequently there is a cause for every commandment ; every positive or negative precept serves a useful object. In some cases the usefulness is evident,

e.g., the prohibition of murder and theft ; in others
the usefulness is not so evident, e.g., the prohibition of
enjoying the fruit of a tree in the first three years
(Lev. xix. 23), or of a vineyard in which other seeds
have been growing (Deut. xxii. 9). Those commandments, whose object is generally evident, are called
' judgments ' (mishpatim) ; those whose object is not
generally clear are called ' ordinances ' (ḥukkim). . . .

" I will now tell you what intelligent persons ought
to believe in this respect ; viz., that each commandment has necessarily a cause, as far as its general
character is concerned, and serves a certain object ;
but as regards its details we hold that it has no
ulterior object. Thus killing animals for the purpose
of obtaining good food is certainly useful ; that, however, the killing should not be performed by poleaxing
but by cutting the neck, and by dividing the œsophagus
and the windpipe in a certain place30—these regulations
and the like are nothing but tests for man's obedience "
(Guide III, 26).

" The reason of a commandment, whether positive
or negative, is clear and its usefulness evident, if it
directly tends to remove injustice, or to teach good
conduct that furthers the well-being of society, or to
impart a truth which ought to be believed either on
its own merit or as being indispensable for facilitating
the removal of injustice or the teaching of good morals.
There is no occasion to ask for the object of such
commandments ; for no one can, e.g., be in doubt as
to the reason why we have been commanded to believe
that God is one ; why we are forbidden to murder, to
steal, and to take vengeance, or to retaliate, or why we
are commanded to love one another.

" But there are precepts concerning which people
are in doubt and of divided opinions, some believing

that they are mere commands and serve no purpose whatever, whilst others believe that they serve a certain purpose which, however, is unknown to man. Such are those precepts which in their literal meaning do not seem to further any of the three above-named results : to impart some truth, to teach some moral or to remove injustice. They do not seem to have any influence upon the well-being of the soul by imparting any truth, or upon the well-being of the body by suggesting such ways and rules as are useful in the government of a state, or in the management of a household. Such are the prohibitions of wearing garments containing wool and linen ; of sowing divers seeds, or of boiling meat and milk together ; the commandment of covering the blood of slaughtered beasts and birds, the ceremony of breaking the neck of a calf in case of a person being found slain, and the murderer being unknown ; the law concerning the first-born of an ass, and the like. I am prepared to tell you my explanation of all these commandments, and to assign for them a true reason supported by proof, with the exception of some minor rules and of a few commandments. I will show that all these and similar laws must have some bearing upon one of the following three things, viz., the regulation of our opinions, or the improvement of our social relations, which implies two things, the removal of injustice and the teaching of good morals " (*Guide* III, 28).

Here follow some examples of the method by which Maimonides endeavoured to assign reasons to the commandments :

Circumcision. Two purposes are suggested for this rite : (i) " I think that one of its objects is to limit sexual intercourse and to weaken the organ of genera-tion as far as possible, and thus cause man to be moderate. Some people believe that circumcision is to remove a defect in man's formation[31] ; but every one can easily reply : How can products of Nature be deficient so as to require external completion, especially as the use of the foreskin to that organ is evident. This commandment has not been enjoined as a complement to a deficient physical creation, but as a means for perfecting man's moral shortcomings. The bodily injury caused to that organ is exactly that which is desired ; it does not interrupt any vital function, nor does it destroy the power of generation. Circumcision simply counteracts excessive lust ; for there is no doubt that circumcision weakens the power of sexual excitement and sometimes lessens the natural enjoyment ; the organ necessarily becomes weak when it loses blood and is deprived of its covering from the beginning. . . .

(ii) " It gives to all members of the same faith, i.e., to all believers in the Unity of God, a common bodily sign, so that it is impossible for any one that is a stranger to say that he belongs to them.[32] For sometimes people say so for the purpose of obtaining some advantage, or in order to make some attack upon the Jews. No one, however, should circumcise himself or his son for any other reason but pure faith ; for circumcision is not like an incision on the leg, or a burning in the arm, but a very difficult operation. It is also a fact that there is much mutual love and assistance among people that are united by the same sign when they consider it as the symbol of a covenant. Circumcision is likewise the symbol of the covenant which Abraham made in connection with the belief in God's Unity. So also every one that is circumcised enters the covenant of Abraham to believe in the Unity of God, in accordance with the words of the Torah,

' To be a God unto thee and to thy seed after thee ' (Gen. xvii. 7). This purpose of the circumcision is as important as the first, and perhaps more important.

" This law can only be kept and perpetuated in its perfection, if circumcision is performed when the child is very young, and this for three good reasons. First, if the operation were postponed till the boy had grown up, he would perhaps not submit to it.33 Secondly, the young child has not much pain, because the skin is tender and the imagination weak ; for grown-up persons are in dread and fear of things which they imagine are coming, some time before these actually occur. Thirdly, when a child is very young, the parents do not think much of him ; because the image of the child, that leads the parents to love him, has not yet taken a firm root in their minds. That image becomes stronger by the continual sight ; it grows with the development of the child, and later on the image begins again to decrease and to vanish. The parents' love for a new-born child is not so great as it is when the child is one year old ; and when one year old, it is less loved by them than when six years old. The feeling and love of the father for the child would have led him to neglect the law if he were allowed to wait two or three years, whilst shortly after birth the image is very weak in the mind of the parent, especially of the father who is responsible for the execution of this commandment "34 (*Guide* III, 49).

Prohibition against eating blood. " In ancient days people were very eager and anxious to eat blood as a kind of idolatrous ceremony as is explained in the book Tomtom35 ; and therefore the prohibition of eating blood is made very stringent " (*Guide* III, 41).

" Although blood was very unclean in the eyes of the Sabeans,36 they nevertheless partook of it, because they thought it was the food of the spirits[37] ; by eating it man has something in common with the spirits, which join him and tell him future events, according to the notion which people generally have of spirits. There were, however, people who objected to eating blood, as a thing naturally disliked by man ; they killed a beast, received the blood in a vessel or in a pot, and ate of the flesh of that beast whilst sitting round the blood. They imagined that in this manner the spirits would come to partake of the blood which was their food, whilst the idolaters were eating the flesh ; that love, brotherhood and friendship with the spirits were established,[38] because they dined with the latter at one place and at the same time ; that the spirits would appear to them in dreams, inform them of coming events, and be favourable to them. Such ideas people liked and accepted in those days ; they were general, and their correctness was not doubted by any one of the common people. The Torah, which is perfect in the eyes of those who know it and seeks to cure mankind of these lasting diseases, forbade the eating of blood, and emphasised the prohibition exactly in the same terms as it emphasises idolatry " (*Guide* III, 46).

Dietary Laws. " I maintain that the food which is forbidden by the Torah is unwholesome. There is nothing among the forbidden kinds of food whose injurious character is doubted, except pork (Lev. xi. 7) and fat (*ibid.* vii. 23). But also in these cases the doubt is not justified. For pork contains more moisture than necessary for human food, and too much of superfluous matter. The principal reason why the Torah forbids swine's flesh is to be found in the circumstance that its habits and its food are very dirty and loathsome. It has already been pointed out how emphatically

the Torah enjoins the removal of the sight of loathsome objects, even in the field and in the camp[39];
how much more objectionable is such a sight in towns.
But if it were allowed to eat swine's flesh, the streets
and houses would be more dirty than any cesspool,
as may be seen at present in the country of the
Franks.[40]   A saying of our Sages declares, ' The mouth
of a swine is as dirty as dung itself '.[41]

" The fat of the intestines makes us full, interrupts
our digestion and produces cold and thick blood ; it
is more fit for fuel than for human food.

" Blood (Lev. xvii. 12) and *nebélah*, i.e., the flesh
of an animal that died of itself (Deut. xiv. 21), are
indigestible and injurious as food.   *Tréfah*, an animal
in a diseased state (Exod. xxii. 30) is on the way of
becoming a *nebélah*.

" The characteristics given in the Torah (Lev. xi.
and Deut. xiv.) of the permitted animals, viz., chewing
the cud and divided hoofs for cattle, and fins and scales
for fish, are in themselves neither the cause of the
permission when they are present, nor of the prohibition when they are absent ; but merely signs by which
the recommended species of animals can be discerned
from those that are forbidden. . . .

" It is prohibited to cut off a limb of a living animal
and eat it,[42] because such act would produce cruelty
and develop it.   Besides, the heathen kings used to
do it ; it was also a kind of idolatrous worship to cut
off a certain limb of a living animal and to eat it.[43]

" Meat boiled in milk is undoubtedly gross food
and makes overfull ; but I think that most probably
it is also prohibited because it is somehow connected
with idolatry, forming perhaps part of the service, or
being used on some festival of the heathen.[44] . . .

" The commandment concerning the killing of

animals[45] is necessary, because the natural food of man consists of vegetables and of the flesh of animals ; the best meat is that of animals permitted to be used as food.   No doctor has any doubts about this.   Since, therefore, the desire of procuring good food necessitates the slaying of animals, the Torah enjoins that the death of the animal should be the easiest.   It is not allowed to torment the animal by cutting the throat in a clumsy manner, by poleaxing or by cutting off a limb whilst the animal is alive " (*Guide* III, 48).

Miscellaneous Laws.   " It is prohibited to round the corners of the head and to mar the corners of the beard,[46] because it was the custom of idolatrous priests.[47]   For the same reason, the wearing of garments made of linen and wool is prohibited[48] ; the heathen priests adorned themselves with garments containing vegetable and animal material,[49] whilst they held in their hand a seal made of a mineral.   This you find written in their books.   The same is also the reason of the precept, ' A woman shall not wear that which pertaineth unto a man ' (Deut. xxii. 5).   You find it in the book Tomtom that a male person should wear coloured woman's dress when he stands before Venus, and a female, when standing before Mars, should wear a buckler and other armour.[50]   I think that this precept has also another reason, viz., that the interchange of dress creates lust and leads to immorality " (*Guide* III, 37).

" He who strikes his father or his mother is killed on account of his great audacity, and because he undermines the constitution of the family, which is the foundation of the state " (*Guide* III, 41).

" The great men among our Sages would not uncover their heads because they believed that God's glory was round them and over them "[51] (*Guide* III, 52).

§9. *The Sacrifices*. Maimonides makes the bold statement that " burnt-offering and sacrifice are of secondary importance " (*Guide* III, 32) ; and in this Chapter of the *Guide* he works out his theory that the sacrifices were not an end in themselves, but a means to an end.[52]

" It is impossible to go suddenly from one extreme to the other ; it is therefore according to the nature of man impossible for him suddenly to discontinue everything to which he has been accustomed. Now God sent Moses to make the Israelites a kingdom of priests and a holy nation (Exod. xix. 6) by means of the knowledge of God. . . . But the custom which was in those days general among all men, and the general mode of worship in which the Israelites were brought up, consisted in sacrificing animals in those temples which contained certain images, to bow down to those images and to burn incense before them ; religious and ascetic persons were in those days the persons that were devoted to the service in the temples erected to the stars.

" It was in accordance with the wisdom and plan of God, as displayed in the whole Creation, that He did not command us to give up and to discontinue all these manners of service, for to obey such a commandment would have been contrary to the nature of man, who generally cleaves to that to which he is used ; it would in those days have made the same impression as a Prophet would make at present if he called us to the service of God and told us in His name that we should not pray to Him, not fast, not seek His help in time of trouble ; that we should serve Him in thought and not by any action. For this reason God allowed these kinds of service to continue ; He transferred to His service that which had formerly served as a worship of created beings, and of things imaginary and unreal, and commanded us to serve Him in the like manner, viz., to build unto Him a temple, to have the altar erected to His name, to offer the sacrifices to Him, to bow down to Him and to burn incense before Him. . . .

" By this divine plan it was effected that the traces of idolatry were blotted out, and the truly great principle of our Faith, the Existence and Unity of God, was firmly established ; this result was thus obtained without deterring or confusing the minds of the people by the abolition of the service to which they were accustomed and which alone was familiar to them.

" I know that you will at first thought reject this idea and find it strange ; you will put the following question to me in your heart : How can we suppose that divine commandments, prohibitions and import- ant acts, which are fully explained and for which certain seasons are fixed, should not have been commanded for their own sake, but only for the sake of some other thing ; as if they were only the means which He employed for His primary object ? What prevented Him from making His primary object a direct commandment to us, and to give us the capacity of obeying it ? Those precepts which in your opinion are only the means and not the object would then have been unnecessary.

" Hear my answer, which will cure your heart of this disease and will show you the truth of that which I have pointed out to you. There occurs in the Torah a passage which contains exactly the same idea ; it is the following : ' God led them not by the way of the land of the Philistines, although that was near ; for God said, Lest peradventure the people repent when they see war, and they return to Egypt ; but God led the people about by the way of the wilderness by the Red Sea ' (Exod. xiii. 17f). Here God led the people about, away from the direct road which He originally intended, because He feared they might meet on that way with hardships too great for their ordinary strength ; He took them by another road in order to obtain thereby His original object.

" In the same manner God refrained from prescribing what the people by their natural disposition would be incapable of obeying, and gave the above-mentioned commandments as a means of securing His chief object, viz., to spread a knowledge of Him among the people, and to cause them to reject idolatry. It is contrary to man's nature that he should suddenly abandon all the different kinds of Divine service and the different customs in which he has been brought up, and which have been so general, that they were considered as a matter of course. It would be just as if a person trained to work as a slave with mortar and bricks, or similar things, should interrupt his work, clean his hands, and at once fight with real giants. . .

" As the sacrificial service is not the primary object of the commandments about sacrifice, whilst supplications, prayers, and similar kinds of worship are nearer to the primary object, and indispensable for obtaining it, a great difference was made in the Torah between these two kinds of service. The one kind, which consists in offering sacrifices, although the sacrifices are offered to the name of God, has not been made obligatory for us to the same extent as it had been before. We were not commanded to sacrifice in every place, and in every time, or to build a temple in every place or to permit any one who desires to become priest and to sacrifice. On the contrary, all this is prohibited unto us. Only one temple has been appointed, ' in the place which the Lord shall choose ' (Deut. xii. 26) ; in no other place is it allowed to sacrifice ; and only the members of a particular family were allowed to officiate as priests. All these restrictions served to limit this kind of worship, and keep it within those bounds within which God did not think it necessary to abolish sacrificial service altogether. But prayer and supplication can be offered anywhere and by every person " (*Guide* III, 32).

Maimonides occasionally points out that the sacrifices and other ceremonial acts have a moral significance which is capable of wide application. Dealing with the ritual of the scapegoat on the Day of Atonement (Lev. xvi.), he declares : " There is no doubt that sins cannot be carried like a burden, and taken off the shoulder of one being to be laid on that of another being But these ceremonies are of a symbolic character, and serve to impress men with a certain idea and to induce them to repent ; as if to say, we have freed ourselves of our previous deeds, have cast them behind our backs, and removed them from us as far as possible " (*Guide* III, 46).

As the offering had to be perfect and of the best of its species, " the same principle applies to everything that is done in the name of God—it must be of the best. If a man build a house of prayer, it must be more beautiful than his place of residence. When he feeds the hungry, it must be of the finest and most tasty that is on his table. When he clothes the naked, it must be with the best of his garments. When he devotes a thing to a holy purpose, it must be from the best of his possessions " (*Yad, Issuré ha-Mizbéaḥ* VII, 11).

Dealing with the laws of impurity, he remarks : " It is quite obvious that the regulations concerning impurities and purities come within the category of 'statutes' and do not belong to subjects which can be rationally explained. Thus the act of immersion, to rid oneself of impurity, is in that class, because the defilement is not material filth which can depart from the body ; but the rite is dependent upon the intention of the heart. On that account the Sages declared, ' If a man took the immersion without the intention of becoming ritually clean, it is as though he had not taken it '.53 Nevertheless there is symbolical significance in this matter. In the same way that a person directs his heart to self-purification and attains cleanliness by immersion although there has been no physical change, so the person who directs his heart to purify his soul from spiritual impurities, viz., wrong thoughts and bad morals, becomes clean when he determines in his heart to hold aloof from those courses and bathe his soul in the waters of knowledge " (*Yad, Mikwaot* XI, 12).

§10. *The Sabbath and Festivals.* The following are passages which deal with the holy days of the year, and treat of their significance and the proper spirit in which they are to be observed :

" The purpose of the Sabbath is none other than to teach us to rest and abstain from the matters which trouble us during the working-days and withhold us from communing with God, viz., the affairs of the material world. It urges us to attach ourselves to His service in place of bondage to a Pharaoh ; as it is stated in the Decalogue in Deuteronomy, ' And thou shalt remember that thou wast a servant in the land of Egypt, and the Lord thy God brought thee out thence by a mighty hand and by an outstretched arm ; therefore the Lord thy God commanded thee to keep the

Sabbath day ' (Deut. v. 15). The other reason upon which the observance is based is that mentioned in the other passage, ' For in six days the Lord made heaven and earth ', etc. (Exod. xx. 11). The mystic intention here is this : You shall attain sanctification through My work, and it shall be on the day when I perfected My creation. On that day shall you perfect your souls by abstaining from mundane affairs, to rest from activities and labours to serve and commune with Me —that being the truly perfect rest. Then shall your rest be twofold, of the body and the soul " (*Ethical Will, Responsa* II, 39b).

" The commandments relating to the observance of the Sabbath and abstention from idolatry are each equal in weight to all the other ordinances of the Torah put together. The Sabbath is the sign between the Holy One, blessed be He, and between us for ever. Therefore, whoever transgresses any of the ordinances comes within the class of ' the wicked of Israel ' ; but he who publicly desecrates the Sabbath is similar in every respect to an idolater.

" Everyone who observes the Sabbath in the proper manner, honouring it and delighting in it in accordance with his means, the reward which is attributed to him by the Prophet is greater in this world than even that reserved for the world to come ; as it is said, ' Then shalt thou delight thyself in the Lord, and I will make thee to ride upon the high places of the earth, and I will feed thee with the heritage of Jacob thy father ; for the mouth of the Lord hath spoken it ' (Isa. lviii. 14) " (*Yad, Shabbat* XXX, 15).

Of the proper way to observe the Festivals, he writes :

" When a man eats and drinks on the Festival, he is under the obligation to feed the stranger, the orphan and the widow, together with the other destitute poor. But if he locks the door of his court and eats and drinks in the company of his wife and children, without providing for the poor and distressed, that is not 'the joy of the commandment' but the joy of his stomach. To such as him do the Prophet's words apply, 'Their sacrifices shall be unto them as the bread of mourners, all that eat thereof shall be polluted ; for their bread shall be for their appetite' (Hos. ix. 4). Rejoicing of this kind is a disgrace to such people. . . .

"Although eating and drinking on the Festivals comes within the class of positive commandments, a man should not eat and drink throughout the day. But such is the proper procedure : In the morning, all the people repair early to the places of worship, read from the Torah the portion of the day, return home from their meal, then go back to the House of Study to read and learn until midday. When midday has passed, they say the afternoon prayer (*Minḥah*) and then wend their way to their homes, and eat and drink for the rest of the day until night.

"When a man eats and drinks and rejoices on a Festival, he is not to indulge immoderately in wine and laughter and levity, saying that to increase in these things is to increase in the fulfilment of the command. to rejoice. Drunkenness and excessive joviality are not rejoicing, but 'madness and folly' (Eccles. i. 17). It was not for this we were commanded, but for that rejoicing in which there is the service of the Creator" (*Yad, Yom Tob* VI, 18-20 ; *Mitswot*, Command. LIV).

"They (the Festivals) promote the good feeling that men should have to each other in their social and political relations" (*Guide* III, 43).

The Passover. " It is kept seven days, because the period of seven days is the unit of time intermediate between a day and a month. It is also known how great is the importance of this period in Nature54 and in many religious duties.55 For the Torah always follows Nature and in some respects brings it to perfection ; for Nature is not capable of designing and thinking, whilst the Torah is the result of the wisdom and guidance of God, Who is the Author of the intellect of all rational beings " (*Guide*, loc. cit.).

Another reason is suggested for the seven days' observance. " If the eating of unleavened bread on Passover were only commanded for one day, we should not have noticed it, and its object would not have been manifest. For it frequently happens that we take the same kind of food for two or three days. But by our continuing for a whole period of seven days to eat unleavened bread, its object becomes clear and evident " (*ibid*).

The Torah ordains the counting of the days that intervene between Passover and the next Festival, viz., the Feast of Weeks.56 The explanation which Maimonides suggests for this counting is : " In order to raise the importance of this day, we count the days that pass since the preceding Festival, just as one who expects his most intimate friend on a certain day counts the days and even the hours. This is the reason why we count the days that pass since the offering of the Omer, between the anniversary of our departure from Egypt and the anniversary of the Lawgiving. The latter was the aim and object of the exodus from Egypt " (*ibid*).

The New Year. " It is a day of repentance, on which we are stirred up from our forgetfulness. For this reason the *Shofar*57 is blown on this day " (*ibid*).

185

The message of the *Shofar* is thus explained by him :
" Awake, ye sleepers, from your sleep ; and ye who are
sunk in slumber, arouse yourselves and examine your
actions. Turn in repentance and remember your
Creator, ye who are forgetful of the truth because of
transient vanities, and go astray the whole year after
vain and idle things which are of no use and cannot
deliver you. Look to your souls, amend your ways
and deeds, and let every one of you forsake his evil
way and his impure thoughts !

" Therefore every man should regard himself during
the whole year as though he were half innocent and
half guilty, and also to regard the entire world in the
same light ; so that were he to commit but one sin
more, he would incline himself and the entire world
towards the scale of guilt and cause its destruction.
On the other hand, were he to perform one commandment, he would incline himself and the entire world
towards the scale of merit and bring salvation and
deliverance to himself as well as to others ; for it is
said, ' The righteous is an everlasting foundation '
(Prov. x. 15)—i.e., the man who acts righteously
inclines the entire world towards merit and secures its
deliverance. On this account the House of Israel has
made it a practice to increase charity and good deeds,
and to engage in pious acts from the New Year to the
Day of Atonement, to a greater extent than during the
rest of the year. The custom has likewise been
established for all to rise in the night during these
ten days, and to pray in the Synagogues with words
of supplication and earnest pleading until daylight "
(*Yad, Teshubah* III, 4).

Day of Atonement. " The Fast creates the sense
of repentance. It is the same day on which the chief
of all the Prophets came down from Sinai with the

second tables, and announced to the people the divine pardon of their great sin.[58] The day was therefore appointed for ever as a day devoted to repentance and true worship of God.   For this reason all material enjoyment, all trouble and care for the body, are interdicted, no work may be done ; the day must be spent in confession ; every one shall confess his sins and abandon them " (*Guide* III, 43).

" He commanded us to confess the sins which we had committed before God, giving utterance to them with contrition.   This is the form of the confession and its intention : He should say, ' O God, I have sinned, I have committed iniquity, I have transgressed,[59] and I have done so and so '.   He should prolong the utterance and beg forgiveness in this intention with all the eloquence his tongue can command " (*Mitswot*, Command. LXXIII).

Feast of Tabernacles.   " The Feast of Tabernacles, which is a feast of rejoicing and gladness, is kept seven days, in order that the idea of the Festival may be more noticeable.   The reason why it is kept in the autumn is stated in the Torah, ' when thou gatherest in thy labours out of the field ' (Exod. xxiii. 16) ; that is to say, when you rest and are free from pressing labours.   Aristotle, in the ninth book of his *Ethics*, mentions this as a general custom among the nations. He says, ' In ancient times the sacrifices and assemblies of the people took place after the ingathering of the corn and the fruit, as if the sacrifices were offered on account of the harvest '.[60]   Another reason is this : in this season it is possible to dwell in tabernacles, as there is neither great heat nor troublesome rain.

" The two Festivals, Passover and the Feast of Tabernacles, imply also the teaching of certain truths and certain moral lessons.   Passover teaches us to remember the miracles which God wrought in Egypt, and to perpetuate their memory; the Feast of Tabernacles reminds us of the miracles wrought in the wilderness. The moral lesson derived from these Feasts is : man ought to remember his evil days in his days of prosperity. He will thereby be induced to thank God repeatedly, to lead a modest and humble life. We eat, therefore, unleavened bread and bitter herbs on Passover in memory of what has happened unto us, and leave our houses on *Succot* in order to dwell in tabernacles, as inhabitants of deserts do that are in want of comfort. We shall thereby remember that this has once been our condition, although we dwell now in elegant houses, in the best and most fertile land, by the kindness of God and because of His promises to our forefathers. . . .

" I believe that the four species[61] are a symbolical expression of our rejoicing that the Israelites changed the wilderness, ' no place of seed or of figs, or of vines, or of pomegranates, or of water to drink ' (Num. xx. 5), for a country full of fruit-trees and rivers. In order to remember this we take the fruit which is the most pleasant of the fruit of the land, branches which smell best, most beautiful leaves, and also the best of herbs, i.e., the willows of the brook. These four kinds have also those three purposes : First, they are plentiful in those days in Palestine, so that every one could easily get them. Secondly, they have a good appearance, they are green ; some of them, viz., the citron and the myrtle, are also excellent as regards their smell, the branches of the palm-tree and the willow having neither good nor bad smell. Thirdly, they keep fresh and green for seven days, which is not the case with peaches, pomegranates, asparagus, nuts and the like " (*Guide* III, 43).

CHAPTER VII

DIVINE PROVIDENCE

§1. *God is cognisant of man.* The tenth Principle of
Faith declares :
"That He, the exalted One, knows the works of
men and is not unmindful of them. Not as they
thought who said, ' The Lord hath forsaken the land '
(Ezek. viii. 12 ; ix. 9), but as he declared who
exclaimed ' Great in counsel, and mighty in work ;
Whose eyes are open upon all the ways of the sons of
men ' (Jer. xxxii. 19). It is further said, ' And the
Lord saw that the wickedness of man was great in the
earth ' (Gen. vi. 5) ; and again, ' the cry of Sodom and
Gomorrah is great ' (*ibid.* xviii. 20) " (C.M., Introd. to
Ḥélek).
    Although this dogma is stated thus baldly,
Maimonides was aware that it raises difficult problems
on the meaning and scope of Divine Providence. He
declares that " on this question the words of those who
are expert in philosophy are wonderful and very
profound ; and he who is familiar with the sciences,
and the intelligent men eager for understanding,
should pay attention to their arguments, and unite
their opinions with the words of Scripture, ' Behold I
have set before thee this day life and good ' (Deut.
xxx. 15) " (C.M., *Berachot* IX, end). He devotes
three chapters to this discussion in Part III of the
Guide.

189

§2. *The Problem of Divine Providence.* He states the problem with his usual fairness and analytical skill :

" At first thought we notice an absence of system in human affairs. Some pious men live a miserable and painful life, whilst some wicked people enjoy a happy and pleasant life. On this account the philosophers assumed as possible the cases which you will now hear. They said that only one of two things is possible, either God is ignorant of the individual or particular things on earth and does not perceive them, or He perceives and knows them. These are all the cases possible. They then continued thus : If He perceives and knows all individual things, one of the following three cases must take place : (i) God arranges and manages human affairs well, perfectly and faultlessly ; (ii) He is overcome by obstacles and is too weak and powerless to manage human affairs ; (iii) He knows all things and can arrange and manage them, but leaves and abandons them, as too base, low, and vile, or from jealousy ; as we may also notice among ourselves some who are able to make another person happy, well knowing what he wants for his happiness, and still in consequence of their evil disposition, their wickedness and jealousy against him, they do not help him to his happiness.

" This is likewise a complete enumeration of all possible cases. For those who have a knowledge of a certain thing necessarily either (i) take care of the thing which they know and manage it, or (ii) neglect it (as we, e.g., neglect and forget the cats in our house, or things of less importance) ; or (iii) while taking care of it, have not sufficient power and strength for its management, although they have the will to do so.

" Having enumerated these different cases, the philosophers emphatically decided that of the three cases possible as regards the management of a thing by one who knows that thing, two are inadmissible in reference to God—viz., want of power or absence of will; because they imply either evil disposition or weakness, neither of which can by any means be attributed to Him. Consequently there remains only the alternative that God is altogether ignorant of human affairs, or that He knows them and manages them well. Since we, however, notice that events do not follow a certain order, that they cannot be determined by analogy, and are not in accordance with what is wanted, we conclude that God has no knowledge of them in any way or for any reason. This is the argument which led the philosophers to speak such blasphemous words. . . .

" You must notice with surprise that the evil into which these philosophers have fallen is greater than that from which they sought to escape, and that they ignore the very thing which they constantly pointed out and explained to us. They have fallen into a greater evil than that from which they sought to escape, because they refuse to say that God neglects or forgets a thing, and yet they maintain that His knowledge is imperfect, that He is ignorant of what is going on here on earth, that He does not perceive it. They also ignore what they constantly point out to us, inasmuch as they judge the whole Universe by that which befalls individual men, although, according to their own view, frequently stated and explained, the evils of man originate in himself or form part of his material nature. We have already discussed this sufficiently.[1] After having laid this foundation, which is the ruin of all good principles and destroys the majesty of all true knowledge, they sought to remove the opprobrium by declaring that for many reasons it is impossible that God should have a knowledge of earthly things, for the individual members of a species can only be perceived by the senses, and not by reason ; but God does not perceive by means of any of the senses" (*Guide* III, 16).

§3. *Five Theories on Providence.* This subject was keenly debated not only by the Greek philosophers but also by Mohammedan theologians who split into two sects on the question. Maimonides is accordingly able to enumerate five distinct theories respecting the problem :

(i) " There is no Providence at all for anything in the Universe ; all parts of the Universe, the heavens and what they contain, owe their origin to accident and chance ; there exists no being that rules and governs them or provides for them. This is the theory of Epicurus, who assumes also that the Universe consists of atoms, that these have combined by chance, and have received their various forms by mere accident.[2] There have been atheists among the Israelites who have expressed the same view ; it is reported of them, ' They have denied the Lord and said He is not ' (Jer. v. 12). Aristotle has proved the absurdity of the theory that the whole Universe could have originated by chance.[3] He has shown that, on the contrary, there is a being that rules and governs the Universe ".[4]

(ii) " Whilst one part of the Universe owes its existence to Providence, and is under the control of a ruler and governor, another part is abandoned and left to chance. This is the view of Aristotle about Providence, and I will now explain to you his theory. He holds that God controls the Spheres and what they contain : therefore the individual beings in the Spheres remain permanently in the same form. . . . From the existence of the Spheres other beings derive existence, which are constant in their species but not in their individuals. In the same manner it is said that Providence sends forth from the Spheres to the earth sufficient influence to secure the immortality and constancy of the species, without securing at the same time permanence for the individual beings of the species. But the individual beings in each species have not been entirely abandoned ; that portion of the *materia prima* which has been purified and refined, and has received the faculty of growth, is endowed with properties that enable it to exist a certain time, to attract what is useful and to repel what is useless.

"That portion of the *materia prima* which has been subject to a further development, and has received the faculty of sensation, is endowed with other properties for its protection and preservation ; it has a new faculty of moving freely toward that which is conducive to, and away from that which is contrary to, its well-being. Each individual being received besides such properties as are required for the preservation of the species to which it belongs. The portion of the *materia prima* which is still more refined, and is endowed with the intellectual faculty, possesses a special property by which each individual, according to the degree of his perfection, is enabled to manage, to calculate, and to discover what is conducive both to the temporary existence of the individual and to the preservation of the species. All other movements, however, which are made by the individual members of each species, are due to accident ; they are not, according to Aristotle, the result of rule and management.

"E.g., when a storm or gale blows, it causes undoubtedly some leaves of a tree to drop, breaks off some branches of another tree, tears away a stone from a heap of stones, raises dust over herbs and spoils them, and stirs up the sea so that a ship goes down with the whole or part of her contents. Aristotle sees no difference between the falling of a leaf or a stone and the death of the good and noble people in the ship; nor does he distinguish between the destruction of a multitude of ants caused by an ox depositing on them his excrement and the death of worshippers killed by the fall of the house when its foundations give way; nor does he discriminate between the case of a cat killing a mouse that happens to come in her way, or that of a spider catching a fly, and that of a hungry lion meeting a Prophet and tearing him.[5]

" In short, the opinion of Aristotle is this : Everything is the result of management which is constant, which does not come to an end and does not change any of its properties, as, e.g., the heavenly beings, and everything which continues according to a certain rule, and deviates from it only rarely and exceptionally, as is the case in objects of Nature. All these are the result of management, i.e., in a close relation to Divine Providence. But that which is not constant and does not follow a certain rule, as, e.g., incidents in the existence of the individual beings in each species of plants or animals, whether rational or irrational, is due to chance and not to management; it is in no relation to Divine Providence.[6] Aristotle holds that it is even impossible to ascribe to Providence the management of these things."

(iii) " This theory is the reverse of the second. According to this theory, there is nothing in the whole Universe, neither a class nor an individual being, that is due to chance ; everything is the result of will, intention and rule. It is a matter of course that he who rules must know that which is under his control. The Mohammedan Ash'ariyah[7] adhere to this theory, notwithstanding evident absurdities implied in it; for they admit that Aristotle is correct in assuming one and the same cause (viz., the wind) for the fall of leaves from the tree, and for the death of a man drowned in the sea. But they hold at the same time that the wind did not blow by chance; it is God that caused it to move; it is not therefore the wind that caused the leaves to fall; each leaf falls according to the Divine decree; it is God Who caused it to fall at a certain time and in a certain place; it could not have fallen before or after that time or in another place, as this has previously been decreed.

" The Ash'ariyah were therefore compelled to assume that motion and rest of living beings are predestined, and that it is not in the power of man to do a certain thing or leave it undone. The theory further implies a denial of possibility in these things; they can only be either necessary or impossible. The followers of this theory accepted also the last-mentioned proposition, and say that we call certain things possible, as, e.g., the facts that A stands and that B is coming; but they are only possible for us, whilst in their relation to God they cannot be called possible; they are either necessary or impossible.

" It follows also from this theory that precepts are perfectly useless, since the people to whom any law is given are unable to do anything : they can neither do what they are commanded nor abstain from what they are forbidden. The supporters of this theory hold that it was the will of God to send Prophets, to command, to forbid, to promise and to threaten, although we have no power over our actions. A duty would thus be imposed upon us which is impossible for us to carry out, and it is even possible that we may suffer punishment when obeying the command and receive reward when disobeying it. According to this theory, it must also be assumed that the actions of God have no final cause. . . . When we see a person born blind or leprous, who could not have merited a punishment for previous sins, they say, It is the will of God ; when a pious worshipper is tortured and slain, it is likewise the will of God ; and no injustice can be asserted of Him for that, for according to their opinion it is proper that God should afflict the innocent and do good to the sinner."

(iv) " Man has free will ; it is therefore intelligible that the Torah contains commands and prohibitions, with announcements of reward and punishment. All acts of God are due to wisdom ; no injustice is found in Him and He does not afflict the good. The Mu'tazila[8] profess this theory, although they do not believe in man's absolute free will.[9] They hold also that God takes notice of the falling of the leaf and the destruction of the ant, and that His Providence extends over all things.

" This theory likewise implies contradictions and absurdities. The absurdities are these : The fact that some persons are born with defects, although they have not sinned previously, is ascribed to the wisdom of God, it being better for those persons to be in such a condition than to be in a normal state, though we do not see why it is better ; and they do not suffer thereby any punishment at all, but, on the contrary, enjoy God's goodness. In a similar manner the slaughter of the pious is explained as being for them the source of an increase of reward in future life. They go even further in their absurdities. We ask them why is God only just to man and not to other beings, and how has the irrational animal sinned that it is condemned to be slaughtered, and they reply it is good for the animal, for it will receive reward for it in the world to come ; also the flea and the louse will there receive compensation for their untimely death. The same reasoning they apply to the mouse torn by a cat or vulture ; the wisdom of God decreed this for the mouse, in order to reward it after death for the mishap. . . .

" I do not consider it proper to blame the followers of any of the last-named three theories on Providence, for they have been driven to accept them by weighty considerations. Aristotle was guided by that which appears to be the nature of things. The Ash'ariyah refused to ascribe to God ignorance about anything and to say that God, whilst knowing one individual being or one portion of the Universe, is ignorant of another portion ; they preferred to admit the above-mentioned absurdities. The Mu'tazilites refused to assume that God does what is wrong and unjust ; on the other hand, they would not contradict common sense and say that it was not wrong to inflict pain on the guiltless, or that the mission of the Prophets and the giving of the Torah had no intelligible reason. They likewise preferred to admit the above-named absurdities. But they even contradicted themselves, because they believe on the one hand that God knows everything, and on the other hand that man has free will."

(v) " This is our[10] theory, or that of our Torah. . . . The theory of man's perfectly free will is one of the fundamental principles of the Torah of our teacher Moses, and of those who follow the Torah. According to this principle, man does what is in his power to do, by his nature, his choice and his will ; and his action is not due to any faculty created for the purpose.[11]   All species of irrational animals likewise move by their own free will.   This is the Will of God : that is to say, it is due to the eternal divine will that all living beings should move freely, and that man should have power to act according to his will or choice within the limits of his capacity.   Against this principle we hear, thank God, no opposition on the part of our nation.

"Another fundamental principle taught by the Torah of Moses is this : Wrong cannot be ascribed to God in any way whatever ; all evils and afflictions as well as all kinds of happiness of man, whether they concern one individual person or a community, are distributed according to justice ; they are the result of a strict judgment that admits of no wrong whatever. Even when a person suffers pain in consequence of a thorn having entered into his hand, although it is at once drawn out, it is a punishment that has been inflicted upon him for sin, and the least pleasure he enjoys is a reward for some good action.   All this is meted out by strict justice ; as is said in Scripture, ' All His ways are judgment ' (Deut. xxxii. 4) ; we are only ignorant of the working of that judgment " (*Guide* III, 17).

§4. *Maimonides' views.*[12]   " My opinion on this principle of Divine Providence I will now explain to you.   In the principle which I now proceed to expound I do not rely on demonstrative proof, but on my conception of the spirit of the Divine Torah and the writings of the Prophets.   The principle which I accept is far less open to objections, and is more reasonable than the opinions mentioned above.   It is this : In the lower or sublunary portion of the Universe, Divine Providence does not extend to the individual members of species except in the case of mankind. It is only in this species that the incidents in the existence of the individual beings, their good and evil fortunes, are the result of justice, in accordance with the words, ' For all His ways are judgment '.

" But I agree with Aristotle as regards all other living beings, and *a fortiori* as regards plants and all the rest of earthly creatures. For I do not believe that it is through the interference of Divine Providence that a certain leaf drops from a tree, nor do I hold that when a certain spider catches a certain fly, that this is the direct result of a special decree and will of God in that moment ; it is not by a particular divine decree that the spittle of a certain person moved, fell on a certain gnat in a certain place, and killed it ; nor is it by the direct will of God that a certain fish catches and swallows a certain worm on the surface of the water. In all these cases the action is, according to my opinion, entirely due to chance, as taught by Aristotle.

" Divine Providence is connected with divine intellectual influence, and the same beings which are benefited by the latter so as to become intellectual, and to comprehend things comprehensible to rational beings, are also under the control of Divine Providence, which examines all their deeds in order to reward or punish them. It may be by mere chance that a ship goes down with all her contents, as in the above-mentioned instance, or the roof of a house falls upon those within ; but it is not due to chance, according to our view, that in the one instance the men went into the ship, or remained in the house in the other instance ; it is due to the will of God and is in accordance with the justice of His judgments, the method of which our mind is incapable of understanding. I have been induced to accept this theory by the circumstance that I have not met in any of the prophetical books with a description of God's Providence otherwise than in relation to human beings. The Prophets even express their surprise that God should take notice of man, who is too little and too unimportant to be worthy of the attention of the Creator ; how, then, should other living creatures be considered as proper objects for Divine Providence ! [13] . . .

" It cannot be objected to this theory, Why should God select mankind as the object of His special Providence, and not other living beings ? For he who asks this question must also inquire, Why has man alone, of all species of animals, been endowed with intellect ? The answer to the second question must be, according to the three afore-mentioned theories : It was the Will of God, it is the decree of His wisdom, or it is in accordance with the laws of Nature. The same answers apply to the first question.

" Understand thoroughly my theory, that I do not ascribe to God ignorance of anything or any kind of weakness. I hold that Divine Providence is related and closely connected with the intellect, because Providence can only proceed from an intelligent being, from a being that is itself the most perfect Intellect. Those creatures, therefore, which receive part of that intellectual influence, will become subject to the action of Providence in the same proportion as they are acted upon by the Intellect. . . .

" Hence it follows that the greater the share is which a person has obtained of this divine influence, on account of both his physical predisposition and his training, the greater must also be the effect of Divine Providence upon him, for the action of Divine Providence is proportional to the endowment of intellect.[14] The relation of Divine Providence is therefore not the same to all men ; the greater the human perfection a person has attained, the greater the benefit he derives from Divine Providence. . . .

" When we see that some men escape plagues and mishaps whilst others perish by them, we must not attribute this to a difference in the properties of their bodies, or in their physical constitution, ' for not by strength shall man prevail ' (1 Sam. ii. 9) ; but it must be attributed to their different degrees of perfection, some approaching God, whilst others move away from Him. Those who approach Him are best protected, and 'He will keep the feet of His holy ones' (*ibid.*) ; but those who keep far away from Him are left exposed to what may befall them ; there is nothing that could protect them from what might happen ; they are like those who walk in darkness and are certain to stumble. . . .

" Now consider how by this method of reasoning we have arrived at the truth taught by the Prophets, that every person has his individual share of Divine Providence in proportion to his perfection. For philosophical research leads to this conclusion, if we assume, as has been mentioned above, that Divine Providence is in each case proportional to the person's intellectual development. It is wrong to say that Divine Providence extends only to the species and not to individual beings, as some of the philosophers teach. For only individual beings have real existence, and individual beings are endowed with Divine Intellect ; Divine Providence acts, therefore, upon these individual beings " (*Guide* III, 17f).

Chapter VIII

REWARD AND PUNISHMENT

§1. *God's Justice.* Closely allied to the subject of Divine Providence is that of Reward and Punishment. It formed an important feature in Maimonides' theory as expounded in the last Chapter. It is the theme of his eleventh Principle of Faith :

" That He, the exalted One, rewards him who obeys the commands of the Torah, and punishes him who transgresses His prohibitions. That God's greatest reward to man is ' the future world ', and that His strongest punishment is ' cutting off '. . . . The Scriptural verses in which the Principle is pointed out are : ' Yet now if Thou wilt forgive their sin— ; and if not, blot me out of Thy book ' (Exod. xxxii. 32). And God replied to him, ' Whosoever hath sinned against Me, him will I blot out of My book ' (*ibid.* 33). This is a proof of what the obedient and the rebellious each obtain. God rewards the one and punishes the other " (C.M., Introd. to *Ḥélek*).

" When the Scriptures state of God, ' Who respecteth not persons nor taketh a bribe ' (Deut. x. 17), the reference cannot be to His acceptance of a bribe to avert justice, for that would be nonsense and an impossibility with God, something that could not in any way be imagined. For how can bribery be ascribed to Him ? What form could it take ? The meaning is that He will not accept good deeds as a bribe to overlook the bad. If, e.g., a man should perform a thousand good acts and a single bad deed, God will not pardon the one transgression because of the numerous good acts, even by deducting one or more of them ; but He will punish him for this one wrong action and reward him for the good " (C.M., *Abot* IV, 29).

So firm is his belief in God's strict justice, that Maimonides feels certain that He would bestow reward on an Israelite for secret obedience of the Torah, even if he were compelled in time of persecution outwardly to profess another religion. " If, according to the Rabbis,[1] notorious evil-doers (like Esau, Ahab and Nebuchadnezzar) are rewarded by God for a trifling good deed which they performed, when Jews are forced to apostasise and perform the commandments in secret, how is it possible that He will not reward them ! " (*Kiddush ha-Shém, Responsa* II, 13c).

" The man whose sins exceed his merits dies at once in consequence of his wickedness. Similarly a country whose sins are in excess perishes. So it is also with regard to the whole world ; if its sins exceed its merits, it is doomed to immediate destruction. The balancing of sins and merits is not quantitative but qualitative. There may be one good deed which outweighs many sins ; and again there may be one sin which outweighs many meritorious actions.[2] The deeds can therefore only be balanced by the mind of the God of all knowledge, and He alone is cognisant how good deeds are to be estimated against sins " (*Yad, Teshubah* III, 2).

§2. *Why Rewards and Punishments are promised.* The doctrine of Reward and Punishment is apparently at variance with that great ideal of Judaism that God should be served purely from love and without ulterior motive.3   Maimonides therefore explains that the Torah instituted Rewards for the incentive of those who have not reached the stage of perfection where they avoid the bad and adhere to the good on ethical grounds only. Rewards and Punishments were intended merely as a temporary expedient ; and he illustrates this thought by means of a parable :4

" Figure to yourself a child young in years brought to a teacher to be instructed by him in the Torah. But the child, on account of the fewness of his years and the weakness of his intellect, does not grasp the measure of that benefit, or the extent to which it leads him towards the attainment of perfection. The teacher must therefore necessarily stimulate him to learning by means of things in which he delights by reason of his youth. Thus he says to him, ' Read, and I shall give you nuts or figs, or a bit of sugar '. The child yields to this. He learns diligently, not indeed for the sake of the knowledge itself, as he does not know the importance of it, but merely to obtain that particular dainty (the eating of that dainty being more relished by him than study, and regarded as an unquestionably greater boon). And consequently he considers learning as a labour and a weariness to which he gives himself up in order by its means to gain his desired object, which consists of a nut, or a piece of sugar.

"When he grows older and his intelligence strengthens, he thinks lightly of the trifle in which he formerly found joy and begins to desire something new. He longs for this newly-chosen object of his, and his teacher now says to him, ' Read, and I shall buy you pretty shoes, or a coat of this kind ! ' Accordingly he again exerts himself to learn, not for the sake of the knowledge, but to acquire that coat ; for the garment ranks higher in his estimation than the learning and constitutes the final aim of his studies. When, however, he reaches a higher stage of mental perfection, this prize also ranks little with him, and he sets his heart upon something of greater moment. So that when his teacher bids him, ' Learn this section or that chapter and I will give you a *dinar*5 or two ', he learns with zest in order to obtain that money which to him is of more value than the learning, seeing that it constitutes the final aim of his studies.

" When, further, he reaches the age of greater discretion, this prize also loses its worth for him. He recognises its paltry nature and sets his heart upon something more desirable. His teacher then says to him, ' Learn, in order that you may become a Rabbi or a Judge ; the people will honour you and rise before you ; they will be obedient to your authority, and your name will be great, both in life and after death, as in the case of so and so '. The pupil throws himself into ardent study, striving all the time to reach this stage of eminence. His aim is that of obtaining the honour of men, their esteem and commendation.

" But all these methods are blameworthy. For in truth it is incumbent upon man, considering the weakness of the human mind, to make his aim in his acquisition of learning something which is extraneous to learning. And he should say of anything which is studied for the sake of gaining reward, ' Of a truth this is a silly business '. This is what the Sages meant when they used the expression *shello lishmah* ' not for its own sake '. They meant to tell us that men obey the laws of the Torah, perform its precepts, and study and strive, not to obtain the thing itself, but for a further object. The Sages prohibited this to us in the remark, ' Make not of the Torah a crown wherewith to aggrandize thyself, nor a spade wherewith to dig '.[6] They allude to that which I have made clear to you, viz., not to make the be-all and end-all of learning either the glorification of man or the acquisition of wealth. Also not to adopt the Torah of God as the means of a livelihood,[7] but to make the goal of one's study the acquisition of knowledge for its own sake.

" Similarly, the aim of one's study of truth ought to be the knowing of truth. The laws of the Torah are truth, and the purpose of their study is obedience to them. The perfect man must not say, ' If I perform these virtues and refrain from these vices which God forbade, what reward shall I receive ? ' For this would resemble the case of the lad who says, ' If I read, what present will be given me ? ' and he receives the reply that he will get such and such a thing . . . The Sages warned us against this also, viz., against a man making the attainment of some worldly object the end of his service to God, and his obedience to His precepts. And this is the meaning of the dictum of that distinguished and perfect man who understood the fundamental truth of things— Antigonus of Socho—' Be not like servants who minister to their master upon the condition of receiving a reward ; but be like servants who minister to their master without the condition of receiving a reward '.[8] They really meant to tell us by this that a man should believe in truth for truth's sake " (C.M., Introd. to Ḥélek).

However worthy this principle may be as an ideal, it can only be reached by a comparative few. The multitude can only be withheld from wrong-doing by means of threats and induced to obedience of the commandments by the hope of reward.

" Our Sages knew how difficult a thing this was (to be ' a server of God from motives of pure love ') and that not every one could act up to it. They knew that even the man who reached it would not at once accord with it and think it a true article of faith. For man only does those actions which will either bring him advantage or ward off loss. All other actions he holds vain and worthless. Accordingly, how could it be said to one who is learned in the Torah, ' Do these things, but do them not out of fear of God's punishment, nor out of hope for His reward ' ? This would be exceedingly hard, because it is not every one that comprehends truth, and becomes like Abraham our father.9 Therefore, in order that the common folk might be established in their convictions, the Sages permitted them to perform meritorious actions with the hope of reward, and to avoid the doing of evil out of fear of punishment. They encourage them to these conceptions and their opinions become firmly rooted, until eventually the intelligent among them come to comprehend and know what truth is and what is the most perfect mode of conduct.

" It is exactly the way in which we deal with the lad in his studies, as we have explained in our foregoing simile. . . . The people at large are not one jot the worse off through their performance of the precepts of the Torah by reason of their fear of punishment and expectation of reward ; for they are in a state of imperfection. On the contrary, they are by this means drawn to cultivate the necessary habits and training for acting in loyalty to the Torah. They bring themselves over to an understanding of

truth, and become 'servers out of pure love'. And
this is what the Sages meant by their remark, 'Man
should ever engage himself in the Torah, even though
it be not for the Torah's sake. Action regardless of
the Torah's sake will lead on to action regardful of
it' "[10] (op. cit.).

§3. *The Highest Form of Reward and Punishment.*
For the man who has passed the stage where he is
attracted by material reward or deterred by fear
of penalty, there is a sense in which he may still be
spurred on by recompense to do what is right.

" As regards the promises and threats alluded to
in the Torah, their interpretation is that which I
shall now tell you. It says to you, 'If you obey
these precepts, I will help you to a further obedience
of them and perfection in the performance of them.
And I shall remove all hindrances from you'. For
it is impossible for man to do the service of God when
sick or hungry or thirsty or in trouble, and this is
why the Torah promises the removal of all these
disabilities and gives man also the promise of health
and quietude until such a time as he shall have
attained perfection of knowledge and be worthy of
the life of the world to come.

" The final aim of the Torah is not that the earth
should be fertile, that people should live long, and that
bodies should be healthy. It simply helps us to the
performance of its precepts by holding out the
promise of all these things. Similarly, if men
transgress, their punishment will be that all these
hindrances will come into being, rendering them
powerless to do righteousness; as we read,
'Because thou didst not serve the Lord thy God
with joyfulness. . . . Therefore shalt thou serve

thine enemy whom the Lord shall send against thee '
(Deut. xxviii., 47).

" If you give this matter more than ordinary
consideration, you will find it to be equivalent to being
told, ' If you carry out a portion of these laws with
love and diligence, we shall help you to a performance of all of them by removing from you all difficulties and obstacles ; but if you abandon any of
them out of disdain we shall bring hindrances into
your path that will prevent you from doing any of
them, so that you will gain neither perfection nor
eternity '. This is what is meant by the assertion of
the Rabbis, ' The recompense of a precept is a precept,
and the recompense of transgression is transgression ' "[11]
(C.M., Introd. to *Ḥélek*).

" When we perform all the commandments of the
Torah, the good things of this world will fall to our
lot ; and when we transgress them, the calamities
recorded in the Torah will befall us. Nevertheless,
those good things are not the ultimate reward of
obeying the commandments ; nor are those calamities the ultimate punishment for transgressing all
the commandments. The solution of the matter is
as follows.

" The Holy One, blessed be He, has given us this
Torah, which is a tree of life to everyone who performs
all that is written therein. Whoever knows it with
a perfect and correct knowledge thereby merits
the life of the world to come, and does so in proportion
to the greatness of his deeds and the abundance
of his wisdom. God has assured us in the Torah
that if we perform it joyfully and with a willing spirit,
constantly meditating on its wisdom, He will remove
from us everything which withholds us from performing its ordinances, such as illness, war, famine

and the like ; and He will grant us all the good things which strengthen our hands to perform the Torah, such as plenty, peace, and abundance of silver and gold ; to the end that we shall not, throughout our life, occupy ourselves with the needs of the body, but dwell in leisure to study wisdom and perform the commandments, thereby meriting the life of the world to come. . . .

" He has likewise informed us in the Torah that if we wilfully abandon it and occupy ourselves with the vanities of the time, the true Judge will remove from those who abandon the Torah all the good things of this world which strengthened their hands to spurn it ; and He will bring upon them all the calamities which prevent them from acquiring the world to come, to the end that they may perish in their wickedness " (*Yad, Teshubah* IX, 1).

The form which the penalty inflicted upon the wicked will take is thus described :

" The consummate evil (of punishment) consists in the cutting off of the soul, its perishing and its failure to attain durability. This is the meaning of ' cutting off ' mentioned in the Torah. The meaning is the cutting off of the soul, as the Torah manifestly declares, ' That soul shall surely be cut off ' (Num. xv. 31). And the Sages remarked : ' cut off ' in this world, ' surely cut off ' in the world to come[12] . . . All those who devote themselves to bodily pleasures, rejecting truth and choosing falsehood, are cut off from participation in that exalted state of things and remain as detached matter merely " (C.M., Introd. to *Ḥélek*).

" This ' cutting off ' will apparently take place after the sinner has suffered punishment for his misdeeds. But Maimonides is very vague—deliberately

so, no doubt—on this point. All he tells us is:
" Gehinnom is an expression for the suffering that will
befall the wicked. The nature of this suffering is not
expounded in the Talmud. One authority there
states that the sun will draw near the wicked and
burn them.[13] He gets his proof from the verse,
' For behold the day cometh, it burneth as a furnace '
(Mal. iii. 19). Another asserts that a strange heat
will arise in their bodies and consume them. He
derives proof for this from the phrase, ' Your breath
is a fire that shall devour you.' (Isa. xxxiii. 11) "
(*ibid.*).

§4. *Repentance.* Man is granted one means of escape
from punishment for his evil deeds, and that is sincere
repentance.

" Repentance is one of those principles which are
an indispensable element in the creed of the followers
of the Torah. For it is impossible for man to be
entirely free from error and sin ; he either does not
know the opinion which he has to choose, or he adopts
a principle, not for its own merits, but in order to
gratify his desire or passion. If we were convinced
that we could never make our crooked ways straight,
we should for ever continue in our errors, and perhaps
add other sins to them since we did not see that any
remedy was left to us. But the belief in the effect
of repentance causes us to improve, to return to the
best of the ways, and to become more perfect than
we were before we sinned " (*Guide* III, 36).

" At this time, when the Temple no longer
exists and we have no atoning altar, there remains
nothing but repentance. Repentance atones for
all transgressions. Even he who has been wicked
throughout his life, and at last |repents, has not

the least part of his wickedness recorded against him. . . .

"What constitutes perfect repentance? It is when a temptation befalls him who has previously succumbed to it and he has the possibility of repeating his offence, but he abstains from doing so from repentance, and not from fear or lack of ability. If one repent only in old age, at a time when it is not possible for him to do what he has been in the habit of doing, although this is not an ideal form of repentance, it avails him and he is a penitent. Even if he had been a sinner all his life, and repented on the day of his death so that he die in penitence, all his sins are pardoned. . . .

"What is repentance? It is that the sinner abandon his sin, remove it from his mind, and also resolve in his heart never to do it again. He must likewise feel contrition for having transgressed, and call Him Who knoweth all secrets to witness that he will never repeat this sin. He must also make a verbal confession and give utterance to the resolutions which he had determined in his heart. Whoever confesses with words, without resolving in his heart to abandon his sins, is like one who undergoes immersion while clutching the unclean thing in his hand.[14] The immersion is useless to him until he throw away the unclean thing. . . .

"It is of the manifestations of repentance that the penitent should cry unremittingly before God with weeping and supplications, practise charity according to his means, keeping himself far from the object of his sin, and alter his name—as though to say, I am a different person and not the same man who committed those actions. He must amend his whole conduct and turn towards the right path. Another thing he should do is to leave the place of his domicile, because exile atones for iniquity,[15] since it causes a man to be humbled and thus become meek and lowly of spirit.

" It is most commendable for the penitent to make his confession publicly, and proclaim his transgressions, disclosing to others the offences existing between himself and his fellow-creatures in such terms as these, ' In truth I have sinned against so and so ; such and such have I done to him ; but to-day I repent and regret it '. As for the man who is proud and refuses to proclaim his transgressions but conceals them, his repentance is not genuine. This, however, applies only to transgressions between man and man ; but with regard to transgressions between man and God, he need not make them public. Rather would it be effrontery on his part, if he were to disclose them ; but he should repent only to God and enumerate his sins before Him, only making a general confession in public. It is preferable that his sin be not published " (*Yad, Teshubah* I, 3, II, 1-5).

Maimonides maintains that sometimes God penalises a heinous sinner by checking his will to repent so that he should die in his wickedness and receive punishment for his misdeeds.

" God at times punishes man by withholding repentance from him, thus not allowing him free will as regards repentance,[15a] for God, blessed be He, knows the sinners, and His wisdom and equity mete out their punishment. Sometimes He punishes only in this world, sometimes only in the world to come, sometimes in both. Furthermore, His punishment in this world is varied, sometimes being bodily, sometimes pecuniary, and sometimes both at once. . . . It is not necessary for us to know about God's wisdom so as to be able to ascertain why He inflicts precisely such punishment as He does and no other, just as little as we know why one species has a certain particular form and not another. It is sufficient for us to know the general principle, that God is righteous in all His ways, that He punishes the sinner according to his sin, and rewards the pious according to his righteousness " (C.M., *Eight Chapters* VIII.).

§5. *Free Will.* The whole doctrine of Reward and Punishment rests upon the supposition that man is endowed with free will and has unhampered choice of action to do good or evil, Maimonides accordingly emphasises human freedom in this respect.

" Free will is granted to every man. If he wish to direct himself to the good way and become righteous, the will to do so is in his hand ; and if he wish to direct himself to the bad way and become wicked, the will to do so is in his hand. That is what is written in the Torah, ' Behold, the man is become as one of us, to know good and evil ' (Gen. iii. 22)— that is to say, the human species has become unique in the world and there is no other species like it in this respect, viz., in knowing by itself, by its own knowledge and reflection, what is good and what is evil, and in doing whatever it wishes without there being anyone to withhold it from doing the good or the evil.

" Let there not enter your mind the assertion of the fools of other peoples and also of the many uninformed men among the Israelites, viz., that the Holy One, blessed be He, decrees concerning the human being, from his birth, whether he is to be righteous or wicked. The matter is not so ; but every man has the possibility of becoming as righteous as Moses our teacher or as wicked as Jeroboam, wise or stupid, kind or cruel, miserly or generous, and similarly with all the other qualities. There is no one to compel, decree or determine him as to either of the two ways ; but it is he, of his own accord and mind, who inclines towards whichever way he prefers. That is what Jeremiah said, ' Out of the mouth of the Most High proceedeth not evil and good ' (Lam. iii. 38)[16], meaning, the Creator does not decree concerning a man that he should be either good or bad. It consequently follows that the sinner caused his own downfall. It therefore behoves him to weep and lament over his sins and for having done violence to his soul. Hence the quotation proceeds, ' Wherefore doth a living man complain ', etc. ; and Jeremiah goes on to say, since our will is under our control and we have consciously committed all the wicked deeds, it behoves us to turn in repentance and abandon our wickedness, because the choice is now in our hands. That is what the text continues, ' Let us search and try our ways, and return to the Lord ' (ibid. 40).

"This subject is a most important Principle of Faith ; it is a pillar of the Torah and of the commandments. . . . If God were to decree concerning man whether he is to be righteous or wicked, or if there were anything in the nature of his nativity which impelled him to either of the two ways, or to a particular quality, or to a particular disposition, or to a particular action, as the foolish astrologers invent in their minds, how could He have commanded us through the Prophets, Do this and avoid that, mend your ways and go not after your wickedness, if from the outset of his existence his fate had been decreed for him or his nativity impels him to something from which he cannot possibly desist ? What place would there have been for the whole of the Torah ? And by what justice, or by what right, could He punish the wicked or reward the righteous ? ' Shall not the Judge of all the earth do justly ? ' (Gen. xviii. 25).

" Do not say in surprise, How can a man do all that he desires and his actions be under his control ? Can he do anything in the world without the permission and will of his Creator ; as Scripture declares, ' Whatsoever the Lord pleased, that hath He done in heaven and in earth ' (Ps. cxxxv. 6) ? Know that everything is done according to His will, although our actions are under our control. How is this ? In the same way that the Creator willed that fire and air should move upward, that water and earth should move downward, that the Sphere revolve in a circle, and that all other things which were created in the Universe should have the tendency which He desired, so did He desire that a man should be possessed of free will, that all his actions should be under his control, and that there should not be anything to compel or withhold him, but that of his own accord and by the mind with which God had endowed him, he should do all that man is able to do. For this reason is man judged according to his actions ; if he has done what is good, good is done to him ; and if he has done what is evil, evil is done to him " (*Yad, Teshubah* V, 1-4).

" The Rabbis expatiate very much upon this subject in the *Midrash Kohélet* and in other writings, one of their statements in reference to this matter being, ' Everything follows its natural course '.[17] In everything that they said, you will always find that the Rabbis, peace be upon them, avoided referring to the Divine Will as determining a particular event at a particular time. When, therefore, they said that man rises and sits down in accordance with the will of God, their meaning was that, when man was first created, his nature was so determined that rising up and sitting down were to be optional to him ; but they as little meant that God wills at any special moment that man should or should not get up, as He determines at any given time that a certain stone should or should not fall to the ground.[18]

" The sum and substance of the matter is, then, that thou shouldst believe that just as God willed that man should be upright in stature, broadchested, and have fingers, likewise did He will that man should move or rest of his own accord, and that his actions should be such as his own free will dictates to him, without any outside influence or restraint " (C.M., *Eight Chapters* VIII).

A correspondent, however, questioned him as to how it was possible to reconcile the doctrine of free will with the Rabbinic statement that " marriages were made in heaven ".[19] His reply is rather curious :

" When the Sage stated that the daughter of *A* is the predestined bride of *B*, this comes under the heading of Reward and Punishment ; for if this man or woman acted meritoriously entitling them to the reward of a fine and praiseworthy marriage, He couples them together. Similarly if He has to punish them with a marriage which is to be productive of constant strife, He couples them " (*Responsa* I, 34c).

§6. *Prescience and Determinism.* Free will raises the difficult problem of God's foreknowledge of events. Maimonides' treatment of the subject was considered by subsequent Jewish philosophers as weak and unphilosophical, since he takes refuge in an agnostic attitude and avoids the issue. His solution is as follows :

" The reason for their belief (that man is determined in his actions) they base on the following statement. ' Does God know or does He not know that a certain individual will be good or bad ? If thou sayest He knows, then it necessarily follows that man is compelled to act as God knew beforehand he would act, otherwise God's knowledge would be imperfect. If thou sayest that God does not know in advance, then great absurdities and destructive religious theories will result '. Listen, therefore, to what I shall tell thee, reflect well upon it, for it is unquestionably the truth.

" It is, indeed, an axiom of the science of the divine, i.e., metaphysics, that God, may He be blessed, does not know by means of knowledge, and does not live by means of life, so that He and His knowledge may be considered two different things in the sense that this is true of man[20]; for man is distinct from knowledge, and knowledge from man, in consequence of which they are two different things. If God knew by means of knowledge, He would necessarily be a plurality, and the primal essence would be composite, that is, consisting of God Himself, the knowledge by which He knows, the life by which He lives, the power by which He has strength, and similarly of all His attributes. I shall only mention one argument, simple and easily understood by all, though there are strong and convincing arguments and proofs that solve this difficulty. It is manifest that God is identical with His attributes and His attributes with Him, so that it may be said that He is the knowledge, the knower and the known, and that He is the life, the living and the source of His own life, the same being true of His other attributes. . . .

"Another accepted axiom of metaphysics is that human reason cannot fully conceive God in His true essence, because of the perfection of God's essence and the imperfection of our reason, and because His essence is not due to causes through which it may be known. Furthermore, the inability of our reason to comprehend Him may be compared to the inability of our eyes to gaze at the sun,[21] not because of the weakness of the sun's light, but because that light is more powerful than that which seeks to gaze into it.

"From what we have said, it has been demonstrated also that we cannot comprehend God's knowledge, that our minds cannot grasp it at all, for He is His knowledge and His knowledge is He. . . . Reflect, then, upon all that we have said, viz., that man has control over his actions, that it is by his own determination that He does either the right or the wrong, without, in either case, being controlled by fate, and that, as a result of this divine commandment, teaching, preparation, reward and punishment are proper. Of this there is absolutely no doubt. As regards, however, the character of God's knowledge, how He knows everything, this is, as we have explained, beyond the reach of human ken" (C.M., *Eight Chapters* VIII, end).

CHAPTER IX

ESCHATOLOGY

§1. *The Coming of the Messiah*. Maimonides concludes his formulation of the cardinal principles of Judaism with a reference to Eschatology, i.e., the doctrine of the last things, the final state of humanity as a whole as well as of the individual in the hereafter. His twelfth Principle of Faith deals with :

" The days of the Messiah. This involves the belief and firm faith in his coming, and that we should not find him slow in coming. ' Though he tarry, wait for him ' (Hab. ii. 3). No date must be fixed for his appearance, neither may the Scriptures be interpreted with the view of deducing the time of his coming.[1] The Sages said, ' A plague on those who calculate periods ' (for Messiah's appearance).[2] We must have faith in him, honouring and loving him, and praying for him according to the degree of importance with which he is spoken of by every Prophet, from Moses unto Malachi. He that has any doubt about him or holds his authority in light esteem imputes falsehood to the Torah, which clearly promises his coming in ' the Chapter of Balaam '[3] and in ' Ye stand this day all of you before the Lord your God '[4]. From the general nature of this Principle of Faith we gather that there will be no king of Israel but from David and the descendants of Solomon exclusively. Every one who disputes

220

the authority of this family denies God and the words of His Prophets " (C.M., Introd. to *Ḥélek*).

§2. *The Personality of the Messiah.* The fullest expression of his views on this subject is found in the Letter addressed by him to the Community of Yemen which had been disturbed by the appearance of a claimant to the Messiahship. Maimonides denounces him as an impostor because his qualifications were not those which must be possessed by the true Messiah.

" The Messiah will be a very great Prophet, greater than all the Prophets with the exception of Moses our teacher. . . . His status will be higher than that of the Prophets and more honourable, Moses alone excepted. The Creator, blessed be He, will single him out with features wherewith He had not singled out Moses ; for it is said with reference to him, ' And his delight shall be in the fear of the Lord ; and he shall not judge after the sight of his eyes, neither decide after the hearing of his ears ' (Isa. xi. 3). It is likewise said, ' And the spirit of the Lord shall rest upon him, the spirit of wisdom and understanding, the spirit of counsel and might, the spirit of knowledge and of the fear of the Lord ' (*v.* 2) ; and ' Righteousness shall be the girdle of his loins and faithfulness the girdle of his reins ' (*v.* 5). The Holy One applied six names to him : ' Wonderful, Counsellor, God, Mighty, Everlasting Father, Prince of Peace ' (*ibid.* ix. 5). His being called ' God ' is hyperbolical, and intimates that his greatness will be superior to that of all men.

" It is one of the known conditions with us that every Prophet must have reached mental perfection before God endows him with Prophecy ; for it is a fundamental principle with us that Prophecy only alights upon a man who is wise, mighty and rich, i.e., mighty in self-control, rich in knowledge.5 But when a man arises who is not renowned for wisdom, claiming to be a Prophet, we do not believe him. How much less do we believe one of the common people ('*ammé ha-arets*) who claims to be the Messiah.

" One of the evidences that such a man belongs to ' the common people ' is that he commands his fellowman to part with all his money by distributing it among the poor.6 All who obey him are fools, and he is a sinner who acts contrary to the Torah. According to our Torah it is not proper to spend all one's possessions in charity but only a part of it— not more than one-fifth7 . . .

" As regards the origin of the Messiah and the place of his appearance, he will first manifest himself in the land of Israel ; as it is said, ' And the Lord, whom ye seek, will suddenly come to His temple ; and the messenger of the covenant, whom ye delight in, behold, he cometh ' (Mal. iii. 1). But with respect to his origin, you cannot know it beforehand, until it is declared of him that he is the son of so and so and from such and such a family. A man will arise who is unknown before his manifestation, and the signs and marvels which will be seen through him will be proof of the validity of his claim.8 For so has the Holy One, blessed be He, informed us on this matter : ' Behold, a man whose name is the Shoot, and who shall shoot up out of his place ' (Zech. vi. 12). Similarly declared Isaiah, ' For he shot up right forth as a sapling ' (liii. 2). . . .

" The special feature with respect to him is that at the time when he manifests himself, all the kings of the earth will be stirred at the report of him and will be filled with dread ; their kingdoms also will be stirred. They will conspire how to withstand him either by the sword or by other means ; that is to say, they will not be able to dispute his claims or deny him, but they will be stirred by the miracles which will be evidenced by him and place their hand upon their mouth (cf. Isa. lii. 15). He will put to death by his word whoever wishes to kill him without possibility of escape ; as it is said, ' And he shall smite the land with the rod of his mouth, and with the breath of his lips shall he slay the wicked ' (Isa. xi. 4) " (*Iggéret Téman, Responsa* II, 6c-7a).

" Let it not enter thy mind that the King Messiah must necessarily perform signs and wonders, display some novelty in the world, revive the dead, or do something similar. It is not so ; for Rabbi Akiba was among the greatest of the Sages of the Mishnah, yet he was the armour-bearer of Ben Koziba, and acknowledged him as King Messiah.[9] Both he and all the other Sages[10] thought him to be the King Messiah until he was slain for his sins ; when he fell in battle it was known that he was not the Messiah. The Sages never demanded of him a sign or miracle. . . .

" If there arise a king from the house of David who meditates in the Torah, occupies himself with the commandments after the manner of his ancestor David, in accord with both the written and the oral law, induces all Israel to walk therein and repair its breach, and fights the battles of the Lord, it may be presumed of him that he is the Messiah. If he succeed in rebuilding the Temple on its site and gathering the dispersed of Israel, he is certainly the Messiah. But if he does not succeed to this extent or is slain, it is certain that he is not the Messiah promised in the Torah. He is to be considered like all the other pious and upright kings of the house of David who died, and the Holy One, blessed be He, only raised him up to try the multitude ; as it is said, ' And some of them that are wise shall stumble, to refine among them, and to purify, and to make white, even the time of the end ; for it is yet for the time appointed ' (Dan. xi. 35).

" Even of him who imagined that he was the Messiah, but was put to death by the Court,[11] Daniel had previously prophesied ; as it is said, ' Also the children of the violent among thy people shall lift themselves up to establish the vision ; but they shall stumble ' (*ibid.* 14). Has there ever been a greater stumbling than this ? For all the Prophets declared that the Messiah would be the deliverer of Israel and their saviour, gathering their dispersed ones and confirming the commandments. But he caused Israel to perish by the sword, their remnant to be dispersed and humbled. He induced them to change the Torah and led the greater part of the world to err and serve another than God.

" No human being, however, is capable of fathoming the designs of the Creator ; for their ways are not His ways, neither are His thoughts their thoughts. All these events, and even those relating to him who succeeded the one referred to,[12] were nothing else than a means for preparing the way for the King Messiah. It will reform the whole world to worship the Lord with one accord ; as it is said, ' For then will I turn to the peoples a pure language, that they may all call upon the name of the Lord to serve Him with one consent ' (Zeph. iii. 9). How will this be ? The entire world has been filled with the doctrine of the Messiah, the Torah and the commandments. The

doctrines have been propagated to the distant isles
and among many peoples, uncircumcised of heart
and flesh. They discuss these subjects which contradict the Torah. Some declare these commandments were true, but are abrogated at the present
time and have lost their force; while others assert
there are occult significations in them and they are
not plain of meaning—the king has already come
and revealed their hidden significance.[13] But when
the king Messiah will in fact arise and succeed, be
exalted and lifted up, they will immediately all
recant and acknowledge the falsity of their asser
tion " (*Yad, Melachim* XI, 3f).

§3. *The Messianic Era.* " The days of the Messiah
will be the time when the kingdom will revert to
Israel who will return to the Holy Land. The king
who will then reign will have Zion as the capital of
his realm. His name will be great and fill the earth
to its uttermost bounds. It will be a greater name
than that of King Solomon and mightier. The
nations will make peace with him, and lands will
obey him by reason of his great rectitude and the
wonders that will come to light by his means. Any
one that rises up against him God will destroy and
make him fall into his hand. All verses of Scripture
testify to his prosperity and our prosperity in him.

" So far as existing things are concerned, there
will be no difference whatever between now and then,
except that Israel will possess the kingdom. And
this is the sense of the Rabbis' statement, ' There
is no difference between this world and the days of the
Messiah except the subjugation of the kingdom
alone '.[14] In his days there will be both the strong
and the weak in their relations to others. But

225

verily in those days the gaining of their livelihood will be so very easy to men that they will do the lightest possible labour and reap great benefit. It is this that is meant by the remark of the Rabbis, ' The land of Israel will one day produce cakes ready baked, and garments of fine silk '[15] . . .

" The great benefits that will accrue to us at that epoch will consist in our enjoying rest from the work of subjugating the kingdoms of wickedness, a work which prevents us from the full performance of righteous action. Knowledge will increase, as it is said, ' For the earth shall be full of the knowledge of the Lord ' (Isa. xi. 9). Discords and wars will cease, as it is said, ' Nation shall not lift up sword against nation ' (Micah iv. 3). Great perfection will appertain to him that lives in those days, and he will be elevated through it to the ' life of the world to come '. But the Messiah will die, and his son and son's son will reign in his stead. God has clearly declared his death in the words, ' He shall not fail nor be crushed, till he have set the right in the earth ' (Isa. xlii. 4). His kingdom will endure a very long time and the lives of men will be long also, because longevity is a consequence of the removal of sorrows and cares " (C.M., Introd. to Ḥélek).

" The King Messiah will arise and restore the kingdom of David to its former position and original dominion. He will rebuild the Temple and gather the dispersed of Israel. All the ordinances will come into force in his days as they used to be in the olden times ; sacrifices will again be offered ; the year of release and the Jubilee[16] will be again observed according to their commandments as stated in the Torah . . .

" Let it not enter the mind that in the days of the

Messiah anything in the world's system will cease to exist, or any novelty be introduced into the scheme of the Universe ; but the world will go on as usual. The statement of Isaiah, ' The wolf shall dwell with the lamb, and the leopard shall lie down with the kid ' (xi. 6), is a metaphorical expression signifying that Israel will dwell in safety among the wicked of the heathens who are likened to wolves and leopards (cf. Jer. v. 6)[16a]. They will be converted to the true religion, and will no more plunder and destroy, but will live honestly and quietly like Israel. . . .

" The Sages and Prophets did not long for the days of the Messiah for the purpose of wielding dominion over all the world, or of ruling over the heathens, or being exalted by the peoples, or of eating and drinking and rejoicing ; their desire was to be free to devote themselves to the Torah and its wisdom, without anyone to oppress and disturb them, in order that they might merit the life of the world to come.

" In that era, there will not be famine or war, jealousy or strife. Prosperity will be widespread, all comforts found in abundance. The sole occupation throughout the world will be to know the Lord. Hence Israelites will be very wise, learned in things that are now hidden, and will attain a knowledge of the Creator to the utmost capacity of the human being ; as it is said, ' For the earth shall be full of the knowledge of the Lord, as the waters cover the sea ' (Isa. xi. 9) " (Yad, Melachim XI, 1 ; XII, 1, 4f).

" On this account all Israel, their Prophets and their Sages, longed for the days of the Messiah. It was for the purpose of obtaining relief from the kingdoms which do not allow them to occupy themselves with the Torah and the commandments in a proper manner ; to the end that they may experience quietness and increase in wisdom, and so merit the life of the world to come. . . . The ultimate reward and final bliss, to which there is neither cessation nor diminution, is the life of the world to come ; whereas the days of the Messiah belong to this world, and the Universe will continue as usual, except that the sovereignty will revert to Israel " (*Yad, Teshubah* IX, 2).

Maimonides apparently associates the Garden of Eden (Paradise) with the Messianic Era and not with the world to come, because he locates it in the sublunary world.

" As for the Garden of Eden, it is a fertile spot on the earth's Sphere rich in streams and fruits. God will of a certainty disclose it to man one day, and will show him the path leading to it. Man will reap enjoyment within it, and there may possibly be found therein plants of a very extraordinary sort, great in usefulness and rich in pleasure-giving properties, in addition to those which are renowned with us. All this is not impossible nor far-fetched. On the contrary, it is quite near possibility, and would be so even if the Torah failed to allude to it. How much more is it the case seeing that it has a clear and conspicuous place in the Torah ! " (C.M., Introd. to *Ḥélek*).

In addition to the fact that the Torah mentions the Garden of Eden as a place located on earth, Maimonides was doubtless influenced by the thought which he stresses that physical pleasures are unknown in the world to come.[17]

§4. *Calculating the Time of the Advent.* Considerable mischief was sometimes done by attempts to foretell by means of abstruse calculations when the Messiah would come. The approach of the date would create expectation in the hearts of the people, and, what was worse, induce an impostor to put himself forward as the awaited deliverer. It was in circumstances of this kind that, in 1172, Maimonides addressed a Letter to the Jews of Yemen, in which he warned them :

" It is your duty to know that it is not proper for any man to endeavour to ascertain when the ' end ' will truly come ; as Daniel explained, ' The words are shut up and sealed till the time of the end ' (xii. 9). But some of the learned have indulged in much speculation on this question and imagined they had solved it ; as the Prophet foretold, ' Many shall run to and fro, and knowledge shall be increased ' (v. 4)—meaning, the opinions and conjectures on this point will be increased. The Holy One, blessed be He, had previously declared through His Prophets that some men will calculate ' ends ' for the Messiah, but these will pass by without fulfilment. After that, He warned us not to despair on account of this, saying, Do not distress yourselves if their calculation proves wrong, but however long the Messiah delay, heighten your hope in him. Thus it is said, ' For the vision is yet for the appointed time, and it declareth of the end, and doth not lie ; though he tarry, wait for him because he will surely come, he will not delay ' (Hab. ii. 3). . . .

" Daniel has explained to us the profundity of the knowledge concerning the ' end ', and that it was ' shut up ' and concealed. For that reason the Sages withheld us from calculating the advent of the Messiah, since it becomes a stumbling-block to the masses and leads them to make mistakes when the foretold ' end ' arrives, when in fact it has not. And so the Sages exclaimed, ' A plague on those who make such calculations ! ' "[18] (*Iggéret Téman, Responsa* II, 5a).

Despite this strong stand against working out a date for the coming of the Messiah, the same Letter contains a calculation, supposed to have been made by Maimonides himself :

" We have a tradition on this matter that the saying of Balaam, ' Now (*lit.* like the time) is it said of Jacob and of Israel, What hath God wrought ! ' (Num. xxiii. 23), contains a secret that from that time is to be reckoned the same period that had elapsed up to then from the Creation of the world, and then the Prophets will say to them, ' What hath God wrought ! ' This Prophecy was uttered in the fortieth year from the Exodus from Egypt ; and you will find that from the beginning of the era up to that time was 2,488 years. According to this analogy and explanation, the Prophecy will be fulfilled in Israel in the year 4,976 from the Creation of the world " (*op. cit.*, 5b, c).

This date corresponds with the year 1216 of the current era. But it hardly seems possible that Maimonides should have practised in the same letter the very thing which he wrote the letter to denounce. As Dr. Friedländer, the translator of the *Guide*, points out, " The inconsistency is so obvious that it is impossible to attribute this passage to Maimonides himself. It is probably spurious, and has, perhaps, been added by the translator ".[19]

§5. *The World to Come.* It is to be gathered from the quotations in §3 that Maimonides regarded the Messianic Era as a helpful preparation to the attain-

ment of the bliss of the world to come ; but whereas
the former is a condition to be experienced in the
lifetime of man, the latter awaits the righteous after
death.

" The good which is treasured up for the righteous
is the life of the world to come ; it is a life which is
deathless and a happiness free from all adversity.
. . . The reward of the righteous is their meriting
this bliss and enjoying this happy state. The punishment of the wicked is that they do not merit this
higher form of life, but are cut off and die. Whoever
does not merit that life suffers death without ever
recovering life again ; he is cut off in his wickedness
and perishes like the beast " (*Yad, Teshubah* VIII, 1).

" The reason why the Sages called it ' the world to
come ' was not because it does not exist now, and this
world must first perish and after that the other world
comes into being. That is not so ; but it is actually in
existence. The only reason the Sages called it ' the
world to come ' was because that life comes to man
subsequently to the life of this world in which we
exist both with body and soul, and is the first stage of
existence through which all men pass " (*ibid.* §8).

§6. *Who will have a share in the world to come.* " All
the wicked (of Israel), though their sins be numerous,
are judged according to their wrongdoings, but still
have a share in the world to come ; because all Israel
have a share therein, although they have sinned.
. . . Likewise the pious of the nations of the world
have a share in it.[20]

" The following (Israelites) have no share in the
world to come, but are cut off, perish and are condemned for all eternity because of their great
wickedness and sinfulness ; viz., infidels and heretics,

they who deny the Torah, they who deny the resurrection of the dead and the coming of the Redeemer, apostates, they who cause the public to sin, they who deviate from the accepted practices of the Community, he who commits transgressions presumptuously and openly like Jehoiakin, informers, they who overawe the Community, not for a religious purpose, they who shed blood, slanderers, and he who obliterates the mark of his circumcision " (*Yad, Teshubah* III, 5f).

" Our statement that none of these sinners has a share in the world to come applies only when he dies without repentance ; but if he turn from his wickedness and die a penitent, he is of the sons of the world to come, because there is nothing which can stand against repentance. Even if one denied a fundamental principle of religion all his life but finally repented, he has a share in the world to come " (*ibid.* §14).

Martyrdom is a certain qualification for the bliss of the hereafter. " The man whom God makes worthy to ascend to this highest degree, viz., to be slain for the sanctification of the Name, even were his iniquities to be like those of Jeroboam the son of Nebat and his associates, he is destined for the world to come. This is so, even if he were not learned in the Torah ; for thus said the Sages,[21] ' No creature can attain the height which is achieved by those who are slain by an idolatrous government ' " (*Kiddush ha-Shém, Responsa* II, 14c).

The performance of a single commandment from disinterested motives will also secure a person that happiness. " It is a cardinal principle of faith in the Torah that should a man fulfil one of the 613 commandments in a proper manner, without associating with it any worldly motive whatever, but performing it for its own sake from a sentiment of love, he merits by that act the life of the world to come " (C.M., *Makkot* III, end).

§7. *The Immortal Soul.* Maimonides does not specify the immortality of the soul as a separate Principle of Faith, because it is clearly implied in that relating to the Resurrection of the Dead. But with reference to immortality he understands " soul " in a special sense.

" The soul that remains after the death of man is not the soul that lives in a man when he is born. The latter is a mere faculty, while that which has a separate existence after death is a reality.[22] Again, the soul and the spirit[23] of man during his life are two different things ; therefore the souls and the spirits are both named as existing in man ; but separate from the body only one of them exists [24] " (*Guide* I, 70).

Maimonides identifies the immortal soul with the rational faculty.

" The soul of all flesh is the form[25] thereof which God gave to it ; and the superior knowledge which is found in the soul of man is the form of the man who is perfect in his knowledge. Concerning this form it is said in the Torah, ' Let us make man in our image, after our likeness ' (Gen. i. 26),[26] meaning that man should possess a form that is able to know and comprehend the Intelligences which are incorporeal like the Angels, who are form without matter, until he becomes like them. This does not refer to that form which is perceptible to the eye, viz., the mouth, the nose, the cheek-bones, or the other features of the body, the term for which is *toar*, ' shape '. Nor does it refer to the ' soul ' which is common to all living creatures, by which it eats, drinks, propagates, feels and reflects[27] ; but it refers to the knowledge which is the form of the soul,[28] and it is of the form of the soul that Scripture declares ' in our image, after our likeness '. This form is often called *néphesh* and also *ruaḥ*. . . .

" This form of the soul is not composed of the elements, so that it ever could be decomposed into them ; nor does it proceed from the power of the breath of life (*neshamah*), so that it should stand in need of the breath of life in the same manner that the breath of life stands in need of the body. But it issues from God, from Heaven ; therefore when the matter, which is composed of the elements, becomes decomposed, and when the breath of life also perishes—since it cannot exist apart from the body, and is in need of the body in all its functions—this form is not destroyed, because it is not in need of the breath of life in its functions, but knows and comprehends the Intelligences that are separate from matter, and knows the Creator of all things. It endures for all eternity " (*Yad, Yesodé ha-Torah* IV, 8f).

" Whenever the expression *néphesh* is used in this connection, it does not refer to the breath of life which is in need of a body, but to the form of the soul, viz., the intelligence which comprehends the Intelligences that are separate from matter, as well as other created things " (*Yad, Teshubah* VIII, 3).

" When it is established that this soul (which is identical with the rational faculty) is in no way matter and is not dependent on matter, it cannot be doubted that when it parts from the body, it returns to the original source whence it issued and remains immortal for all eternity " (*Ma'amar ha-Yiḥud*, pp. 15f).

§8. *Resurrection of the Dead*. Maimonides' last Principle of Faith contains nothing more than this : " The resurrection of the dead. We have already explained this ". The explanation alluded to is that given earlier in the Introduction to *Ḥélek* in the following terms : " The Resurrection of the Dead is one of the cardinal doctrines of the Torah of Moses. He who does not believe in this has no religion, and no bond with the Jewish Faith. But it is the reward of the righteous only, as is shown by the statement in *Beréshit Rabba* : ' The great benefits of rain are for both the righteous and the wicked, but the resurrection of the dead applies to the righteous only '.[29] And forsooth how shall the evil-doers live after death, seeing that they were dead even in life ; as the Sages said, ' The wicked are called dead even during their lives, but the good are called living even after death '.[30] And know that man is bound to die and become dissolved into his component parts ".

Maimonides' statements with reference to this subject created the impression that he doubted the resurrection of the human being, and in reply to a challenge on the point, he composed in 1191 his *Ma'amar Teḥiyyat ha-Métim*, " Essay on the Resurrection of the Dead ", to refute the charge. But in this essay he insists that there are no material enjoyments after death, and he regards that as a conclusive argument that there are no bodies in the world to come.

" Behold it has been explained that the entire necessity for the existence of the body is for one function, and that is the reception of food for the preservation of the body and the propagation of its kind for the preservation of the species. When that function is removed because its necessity no longer exists, viz., in the world to come—as our Sages have informed us, ' In the world to come there is no eating, drinking or sexual intercourse '[31]—that is clear evidence of the non-existence of the body. Because

God brings nothing into existence to serve no purpose whatsoever, and does nothing only on account of something else.[31a] Far be it from Him that His works should be modelled on those of idol-worshippers whose images have unseeing eyes, unhearing ears and a nose that smells not. Similarly, in the view of these people, God creates bodies, i.e., organs, not to function at all in the way for which they were created, nor for any purpose. And if the people of the world to come are not, in the opinion of these persons, possessed of organs, but are just bodies—perhaps solid globes, or pillars or cubes—this is simply ludicrous " (*Teḥiyyat ha-Métim, Responsa* II, 9c).

He attaches no importance to the matter as a doctrine of religion, and we find him telling a correspondent :

" It will not harm your religious faith to think that in the world to come people will have bodies. . . . Even if you were to hold that they eat and drink and propagate in the high heavens or in the Garden of Eden, as some declare, it would not injure your faith " (*Responsa* II, 16c).

§9. *Happiness in the World to Come.* For all that, Maimonides is very firm in his teaching that bodies do not exist in the hereafter, nor are physical joys experienced.

" Know that just as a blind man can form no idea of colours, nor a deaf man comprehend sounds, nor a eunuch feel the desire for sexual intercourse, so the bodies cannot comprehend the delights of the soul. And even as fish do not know the element fire because they exist ever in its opposite, so are the delights of the world of spirit unknown in this world of flesh. Indeed we have no pleasure in any way except what is bodily, and what the senses can comprehend of eating, drinking and sexual intercourse. Whatever is outside these is non-existent to us. We do not discern it, neither do we grasp it at first thought, but only after deep penetration. And truly this must necessarily be the case. For we live in a material world and the only pleasure we can comprehend must be material.

"But the delights of the spirit are everlasting and uninterrupted, and there is no resemblance in any possible way between spiritual and bodily enjoyments. We are not sanctioned either by the Torah or by the divine philosophers to assert that the Angels, the stars, and the Spheres enjoy no delights. In truth they have exceeding great delight in respect of what they comprehend of the Creator. This to them is an everlasting felicity without a break. They have no bodily pleasures, neither do they comprehend them, because they have no senses like ours, enabling them to have our sense-experiences.

"And likewise will it be with us too. When after death the worthy from among us will reach that exalted stage, he will experience no bodily pleasures, neither will he have any wish for them, any more than would a king of sovereign power wish to divest himself of his imperial sway and return to his boyhood's games with a ball in the street, although at one time he would without doubt have set a higher worth upon a game with a ball than on kingly dominion, such being the case only when his years were few and he was totally ignorant of the real significance of either pursuit, just as we to-day rank the delights of the body above those of the soul.

"And when you will give your consideration to the subject of these two pleasures, you will discover the meanness of the one and the high worth of the other.

And this applies even to this world. For we find in the case of the majority of men that they all burden their souls and bodies with the greatest possible labour and fatigue in order to attain distinction or a great position in men's esteem. This pleasure is not that of eating and drinking. Similarly, many a man prefers the obtaining of revenge over his enemies to many of the pleasures of the body. And many a man, again, shuns the greatest among all physical delights out of fear that it should bring him shame and the reproach of men, or because he seeks a good reputation.

" If such, then, is our condition in this world of matter, how much more will it be our case in the world of the spirit, viz., the world to come, where our souls will attain to a knowledge of the Creator as do the higher bodies, or more. This pleasure cannot be divided into parts. It cannot be described, neither can anything be found to compare with it. It is as the Prophet exclaimed, when admiring its great glories : ' Oh, how abundant is Thy goodness which Thou hast laid up for them that fear Thee, which Thou hast wrought for them that take refuge in Thee, in the sight of the sons of men ' (Ps. xxxi. 20). And in a similar sense the Sages remarked, ' In the world to come there will be no eating and no drinking, no washing and no anointing and no marriage ; but only the righteous sitting with crowns on their heads enjoying the splendour of the Shechinah '.[32] By their remark, ' their crowns on their heads ', is meant that those souls will reap bliss in what they comprehend of the Creator, just as the holy *Ḥayyot* and the other ranks of Angels enjoy felicity in what they understand of His existence.

" And so the felicity and the final goal consist in reaching to this exalted company and attaining to this high pitch. The continuation of the soul is endless, like the continuation of the Creator Who is the cause of its continuation in that it comprehends Him, as is explained in elementary philosophy. This is the great bliss with which no bliss is comparable and to which no pleasure can be likened. For how can the enduring and infinite be likened to a thing which has a break and an end ? This is the meaning of the Scriptural phrase, ' That it may be well with thee and that thou mayest prolong thy days ' (Deut. xxii. 7), for which we possess the traditional interpretation : ' That it may be well with thee—in the world which is all good ; and that thou mayest prolong thy days— in a world which is of unceasing length ' "33 (C.M., Introd. to Hélek).

" In the world to come there is no bodily form, but the souls only of the righteous without body, like the ministering Angels. Since there are no bodies in it, there can likewise be neither eating nor drinking nor any other of the things which the bodies of men need in this world. Nor can any of the accidents to which bodies are subject in this world, such as sitting, standing, sleep, death, pain, laughter, etc., occur there.

" Perhaps that bliss will be lightly esteemed by you, and you will think that the reward for fulfilling the commandments and for being perfect in the ways of truth consists in nothing else than indulging in fine food and drink, enjoying beautiful women, wearing raiment of fine linen and embroidery, dwelling in apartments of ivory, and using vessels of silver and gold or similar luxuries, as those foolish and ignorant Arabs imagine who are steeped in sensuality.34 But wise and intelligent men know that all these things are nonsense and vanity and quite futile ; since with us, in this world, they are only considered as something desirable because we possess bodily forms, and because all these things are needs of the body, whereas the soul neither longs nor yearns for them apart from the cravings of the body, so that its desires may be gratified and it be preserved in a perfect state. At a time, however, when there is no body, all these things must necessarily cease to exist.

" As for the great bliss which the soul is to enjoy in the world to come, there is no possibility of comprehending or knowing it in this world ; because in this world we are only cognisant of the welfare of the body and for that we long. But the bliss of the world to come is exceedingly great and cannot bear comparison with the happiness of this world except in a figurative manner. Actually, however, to compare the bliss of the soul in the world to come with the happiness of the body in this world by means of eating and drinking is quite incorrect. That heavenly bliss is great beyond limit, and there is nothing to be compared or likened to it " (Yad, Teshubah VIII, 2, 6).

CHAPTER X

PSYCHOLOGY

§1. *The Soul and its Faculties.* In his teachings on Psychology, Maimonides closely follows the system of Aristotle as expounded in *De Anima.* By the term " soul " as used with reference to Psychology, Maimonides means something different from that part of the human constitution which makes man God-like and survives death. It is the *néphesh* which human beings, as well as all living creatures, possess. It is " the vitality which is common to all living, sentient beings " (*Guide* I, 41).

The soul is a unity. " Know that the human soul is one, but that it has many diversified activities. Some of these activities have, indeed, been called souls, which has given rise to the opinion that man has many souls, as was the belief of the physicians, with the result that the most distinguished of them[1] states in the introduction to his book that there are three souls, the physical, the vital and the psychical. These activities are called *faculties* and *parts*, so that the phrase ' parts of the soul ', frequently employed by philosophers, is commonly used. By the word ' parts ', however, they do not intend to imply that the soul is divided into parts as are bodies, but they merely enumerate the different activities of the soul as being parts of a whole, the union of which makes up the soul[2] " (C.M., *Eight Chapters* I).

16

Five Faculties of the Soul. " The soul has five faculties : the nutritive, the sensitive, the imaginative, the appetitive, and the rational.3 . . . The nutritive faculty by which man is nourished is not the same, for instance, as that of the ass or the horse. Man is sustained by the nutritive faculty of the human soul, the ass thrives by means of the nutritive faculty of its soul, and the palm-tree flourishes by the nutritive faculty peculiar to its soul. Although we apply the same term *nutrition* to all of them indiscriminately, nevertheless, its signification is by no means the same. In the same way, the term *sensation* is used homonymously4 for man and beast ; not with the idea, however, that the sensation of one species is the same as that of another, for each species has its own characteristic soul distinct from every other, with the result that there necessarily arises from each soul activities peculiar to itself " (*ibid.*).

The Nutritive Faculty. " The nutritive faculty consists of (i) the power of attracting nourishment to the body, (ii) the retention of the same, (iii) its digestion, (iv) the repulsion of superfluities, (v) growth, (vi) procreation, and (vii) the differentiation of the nutritive juices that are necessary for sustenance from those which are to be expelled " (*ibid.*).

The Sensitive Faculty. " The faculty of *sensation* consists of the five well-known senses of seeing, hearing, tasting, smelling and feeling, the last of which is found over the whole surface of the body, not being confined to any special member, as are the other four faculties" (*ibid.*).

The Imaginative Faculty. " The *imagination* is that faculty which retains impressions of things perceptible to the mind, after they have ceased to affect directly the senses which conceived them.

This faculty, combining some of these impressions and separating others from one another, thus constructs out of originally perceived ideas fresh ideas of which it has never received any impression, and which it could not possibly have perceived. For instance, one may imagine an iron ship floating in the air, or a man whose head reaches the heaven and whose feet rest on the earth, or an animal with a thousand eyes, and many other similar impossibilities which the imagination may construct and endow with an existence that is fanciful " (*ibid.*).

On this point Maimonides clashed with a class of Mohammedan philosophers, called *Mutakallimun*,5 who held " that all creations of the imagination were possible" (*ibid.*). This theory he criticises in the following terms :

" If you know the nature of the soul and its properties, and if you have a correct notion of everything which concerns the soul, you will observe that most animals possess imagination. As to the higher classes of animals, that is, those which have a heart, it is obvious that they have imagination. Man's distinction does not consist in the possession of imagination, and the action of imagination is not the same as the action of the intellect, but the reverse of it. For the intellect analyses and divides the component parts of things, it forms abstract ideas of them, represents them in their true form as well as in their causal relations, derives from one object a great many facts, which—for the intellect—totally differ from each other, just as two human individuals appear different to the imagination ; it distinguishes that which is the property of the *genus* from that which is peculiar to the individual—and no proof is correct unless founded on the former ; the intellect further determines whether certain qualities of a thing are essential or non-essential.

" Imagination has none of these functions. It only perceives the individual, the compound in that aggregate condition in which it presents itself to the senses ; or it combines things which exist separately, joins some of them together, and represents them all as one body or as a force of the body. Hence it is that some imagine a man with a horse's head, with wings, etc. This is called a fiction, a phantasm ; it is a thing to which nothing in the actual world corresponds. Nor can imagination in any way obtain a purely immaterial image of an object, however abstract the form of the image may be. Imagination yields therefore no test for the reality of a thing " (*Guide* I, 73 Note to Tenth Proposition).

" Part of the functions of the imaginative faculty is to retain impressions by the senses, to combine them, and chiefly to form images. The principal and highest function is performed when the senses are at rest and pause in their action, for then it receives, to some extent, divine inspiration in the measure as it is predisposed for this influence.[6] This is the nature of those dreams which prove true, and also of Prophecy, the difference being one of quantity, not of quality " (*Guide* II, 36).

The Appetitive Faculty. " The *appetitive* is that faculty by which a man desires or loathes a thing, and from which there arises the following activities : the pursuit of an object or flight from it, inclination and avoidance, anger and affection, fear and courage, cruelty and compassion, love and hate, and many other psychic qualities. All parts of the body are subservient to these activities, as the ability of the hand to grasp, that of the foot to walk, that of the eye to see, and that of the heart to make one bold or timid. Similarly, the other members of the body, whether external or internal, are instruments of the appetitive faculty" (C.M., *Eight Chapters* I).

The Rational Faculty. "*Reason*, that faculty peculiar to man, enables him to understand, reflect, acquire knowledge of the sciences, and to discriminate between proper and improper actions. Its functions are partly *practical* and partly *speculative*, the *practical* being, in turn, either *mechanical* or *intellectual*. By means of the *speculative* power, man knows things as they really are, and which, by their nature, are not subject to change. These are called the sciences in general. The mechanical power is that by which the arts, such as architecture, agriculture, medicine and navigation are acquired. The intellectual power is that by which one, when he intends to do an act, reflects upon what he has premeditated, considers the possibility of performing it, and, if he thinks it possible, decides how it should be done" (*ibid.*).

§2. *The Human Intellect.* The endowment of man which places him in a separate class, and the highest class of creatures, is the intellect.

"Man, before he develops understanding and acquires knowledge, is accounted as the beast. He is only distinguished from the rest of the animal creation by the consciousness that he is a living being possessed of intellect—that is to say, by the consciousness whereby he formulates ideas to his soul. And the supreme idea which he has to formulate to his soul is the Unity of God and all the divine concepts which are associated with that thought" (C.M., Introduction).

"On this account, i.e., on account of the divine intellect with which man has been endowed, he is said

245

to have been made in the form and likeness of the Almighty " (*Guide* I, 1).

Since the supreme purpose of intellect is to direct the soul to God, it must be the connecting link between Him and man.

" The intellect which emanates from God unto us is the link that joins us to God. You have it in your power to strengthen that bond, if you choose to do so, or to weaken it gradually till it breaks, if you prefer this. It will only become strong when you employ it in the love of God and seek that love ; it will be weakened when you direct your thoughts to other things " (*Guide* III, 51).

Maimonides gives the following analysis of the intellectual virtues :

" They are (i) *wisdom*, which is the knowledge of the direct and indirect causes of things based on a previous realisation of the existence of those things, the causes of which have been investigated ; (ii) *reason*, consisting of (a) *inborn, theoretical reason*, that is axioms, (b) the *acquired intellect*, and (c) *sagacity* and *intellectual cleverness*, which is the ability to perceive quickly, and to grasp an idea without delay, or in a very short time " (C.M., *Eight Chapters* II).

As regards *wisdom*, it " is used of four things : (i) it denotes the knowledge of those truths which lead to the knowledge of God ; (ii) also knowledge of any workmanship ; (iii) the acquisition of moral principles ; (iv) cunning and subtlety " (*Guide* III, 54).

What is intended by *inborn reason* is explained in this passage of the *Guide* : " There are many things whose existence is manifest and obvious ; some of these are innate notions or objects of sensation, others are nearly so ; and in fact they would require no proof if man had been left in his primitive state. Such are the existence of motion, of man's free will,7 of phases of production and destruction, and of the natural properties perceived by the senses, e.g., the heat of fire, the coldness of water, and many other similar things " (I, 51).

The *acquired intellect* is " not a power inherent in the body, but a power which is absolutely separate from the body, and is from without brought into contact with the body " (*Guide* I, 72). Since it is a power " absolutely separate from the body ", it is capable of surviving the body's dissolution, and is, in fact, the immortal element in man. As the name suggests, it is acquired by the conversion of potentiality into actuality. It is the result of the addition of " form ", derived from the Intelligences, to the hylic intellect[7a] which is the peculiar possession of the human being. The function of the hylic intellect is thus described :

" An animal does not require for its sustenance any plan, thought or scheme ; each animal moves and acts by its nature, eats as much as it can find of suitable things, it makes its resting-place wherever it happens to be, cohabits with any mate it meets while in heat in the periods of its sexual excitement. In this manner does each individual conserve itself for a certain time, and perpetuates the existence of its species without requiring for its maintenance the assistance or support of any of its fellow-creatures ; for all the things to which it has to attend it performs by itself.

" With man it is different ; if an individual had a solitary existence, and were, like an animal, left without guidance, he would soon perish, he would not endure even one day, unless it were by mere chance, unless he happened to find something upon which he might feed. For the food which man requires for his subsistence demands much work and preparation, which can only be accomplished by reflection and by plan; many vessels must be used, and many individuals, each in his peculiar work, must be employed. It is therefore necessary that one person should organise the work and direct men in such a manner that they should properly co-operate, and that they should assist each other. The protection from heat in summer and from cold in winter, and shelter from rain, snow and wind, require in the same manner the preparation of many things, none of which can properly be done without design and thought.

" For this reason man has been endowed with intellectual faculties which enable him to think, consider and act, and by various labours to prepare and procure for himself food, dwelling and clothing, and to control every organ of his body, causing both the principal and the secondary organs to perform their respective functions. Consequently, if a man, being deprived of his intellectual faculties, only possessed vitality, he would in a short time be lost " (*Guide* I, 72).

Closely allied to man's intellect is his *intuitive faculty*. " All possess it, but in different degrees. Man's intuitive power is especially strong in things which he has well comprehended, and in which his mind is much engaged. Thus you may yourself guess correctly that a certain person said or did a certain thing in a certain matter. Some persons are so strong and sound in their imagination and intuitive faculty that, when they assume a thing to be in existence, the reality either entirely or partly confirms their assumption. Although the causes of this assumption are numerous, and include many preceding, succeeding and present circumstances,[8] by means of the intuitive faculty the intellect can pass over all these causes, and draw inferences from them very quickly, almost instantaneously. This same faculty enables some persons to foretell important coming events " (*Guide* II, 38).

§3. *The Functioning of the Intellect.* Maimonides crystallised the purpose of mind in the statement, " It is the function of the intellect to discriminate between the true and the false " (*Guide* I, 2). He followed the Greek thinkers in his psychological analysis of the working of the intellect.

" Man, before comprehending a thing, comprehends it *in potentia* ;[9] when, however, he comprehends a thing, e.g., the form of a certain tree which is pointed out to him, when he abstracts its form from its substance, and reproduces the abstract form, an act performed by the intellect, he comprehends in reality, and the intellect which he has acquired in actuality is the abstract form of the tree in man's mind. For in such a case the intellect is not a thing distinct from the thing comprehended.[10] It is therefore clear to you that the thing comprehended is the abstract form of the tree, and at the same time it is the intellect in action ; and that the intellect and the abstract form of the tree are not two different things, for the intellect in action is nothing but the thing comprehended, and that agent by which the form of the tree has been turned into an intellectual and abstract object, viz., that which comprehends, is undoubtedly the intellect in action.

" All intellect is identical with its action ; the intellect in action is not a thing different from its action, for the true nature and essence of the intellect is comprehension, and you must not think that the intellect in action is a thing existing by itself, separate from comprehension, and that comprehension is a different thing connected with it ; for the very essence of the intellect is comprehension. In assuming an intellect in action you assume the comprehension of the thing comprehended. This is quite clear to all who have made themselves familiar with the figurative language common to this discipline. You therefore accept it as proved that the intellect consists in its action, which is its true nature and essence. Consequently the very thing by which the form of that tree has been made abstract and intelligible, viz., the intellect, is at the same time the *intelligens*, for the intellect is itself the *agens* which abstracts the form and comprehends it, and that is the action on account of which it is called the *intelligens*[11] ; but itself and its action are identical ; and that which is called intellect in action consists, in the above-mentioned instance, of nothing else but of the form of the tree.

" It must now be obvious to you that whenever the intellect is found in action, the intellect and the thing comprehended are one and the same thing ; and also that the function of all intellect, viz., the act of comprehending, is its essence. The intellect, viz., that which comprehends and that which is comprehended, are therefore the same, whenever a real comprehension takes place. But when we speak of the power of comprehension, we necessarily distinguish two things : the power itself and the thing which can be comprehended ; e.g., that hylic intellect[12] of *A* is the power of comprehension, and this tree is, in like manner, a thing which is capable of being comprehended ; these, undoubtedly, are two different things. When, however, the potential is replaced by the actual, and when the form of the tree has really been comprehended, the form comprehended is the intellect, and it is by that same intellect, by the intellect in action, that the tree has been converted into an abstract idea and has been comprehended.

" For everything in which a real action takes place exists in reality.[13] On the other hand, the power of comprehension and the object capable of comprehension are two things ; but that which is only potential cannot be imagined otherwise than in connexion with an object possessing that capacity, as, e.g., man, and thus we have three things : the man who possesses the power and is capable of comprehending ; that power itself, viz., the power of comprehension ; and the object which presents itself as an object of comprehension and is capable of being comprehended. To use the foregoing example, the man, the hylic intellect and the abstract form of the tree are three different things. They become one and the same thing when the intellect is in action, and you will never find the intellect different from the comprehensible object, unless the power of comprehending and the power of being comprehended be referred to " (*Guide* I, 68).

The powers of the intellect are subject to the same conditions as the physical organs. Overstrain leads to defective functioning.

" Mental perception, because connected with matter,[14] is subject to conditions similar to those to which physical perception is subject. That is to say, if your eye looks around, you can perceive all that is within the range of your vision ; if, however, you overstrain your eye, exerting it too much by attempting to see an object which is too distant for your eye, or to examine writings or engravings too small for your sight, and forcing it to obtain a correct perception of them, you will not only weaken your sight with regard to that special object, but also for those things which you otherwise are able to perceive : your eye will have become too weak to perceive what you were able to see before you exerted yourself and exceeded the limits of your vision.

" The same is the case with the speculative faculties of one who devotes himself to the study of any science. If a person studies too much and exhausts his reflective powers, he will be confused, and will not be able to apprehend even that which had been within the power of his apprehension. For the powers of the body[15] are all alike in this respect.

" The mental perceptions are not exempt from a similar condition. If you admit the doubt, and do not persuade yourself to believe that there is a proof for things which cannot be demonstrated, or to try at once to reject and positively to deny an assertion the opposite of which has never been proved, or attempt to perceive things which are beyond your perception, then you have attained the highest degree of human perfection ; then you are like Rabbi Akiba who ' in peace entered (the study of these theological problems) and came out in peace '.[16] If, on the other hand, you attempt to exceed the limit of your intellectual power, or at once to reject things as impossible which have never been proved to be impossible, or which are in fact possible, though their possibility be very remote, then you will be like Elisha Aḥer ; you will not only fail to become perfect, but you will become exceedingly imperfect. Ideas founded on mere imagination will prevail over you ; you will incline towards defects, and towards base and degraded habits, on account of the confusion which troubles the mind, and of the dimness of its light ; just as weakness of sight causes invalids to see many kinds of unreal images, especially when they have looked for a long time at dazzling or at very minute objects " (*Guide* I, 32).

This psychological fact leads to the practical conclusion that the burden placed upon the intellect must be proportionate to its power of sustaining it. Hence the study of philosophical and theological problems must be graduated and should be commenced in the earlier stage of life.

" It is necessary to initiate the young and to instruct the less intelligent according to their comprehension ; those who appear to be talented and have the capacity for the higher method of study, i.e., that based on proof and true logical argument, should be gradually advanced towards perfection, either by tuition or by self-instruction. He, however, who begins with Metaphysics, will not only become confused in matters of religion, but will fall into complete infidelity. I compare such a person to an infant fed with wheaten bread, meat and wine ; it will undoubtedly die, not because such food is naturally unfit for the human body, but because of the weakness of the child, who is unable to digest the food and cannot derive benefit from it " (*Guide* I, 33).

§4. *Sources of True Knowledge*. There are three channels through which accurate knowledge is derivable :

" Know that it is not proper for a man to believe except one of three things : (i) that for which the mind offers clear proof, as, e.g., arithmetic, geometry and astronomy ; (ii) that which he can grasp through the five senses ; e.g., he knows and sees that this is black

and that red, etc., through the vision of the eye, or
he tastes that this is bitter and that sweet, or he feels
that this is hot and that cold, or he hears that this
sound is clear and that blurred, or he smells that this
is malodorous and that pleasant, and so on ; (iii) that
which is received from the Prophets and righteous
men.[17]

" It is necessary that a man should be mentally
able to classify in his mind and thought all that he
believes, and say, ' This I believe because it is handed
down from the Prophets ; this I believe from my
senses ; and this I believe from reason '. But whoever
believes anything which does not fall within these three
categories, to him applies the dictum, ' The thought-
less believeth every word ' (Prov. xiv. 15) " (*Responsa*
II, 25a).

With regard to the first source, Maimonides
attaches supreme importance to the power of logical
reasoning as a factor in attaining true knowledge of
God. He remarks : " We can only obtain a knowledge
of Him through His works ; His works give evidence
of His existence, and show what must be assumed
concerning Him—that is to say, what must be
attributed to Him either affirmatively or negatively.
It is thus necessary to examine all things according
to their essence, to infer from every species such true
and well-established propositions as may assist us in
the solution of metaphysical problems. . . .
Consequently he who wishes to attain to human
perfection must therefore first study Logic, next the
various branches of Mathematics in their proper
order, then Physics, and lastly Metaphysics "[18] (*Guide*
I, 34).

In placing reliance upon the senses as a source of
knowledge, Maimonides opposed the doctrine of the

Mutakallimun, who held that " the senses mislead, and are in many cases inefficient ; their perceptions, therefore, cannot form the basis of any law, or yield data for any proof " (*Guide* I, 73 Twelfth Proposition).

Finally, the teachings of the Prophets must be a medium of true knowledge since, on his hypothesis, the gift of Prophecy presupposes a perfect intellectual endowment.[19]

§5. *Limits of the Intellect.* Ardent rationalist though he was, Maimonides admits that " a limit is set to human reason where it must halt " (*Guide* I, 32).

" I declare that there is a limit to the knowledge of man, and so long as the soul is in the body, it cannot know what is beyond Nature. Since knowledge resides in Nature, it cannot perceive beyond it. Therefore when the mind essays to contemplate what is beyond, it is unable to do so for the reason that the matter is too high for it ; but whatever is in Nature, it is able to know and reflect upon " (*Responsa* II, 23b).

" Know that for the human mind there are certain objects of perception which are within the scope of its nature and capacity; on the other hand, there are, amongst things which actually exist, certain objects which the mind can in no way and by no means grasp : the gates of perception are closed against it. Further, there are things of which the mind understands one part, but remains ignorant of the other ; and when man is able to comprehend certain things, it does not follow that he must be able to comprehend everything. This also applies to the senses : they are able to perceive things, but not at every distance ; and all other powers of the body are limited in a similar way. . . . How individuals of the same species surpass each other in these sensations and in other bodily faculties in universally known, but there is a limit to them, and their power cannot extend to every distance or to every degree.

" All this is applicable to the intellectual faculties of man. There is a considerable difference between one person and another as regards these faculties, as is well-known to philosophers. While one man can discover a certain thing by himself, another is never able to understand it, even if taught by means of all possible expressions and metaphors, and during a long period ; his mind can in no way grasp it, his capacity is insufficient for it. This distinction is not unlimited. A boundary is undoubtedly set to the human mind which it cannot pass. There are things (beyond that boundary) which are acknowledged to be inaccessible to human understanding, and man does not show any desire to comprehend them, being aware that such knowledge is impossible, and that there are no means of overcoming this difficulty " (*Guide* I, 31).

The imperfect capacity of the human mind is the source of error ; but that is not its only cause. Maimonides enumerates three suggested by Alexander Aphrodisius[20] and himself proposes a fourth :

" There are three causes which prevent men from discovering the exact truth : first, arrogance and vain-glory ; secondly, the subtlety, depth and difficulty of any subject which is being examined ; thirdly, ignorance and want of capacity to comprehend what might be comprehended.

" At the present time there is a fourth cause not mentioned by him, because it did not then prevail, viz., habit and training. We naturally like what we have been accustomed to, and are attracted towards it. This may be observed amongst villagers ; though they rarely enjoy the benefit of a douche or bath, and have few enjoyments, and pass a life of privation, they dislike town-life and do not desire its pleasures, preferring the inferior things to which they are accustomed to the better things to which they are strangers ; it would give them no satisfaction to live in palaces, to be clothed in silk, and to indulge in baths, ointments and perfumes.

"The same is the case with those opinions of man to which he has been accustomed from his youth ; he likes them, defends them, and shuns the opposite views. This is likewise one of the causes which prevent men from finding truth, and which make them cling to their habitual opinions " (*ibid.*).

CHAPTER XI

ETHICS

§1. *Varying Dispositions in Men.* If all men were
exactly the same in physical constitution and temperament, they would act alike in the same set of
circumstances. But dispositions vary widely, and
consequently there is variety in conduct.

" Individuals are possessed of very varying
temperaments, differing widely one from the other to
an extreme degree. Some are passionate and in a
constant state of irritation. Others are composed of
mind and are hardly ever irritated ; and should they
be put out, it will be very slightly during a long period
of time. Some there are of an extremely proud
nature ; others are very humble. Some are addicted
to voluptuousness, whose appetites are never sated ;
while others are of a very pure heart and do not long
even for the few things which the body requires.

" Again, there are men so avaricious that they
would not be satisfied with all the wealth in the world ;
but others curtail their desires, and are contented even
with a little which does not suffice for their needs and
do not strive to obtain all they require. Some there
are who rather afflict themselves with hunger to hoard
wealth, and do not spend the smallest coin on themselves without considerable pain ; whereas others
deliberately squander all their possessions. It is the
same with all other dispositions, e.g., the jovial and

morose, miserly and generous, cruel and kind, faint-hearted and brave, etc.

" Between each disposition and its opposite extreme there are intermediate qualities which also vary one from the other. Of all the dispositions, some are innate in man according to his physical constitution ; others are such that the nature of certain men is more readily inclined to adopt than other dispositions ; and there are still others which are not innate in man but acquired by example, or voluntarily adopted because of his ideas, or through having heard that such a disposition is good and proper for him to follow, and he accustoms himself to it until it is fixed in his heart " (*Yad, Déot* I, 1f).

Maimonides is emphatic that the human being is not born either good or evil. " He is not endowed with perfection at the beginning, but at first possesses perfection only *in potentia*, not in fact.[1] . . . If a man possesses a certain faculty *in potentia*, it does not follow that it must become in him a reality. He may possibly remain deficient either on account of some obstacle, or from want of training in practices which would turn the possibility into a reality " (*Guide* I, 34). In the same way, any evil disposition with which he may have been endowed need not necessarily become an overpoweringly strong force in his life.

" It is impossible for man to be born endowed by nature from his very birth with either virtue or vice, just as it is impossible that he should be born skilled by nature in any particular art. It is possible, however, that through natural causes he may from birth be so constituted as to have a predilection for a particular virtue or vice, so that he will more readily practise it than any other. For instance, a man whose natural constitution inclines towards dryness, whose brain-matter is clear and not overloaded with fluids, finds it much easier to learn, remember, and understand things than the phlegmatic man whose brain is encumbered with a great deal of humidity. But, if one who inclines constitutionally towards a certain excellence is left entirely without instruction, and if his faculties are not stimulated, he will undoubtedly remain ignorant. On the other hand, if one by nature dull and phlegmatic, possessing an abundance of humidity, is instructed and enlightened, he will, though with difficulty, it is true, gradually succeed in acquiring knowledge and understanding.

" In exactly the same way, he whose blood is somewhat warmer than is necessary has the requisite quality to make of him a brave man. Another, however, the temperament of whose heart is colder than it should be, is naturally inclined towards cowardice and fear, so that if he should be taught and trained to be a coward, he would easily become one. If, however, it be desired to make a brave man of him, he can without doubt become one, providing he receive the proper training which would require, of course, great exertion.

" I have entered into this subject so that thou mayest not believe the absurd ideas of astrologers, who falsely assert that the constellation at the time of one's birth determines whether one is to be virtuous or vicious, the individual being thus necessarily compelled to follow out a certain line of conduct. We, on the contrary, are convinced that our Torah agrees with Greek philosophy,[2] which substantiates with convincing proofs the contention that man's conduct is entirely in his own hands, that no compulsion is exerted, and that no external influence is brought to bear upon him that constrains him to be either virtuous or vicious, except inasmuch as, according to what we have said above, he may be by nature so constituted as to find it easy or hard, as the case may be, to do a certain thing ; but that he must necessarily do, or refrain from doing, a certain thing is absolutely untrue " (C.M., *Eight Chapters* VIII).

Hereditary forces, therefore, are not the deciding factor of a man's conduct in life. Ultimately he himself determines the course he follows and the responsibility of choice is his alone. Commenting on the verse, " Be ye not as the horse or as the mule which have no understanding ; whose mouth must be held with bit and bridle " (Ps. xxxii. 9), Maimonides remarks : " This means that what restrains beasts from doing harm is something external, as a bridle and a bit. But not so with man. His restraining agency lies in his very self, I mean in his human framework. When the latter becomes perfected it is exactly that which keeps him away from those things which perfection withholds from him and which are termed vices ; and it is that which spurs him on to what will bring about perfection in him, viz., virtue " (C.M., Introd. to *Hélek*).

" Man's shortcomings and sins are all due to the substance of the body and not to its form3 ; while all his merits are exclusively due to his form. Thus the knowledge of God, the formation of ideas, the mastery of desire and passion, the distinction between that which is to be chosen and that which is to be rejected, all these man owes to his form ; but eating, drinking, sexual intercourse, excessive lust, passion, and all vices have their origin in the substance of his body. Now it was clear that this was the case—it was impossible, according to the wisdom of God, that substance should exist without form, or any of the forms of the bodies without substance, and it was necessary that the very noble form of man, which is the image and likeness of God, as has been shown by us, should be joined to the substance of dust and darkness, the source of all defect and loss. For these reasons the Creator gave to the form of man power, rule and dominion over the substance ; the form can subdue the substance, refuse the fulfilment of its desires, and reduce them, as far as possible, to a just and proper measure " (*Guide* III, 8).

Maimonides discusses the question as to who is on a higher ethical plane : the saintly man who feels no evil desire, or the man who experiences such a desire but refuses to yield to it. The Greek philosophers award the palm to the former ; the Rabbis, apparently, reverse this estimate ; and Maimonides reconciles the conflicting opinions.

" Philosophers[4] maintain that though the man of self-restraint performs moral and praiseworthy deeds, yet he does them desiring and craving all the while for immoral deeds, but, subduing his passions and actively fighting against a longing to do those things to which his faculties, his desires, and his psychic disposition excite him, succeeds, though with constant vexation and irritation, in acting morally. The saintly man, however, is guided in his actions by that to which his inclination and disposition prompt him, in consequence of which he acts morally from innate longing and desire. Philosophers unanimously agree that the latter is superior to, and more perfect than, the one who has to curb his passions, although they add that it is possible for such a one to equal the saintly man in many regards. In general, however, he must necessarily be ranked lower in the scale of virtue, because there lurks within him the desire to do evil, and, though he does not do it, yet because his inclinations are all in that direction, it denotes the presence of an immoral psychic disposition. . .

" When, however, we consult the Rabbis on this subject, it would seem that they consider him who desires iniquity, and craves for it (but does not do it) more praiseworthy and perfect than the one who feels no torment at refraining from evil ; and they even go so far as to maintain that the more praise-worthy and perfect a man is, the greater is his desire to commit iniquity, and the more irritation does he feel at having to desist from it. This they express by saying, ' Whosoever is greater than his neighbour has likewise greater evil inclinations '.5 Again, as if this were not sufficient, they even go so far as to say that the reward of him who overcomes his evil inclination is commensurate with the torture occasioned by his resistance, which thought they express by the words, ' According to the labour is the reward '.6 Further-more, they command that man should conquer his desires, but they forbid one to say, ' I, by my nature, do not desire to commit such and such a transgression, even though the Torah does not forbid it '. Rabbi Simeon ben Gamaliel summed up this thought in the words, ' Man should not say, " I do not want to eat meat together with milk ; I do not want to wear clothes made of a mixture of wool and linen ; I do not want to enter into an incestuous marriage ", but he should say, " I do indeed want to, yet I must not, for my Father in Heaven has forbidden it " '.7

" At first blush, by a superficial comparison of the sayings of the philosophers and the Rabbis, one might be inclined to say that they contradict one another. Such, however, is not the case. Both are correct and, moreover, are not in disagreement in the least, as the evils which the philosophers term such—and of which they say that he who has no longing for them is more to be praised than he who desires them but conquers his passion—are things which all people commonly agree are evils, such as the shedding of blood, theft, robbery, fraud, injury to one who has done no harm, ingratitude, contempt for parents, and the like. The prescriptions against these are called *commandments* (*Mitswot*), about which the Rabbis said, ' If they had not already been written in the Torah, it would be proper to add them '8 . . .

" When, however, the Rabbis maintain that he who overcomes his desire has more merit and a greater reward (than he who has no temptation), they say so only in reference to laws that are ceremonial prohibitions. This is quite true, since, were it not for the Torah, they would not at all be considered transgressions. Therefore, the Rabbis say that man should permit his soul to entertain the natural inclination for these things, but that the Torah alone should restrain him from them " (C.M., *Eight Chapters* VI).

Another question discussed is how is a man's conduct to be estimated—by the number of his good actions, or their quality ? Maimonides decides in favour of the former criterion.9

" Man's virtues do not accrue to him in accordance with the qualitative magnitude of a single action but in accordance with the numerical magnitude of his actions. This is to say, the virtues really accrue by reason of the frequent repetition of good deeds and thereby man attains a strong position ; but not through the performance of merely one great act of goodness does a man attain a strong position.

" This may be illustrated by the case of a man who

gives a deserving person, on a single occasion, a
thousand gold pieces, but to another he gives nothing.
By this one great act he does not acquire the quality
of generosity as does a man who donates a thousand
gold pieces on a thousand occasions, giving away each
gold piece through a generous feeling. The latter has
repeated his generous act a thousand times and
attained a strong position ; but as for the other, on
one occasion only was his heart deeply moved to
perform a kind action, and after that it ceased.
Similarly in the Torah, the reward of a man who
redeemed a captive for a hundred *dinars*,[10] or performed charity to a poor man to the extent of a hundred
dinars sufficient for his needs, is not the same as the
reward of a man who redeemed ten captives or supplied
the needs of ten poor persons, each at a cost of ten
dinars ; and so on. Hence the Sages declared, ' All
is according to the numerical value (*rob*) of the deed ',
not ' according to the greatness (*godel*) of the deed ' "
(C.M., *Abot* III, 19).

§2. *Virtues and Vices.* Of the five soul-faculties
enumerated in Chap. X, §1 only two come within the
purview of Ethics.

" Know that transgressions and observances of the
Torah have their origin only in two of the faculties of
the soul, viz., the *sensitive* and the *appetitive*, and that
to these two faculties alone are to be ascribed all
transgressions and observances. The faculties of
nutrition and *imagination* do not give rise to observance
or transgression, for in connection with neither is there
any conscious or voluntary act. That is, man
cannot consciously suspend their functions, nor can
he curtail any one of their activities. The proof of
this is that the functions of both these faculties, the

nutritive and the imaginative, continue to be operative when one is asleep, which is not true of any other of the soul's faculties.

" As regards the *rational* faculty, uncertainty prevails (among philosophers), but I maintain that observance and transgression may also originate in this faculty, in so far as one believes a true or a false doctrine, though no action which may be designated as an observance or a transgression results therefrom[11]. Consequently, as I said above, these two faculties (the sensitive and the appetitive) alone really produce transgressions and observances. . . .

" Moral virtues belong only to the appetitive faculty to which that of sensation in this connection is merely subservient. The virtues of this faculty are very numerous, being moderation, liberality, honesty, meekness, humility, contentedness, courage, faithfulness, and other virtues akin to these. The vices of this faculty consist of a deficiency or of an exaggeration of these qualities.

" As regards the faculties of nutrition and imagination, it cannot be said that they have vices or virtues, but that the nutritive functions work properly or improperly ; as, for instance, when one says that a man's digestion is good or bad, or that one's imagination is confused or clear. This does not mean, however, that they have virtues or vices " (C.M., *Eight Chapters* II).

Vice is a disease of the soul, while virtue is a manifestation of the soul's healthy state.

" The ancients[12] maintained that the soul, like the body, is subject to good health and illness. The soul's healthful state is due to its condition, and that of its faculties, by which it constantly does what is right, and performs what is proper, while the illness of the soul is occasioned by its condition, and that of its faculties, which results in its constantly doing wrong, and performing actions that are improper.

" The science of medicine investigates the health of the body. Now, just as those, who are physically ill, imagine that, on account of their vitiated tastes, the sweet is bitter and the bitter is sweet—and likewise fancy the wholesome to be unwholesome—and just as their desire grows stronger, and their enjoyment increases for such things as dust, coal, very acidic and sour foods, and the like—which the healthy loathe and refuse, as they are not only not beneficial even to the healthy, but possibly harmful—so those whose souls are ill, that is the wicked and the morally perverted, imagine that the bad is good, and that the good is bad. The wicked man, moreover, continually longs for excesses which are really pernicious, but which, on account of the illness of his soul, he considers to be good " (C.M., *Eight Chapters* III).

§3. *The Mean.* Since a moral vice is defined as " a deficiency or an exaggeration of the moral qualities ", it must follow that virtue consists in the happy medium, or to use Aristotle's term " the Mean " ($\mu\epsilon\sigma\acute{o}\tau\eta s$). This criterion for determining the right path to follow and the right action to perform is advocated by Maimonides.

" The right way is the middle course in every one of the dispositions in man ; it is that disposition which is equidistant between the two extremes, so that it is not nearer to one than to the other. The Sages of old have therefore recommended that a man should always keep estimating his dispositions, calculating and directing them into the middle course,[13] so that he may be perfect in his bodily constitution.

How is this meant? He should not be passionate and easily irritated, nor like a corpse which is without feeling; but he should hold the Mean between the two, not giving way to vexation except in some serious matter where it is proper for him to be vexed, in order that a similar thing may not be repeated" (*Yad, Déot* I, 4).

" Good deeds are such as are equibalanced, maintaining the Mean between two equally bad extremes, the *too much* and the *too little*. Virtues are psychic conditions and dispositions which are mid-way between two reprehensible extremes, one of which is characterised by an exaggeration, the other by a deficiency. Good deeds are the product of these dispositions. To illustrate, abstemiousness is a disposition which adopts a mid-course between inordinate passion and total insensibility to pleasure.[14] Abstemiousness, then, is a proper rule of conduct, and the psychic disposition which gives rise to it is an ethical quality; but inordinate passion, the extreme of excess, and total insensibility to enjoyment, the extreme of deficiency, are both absolutely pernicious. The psychic dispositions, from which these two extremes, inordinate passion and insensibility, result—the one being an exaggeration, the other a deficiency—are alike classed among moral imperfections.

" Likewise, liberality is the Mean between sordidness and extravagance; courage, between recklessness and cowardice; dignity, between haughtiness and loutishness; humility, between arrogance and self-abasement; contentedness, between avarice and slothful indifference; and magnificence, between meanness and profusion. Gentleness is the Mean between irascibility and insensibility to shame and disgrace ; and modesty, between impudence and shamefacedness. So it is with the other qualities.

" It often happens, however, that men err as regards these qualities, imagining that one of the extremes is good, and is a virtue. Sometimes, the extreme of the *too much* is considered noble, as when temerity is made a virtue, and those who recklessly risk their lives are hailed as heroes. Thus, when people see a man, reckless to the highest degree, who runs deliberately into danger, intentionally tempting death, and escaping only by mere chance, they laud such a one to the skies, and say that he is a hero.[15] At other times, the opposite extreme, the *too little*, is greatly esteemed, and the coward is considered a man of forbearance ; the idler, as being a person of a contented disposition ; and he, who by the dullness of his nature is callous to every joy, is praised as a man of moderation. In like manner, profuse liberality and extreme lavishness are erroneously extolled as excellent characteristics. This is, however, an absolutely mistaken view, for the really praiseworthy is the medium course of action to which every one should strive to adhere, always weighing his conduct carefully, so that he may attain the proper Mean " (C.M., *Eight Chapters* IV).

Since Maimonides holds that heredity is not the all-powerful factor in determining a man's actions, he concludes that environment must be that force. Virtues and vices are fixed by constant repetition of acts of goodness or wickedness respectively, and a man's surroundings will be such as to give him scope for good or evil, as the case may be.

" It is the innate characteristic of man to be drawn in his dispositions and in his actions after the example of his friends and associates, and conduct himself according to the customs of his countrymen. A man ought therefore to associate with the righteous and be constantly in the company of the wise, so that he may learn from their actions. He must likewise keep far from the wicked who walk in darkness, so that he should not learn from their actions. . . . Consequently if he is in a country where the customs are evil and the inhabitants do not walk in the right way, he should go to a place where the inhabitants are righteous and conduct themselves in the way of good men.

" If, however, the inhabitants of all the countries which he knows, and the report of which he has heard, conduct themselves in a way which is not good, as in our days, or if he be unable to go to a country where the customs are good, in consequence of hostile troops or illness, he should lead a solitary life. And if his countrymen be so wicked and sinful that they do not allow him to dwell in that land unless he mingle with them and conform to their evil customs, he should repair to caves, thickets, and deserts rather than conform to the way of sinners " (*Yad, Déot* VI, 1).

Association with good and wise men, or the avoidance of the wicked, is, accordingly, the first step to the acquisition of virtues and the eradication of vices. Maimonides included this duty of associating with the wise in his list of the Biblical ordinances :

" The commandment which orders us to mingle with the learned, associate with them, be continually in their society and company in every possible way, in the matter of food and drink and business transaction, that by these means there result to us the imitation of their deeds and belief in true ideas from their words. That is what He, exalted be He, declared, ' To Him shalt thou cleave ' (Deut. x. 20) ; and the ordinance was repeated likewise in the phrase ' to cleave to Him ' (*ibid*. xi. 22). And the explanation of this latter phrase occurs thus : ' Cleave to the wise and their disciples '—this being the expression of the Sifré.[16] They similarly deduce proof of the duty to marry the daughter of a learned man and give one's daughter in marriage to a learned man, to feed the learned and have transactions with them, from the statement ' To Him shalt thou cleave ', declaring, ' Is it then possible for a man to cleave to the *Shechinah* ? For lo, it is written, " The Lord thy God is a devouring fire "! (*ibid*. iv. 24). But whoever marries the daughter of[17] a learned man, transacts business for the learned and allows them to enjoy his possessions, the Scriptures account it to him as though he clave to the *Shechinah* (*Mitswot*, Command. VI).

A second and more drastic method of acquiring virtue and eradicating vice is to undergo " a cure, exactly as he would were his body suffering from an illness. So, just as when the equilibrium of the physical health is disturbed, and we note which way it is tending in order to force it to go in exactly the opposite direction until it shall return to its proper condition, and, just as when the proper adjustment is reached, we cease this operation, and have recourse to that which will maintain the proper balance, in exactly the same way must we adjust the moral equilibrium.

" Let us take, for example, the case of a man in whose soul there has developed a disposition of great avarice on account of which he deprives himself of every comfort in life, and which, by the way, is one of the most detestable of defects, and an immoral act. If we wish to cure this sick man,[18] we must not command him merely to practise deeds of generosity, for that would be as ineffective as a physician trying to cure a patient consumed by a burning fever by administering mild medicines, which treatment would be inefficacious. We must, however, induce him to squander so often, and to repeat his acts of profusion so continuously until that propensity which was the cause of his avarice has totally disappeared. Then, when he reaches that point where he is about to become a squanderer, we must teach him to moderate his profusion, and tell him to continue with deeds of generosity, and to watch out with due care lest he relapse either into lavishness or niggardliness.

" If, on the other hand, a man is a squanderer, he must be directed to practise strict economy, and to repeat acts of niggardliness. It is not necessary, however, for him to perform acts of avarice as many times as the mean man should those of profusion. This subtle point, which is a canon and secret of the science of medicine, tells us that it is easier for a man of profuse habits to moderate them to generosity, than it is for a miser to become generous. Likewise, it is easier for one who is apathetic to be excited to moderate enjoyment, than it is for one, burning with passion, to curb his desires. Consequently, the licentious man must be made to practise restraint more than the apathetic man would be induced to indulge his passions ; and, similarly, the coward requires exposure to danger more frequently than the reckless man should be forced to cowardice. The mean man needs to practise lavishness to a greater degree than should be required of the lavish to practise meanness. This is a fundamental principle of the science of curing moral ills, and is worthy of remembrance " (C.M., *Eight Chapters* IV).

The standard of the Mean is the prudent course to

adopt, but Maimonides concedes the praiseworthiness of those who allow themselves to be deviated in moderation therefrom to the right side.

" He who is extremely punctilious with himself and departs from the middle course slightly towards either side is termed *ḥasid* ' saint '. For instance, whoever holds aloof from haughtiness for the opposite extreme and becomes exceedingly humble earns the title of *ḥasid* ; and that is the quality of saintliness. If, however, he holds aloof from haughtiness for the middle course only and becomes meek, he earns the title of *ḥacham* ' wise ' ; and that is the quality of wisdom. It is the same with all other dispositions. The saints of old used to incline their dispositions from the Mean towards the two extremes. Some dispositions they would incline towards the second extreme (of excess), while others they would incline towards the first extreme (of deficiency). This is the meaning of the phrase ' within the line of the law '. We are commanded to walk in the middle path, which is the good and right path " (*Yad, Déot* I, 5).

He further admits that the Mean is not always the correct attitude to adopt. With some moral qualities a tendency towards excess is desirable.

" There are some dispositions, in regard to which man is forbidden to adopt the middle course, but should rather remove from one extreme to the other. This is the case with haughtiness of mind ; because it is not the good way for a man to be merely meek, but to be of humble mind and exceedingly lowly of spirit. Therefore it is said of Moses our teacher that he was not just meek, but *very* meek (Num. xii. 3). Consequently the Sages exhorted us, ' Be *exceedingly* lowly of spirit '.[19] They further declared, ' Whoever makes his heart haughty denies a cardinal doctrine ; for it is said, " Then thy heart be lifted up and thou forget the Lord thy God " (Deut. viii. 14)'.[20] They also taught, ' Whoever is possessed of haughtiness of spirit deserves excommunication '.[21]

" Anger is likewise a most evil quality, and man should keep aloof from it to the opposite extreme, and train himself not to be vexed even by a thing over which it would be legitimate to be irritated. Should he desire to impress fear upon his children, his household or the community—if he be their leader and wish to display anger against them that they return to good behaviour—he may show himself in their presence as though he were angry for the purpose of reproving them, but he ought nevertheless to be composed within himself, like a man who pretends to be vexed though really he is not. The Sages of old said, ' Whoever gives way to anger is as though he were an idolater ',[22] ' Whoever gives way to anger, if he be a wise man his wisdom departs from him, and if he be a Prophet his Prophecy departs from him ',[23] ' The life of the passionate man is not truly life '.[24] The Sages have therefore ordered that a man should keep far from anger until he accustom himself not to take notice even of things that provoke irritation : this being the good way.

" The way of the righteous is this : they may be insulted but they do not insult, they hear themselves reviled but make no retort. They act from Love of God and are happy under affliction " (*Yad, Déot* II, 3).

§4. *Asceticism.* To one deviation from the mean Maimonides devotes special attention, because it was generally considered to be a characteristic of saintly men, viz., the ascetic life. He distinguishes between true and false asceticism.

" When, at times, some of the pious ones deviated to one extreme by fasting, keeping nightly vigils, refraining from eating meat or drinking wine, renouncing sexual intercourse, clothing themselves in woollen[25] and hairy garments,[26] dwelling in the mountains, and wandering about in the wilderness, they did so, partly as a means of restoring the health of their souls, as we have explained above, and partly because of the immorality of the townspeople. When the pious saw that they themselves might become contaminated by association with evil men, or by constantly seeing their actions, fearing that their own morals might become corrupt on account of contact with them, they fled to the wilderness far from their society. . . .

" When the ignorant observed saintly men acting thus, not knowing their motives, they considered their deeds to be virtuous, and so, blindly imitating their acts, thinking thereby to become like them, chastised their bodies with all kinds of afflictions, imagining that they had acquired perfection and moral worth, and that by this means man would approach nearer to God, as if He hated the human body and desired its destruction. It never dawned upon them, however, that these actions were bad and resulted in moral imperfection of the soul.

" Such men can only be compared to one who, ignorant of the art of healing, when he sees skilful physicians administering to those at the point of death such purgatives as colocynth, scammony, aloe, and the like, and depriving them of food, in consequence of which they are completely cured and escape death, foolishly concludes that since these things cure sickness, they must all the more be efficacious in preserving health, or prolonging life. If a person should take these things constantly, and treat himself as a sick person, then he would really become ill. Likewise, those who are spiritually well, but have recourse to remedies, will undoubtedly become morally ill.

" The perfect Torah which leads us to perfection . . . recommends none of these things. On the contrary, it aims at man's following the path of moderation, in accordance with the dictates of Nature, eating, drinking, enjoying legitimate sexual intercourse, all in moderation, and living among people in honesty and uprightness, but not dwelling in the wilderness or in the mountains, or clothing oneself in garments of hair and wool, or afflicting the body " (C.M., *Eight Chapters* IV).

On this principle Maimonides denounces the spending of all one's possessions on religious objects.

" A man should never devote all his possessions to religious purposes. To act thus is to transgress the intention of the Scriptural verse which states, ' *Of all* that he hath ' (Lev. xxvii. 28)—not ' *all* that he hath ', as the Sages comment.[27] This is not piety but folly, because he deprives himself of all his money and has to resort to assistance from his fellowmen. On such a man we are to have no pity, for he belongs to the class, described by the Sages, ' Pious fools who destroy the world '.[28]

" Whoever wishes to spend his money on religious objects should not exceed one-fifth, and thus resemble the man whom the Prophets commend, ' that ordereth his affairs rightfully ' (Ps. cxii. 5), both in religious and worldly affairs. Even in the matter of the sacrifices which a man was in duty bound to bring, the Torah has consideration for his resources and regulates them according to his means.[29] How much more so, then, in matters where there is not the obligation apart from a vow which he places upon himself, should he not vow more than is commensurate with his means " (*Yad*, *Arachin* VIII, 13).

Luxuries and comforts, if they are not made the be-all and end-all of one's activities and desires, may even serve a beneficial purpose from the ethical standpoint.

" There are, indeed, times when the agreeable may be used from a curative point of view, as, for instance, when one suffers from loss of appetite, it may be stirred up by highly seasoned delicacies and agreeable, palatable food. Similarly, one who suffers from melancholia may rid himself of it by listening to singing and all kinds of instrumental music, by strolling through beautiful gardens and splendid buildings, by gazing upon beautiful pictures, and other things that enliven the mind and dissipate gloomy moods. The purpose of all this is to restore the healthful condition of the body, but the real object in maintaining the body in good health is to acquire wisdom. Likewise, in the pursuit of wealth, the main design in its acquisition should be to expend it for noble purposes, and to employ it for the maintenance of the body and the preservation of life, so that its owner may obtain a knowledge of God, in so far as that is vouchsafed unto man. . . .

" Our Rabbis of blessed memory say, ' It is becoming that a Sage should have a pleasant dwelling, a beautiful wife, and domestic comfort '[30] ; for one becomes weary, and one's mind is dulled by continued mental concentration upon difficult problems. Thus, just as the body becomes exhausted from hard labour, and then by rest and refreshment recovers, so it is necessary for the mind to have relaxation by gazing upon pictures and other beautiful objects, that its weariness may be dispelled " (C.M., *Eight Chapters* V).

On the other hand, Maimonides clearly recognises that self-indulgence is inimical to mental and moral development.

" With the formation of intellectual concepts, one is obliged to abstain from most physical enjoyments, because the beginning of intellect is to formulate the idea that the mortification of the soul is brought about by care for the body and mortification of the body by care for the soul. When a man follows his lusts, allows his desires to master his thoughts, and sets aside his intellect for his cravings, until he returns to the level of the beast which formulates no other longing to its soul than eating, drinking and sexual inter-course, then the divine power, i.e., the intellect, cannot manifest itself, and he becomes a mere creature swimming in the sea of matter " (C.M., Introduction).

§5. *Correct Living (Physical).* The doctrine of *mens sana in corpore sano* is stressed in Maimonides' teaching. The effect of the physical condition upon the functioning of the soul is clearly perceived by him. He lays down the principle : " The well-being of the soul can only be obtained after that of the body has been secured " (*Guide* III, 27).

" Know that the perfection of the body precedes the perfection of the soul, and is like the key which opens the inner chamber. Let, then, the chief aim of your discipline be the perfecting of your body and the correcting of your morals, to open before you the gates of Heaven " (*Ethical Will, Responsa* II, 38a, b)

" Man's only design in eating, drinking, cohabiting, sleeping, waking, moving about, and resting should be the preservation of bodily health; while, in turn,

the reason for the latter is that the soul and its
agencies may be in sound and perfect condition, so
that he may readily acquire wisdom, and gain moral
and intellectual virtues, all to the end that man may
reach the highest goal of his endeavours " (C.M.,
Eight Chapters V).

He advised his son : " Eat that you may live and
condemn excess. Believe not that much eating and
drinking makes the body grow and enlarges the
understanding, like a sack which is filled by what is
put into it. It is just the reverse. By moderate
eating the stomach acquires strength to receive it
and, through the natural heat, to digest it. Then a
man grows in physical health and his mind is settled.
But if he eat more than is necessary, the stomach
cannot receive it and the natural heat cannot digest
it ; it will come out before him. ' It is a vile thing ;
it shall not be accepted ' (Lev. xix. 7). His body will
be emaciated, his understanding negligible, his purse
empty. Take care, then, that you do not eat except
what you can digest, because it is injurious to the body
and purse, and it is the cause of most illnesses "
(*Ethical Will, Responsa* II, 39a).

Such importance did Maimonides attach to this
matter, that he included a long list of dietetic rules
in his codification of Rabbinic law. Some of them
occur in the Talmud, but he considerably elaborated
them. As he was a noted physician, his regulations
are not without interest.

" Since the preservation of the body in a healthy
and perfect state belongs to the way of life prescribed
by God—since it is impossible for a man to understand
or have any knowledge of the Creator when he is in
poor physical condition—it is consequently necessary
that he should keep himself aloof from things which

are injurious to the body and accustom himself to the use of things which are healthful and invigorating.

" They are as follows : A man should never eat except when he is hungry, nor drink except when he is thirsty ; and he should not delay the performance of the act of purgation.[31] . . . He should not keep on eating until his stomach is filled, but leave about a fourth part of his appetite unsatisfied. He is not to drink water during a meal,[32] but only a little water mixed with wine. When the food begins to digest, he may drink as much as is proper ; much water, however, should not be drunk even when the food is digesting. He should not eat until he is completely assured that he has no need of performing his natural functions. He should not eat until he has walked before the meal[33] a sufficient distance for the body to begin feeling warm, or do some kind of work, or undergo another form of exertion. The general rule is, he should exercise his body and tire it daily in the morning, until it begins to feel warm, rest a little until he is refreshed, and then have his meal. To take a hot bath after exercise is a good thing, but after it he should wait a little before having a meal.

" One should always remain seated while eating or recline on his left side ; he should not walk, ride, undergo exertion and induce perspiration. He should not walk about until the food becomes digested ; and whoever walks about or exerts himself immediately after a meal brings on himself serious illnesses.

" Day and night being twenty-four hours, it is enough for a person to sleep a third part thereof, viz., eight hours. These hours should be towards the end of the night, so that there are eight hours from the beginning of his sleep to sun-rise, and he consequently gets up from his bed before the sun rises. It is not proper to sleep lying on one's face or back34, but on the side—at the beginning of the night on the left, and at the end of the night on the right side. He should not retire to sleep immediately after a meal, but wait about three or four hours. He should also not sleep during the day.

" Things which are laxative, e.g., grapes, figs, mulberries, pears, melons and all kinds of cucumbers and gurkins, one may eat as *hors d'œuvre*, not partaking of them together with the food, but waiting a little while and then eating his meal. Things of a costive tendency, such as pomegranates, quinces, apples and Paradise-pears he may eat immediately after a meal, but should not overindulge in them.

" If one wish to partake of poultry and meat at the same meal, he should eat the poultry first. Similarly in the case of eggs and poultry, he should eat the eggs first ; lamb and beef, he should give precedence to the former. A person should always partake of the lighter food first and then the heavier.

" During the Summer he should eat cooling things and not take too much spice ; but he may use vinegar. During the Winter he should eat warmth-giving food, use much spice, and take a little mustard and asafœtida. He should follow these directions in cold countries and hot, in each place according to the local conditions.

" There are foods which are exceedingly harmful and a person should never eat them ; e.g., large, salted and stale fish, salted stale cheese, mushrooms and all fungi, stale salted meat, wine fresh from the press, and cooked food which has been standing until its flavour has gone ; likewise any food which is

malodorous or excessively bitter is to the body like a
deadly poison. There are, on the other hand, foods
which are injurious, though not to the same extent as
the former ; therefore it is right that a person should
indulge in them sparingly and at rare intervals. He
should not accustom himself to the use of them as food,
or frequently eat them with his food. In this
category are large fish, cheese, milk which has stood
more than twenty-four hours from the time of milking,
meat of big bulls and rams, beans, lentils,35 chick-peas,
barley bread, unleavened bread, cabbage, leek, onions,
garlic, mustard and raddish. All these are harmful
food of which one should eat but very little indeed,
and only in Winter. In Summer one ought not to eat
them at all. Beans and lentils by themselves should
not be eaten in Summer or Winter ; gourds, however,
may be eaten in Summer.

"There are some foods which are injurious, though
not to the extent of the above-mentioned ; e.g., water-
fowl, small pigeons, dates,36 bread toasted in oil or
kneaded in oil, fine flour which has been so thoroughly
sifted as to leave not even a particle of bran, brine
and pickle. One should not overindulge in them ;
and the man who is wise, curbs his desire and is not
carried away by his appetite, abstaining from them
altogether unless he requires them as medicine, is
' mighty '.37

"A person should always withhold himself from
fruit of the trees and not eat much of them even dried,
still less fresh ; but before they are thoroughly ripe,
they are like swords to the body. Similarly carobs
are always harmful; likewise all sour fruits are bad and
should only be eaten in small quantities in Summer
and in hot climates. Figs, grapes and almonds are
always beneficial, whether fresh or dried. One may

eat of them as much as he needs ; but he must not keep continually eating them, although they are more beneficial than all other fruits of trees.

" Honey and wine are bad for the young, but beneficial to the old, especially in Winter. One need eat in Summer two-thirds of what he eats in Winter. . . .

" There is another rule stated in connection with the healthy condition of the body : As long as a person works and takes plenty of exercise, does not eat to satiety, and his bowels are regular, no ailment will befall him and his strength keeps developing, even if he eat unwholesome food. But whoever sits idle and does no work, or defers the natural functions or is of a costive nature, even if he eat wholesome food and take care of himself according to medical regulations, will suffer all his life and his strength will grow weaker. Excessive eating is to the body of a man like deadly poison and is the root of all diseases. Most illnesses which befall men arise either from bad food or from immoderate indulgence in food, even of the wholesome kind. . . .

" The rule about the bath[38] is this : A man ought to enter the bath-house each week, but he should not enter it immediately after a meal, nor when he is hungry, but when the food begins to digest. He should bathe the whole of his body in hot water, but not of a heat to scald the body. The head only is to be washed in very hot water. After that he should bathe in luke-warm water, then in water still cooler, until he finally bathes in cold water. The head, however, should not be immersed in luke-warm or cold water. One should not bathe during Winter in cold water, nor take the bath until the whole body is in a state of perspiration and has been shampooed. He should not stay long in the bath, but as soon as his body perspires and has been shampooed, he should have a shower-bath, and go out. . . .

" When he leaves the bath, he should dress and cover his head in the outer room, so as not to catch cold ; even in Summer he must be careful. After leaving the bath, he should wait a while until he has refreshed himself, his body has rested and the heat departed ; then he may take a meal. If he can sleep a little on leaving the bath, before his meal, this is very beneficial. He should not drink cold water when he comes out of the bath, much less drink it while in the bath ; but if he is thirsty on leaving the bath and cannot resist drinking, he should mix the water with wine or honey and drink. If he anoint himself with oil in the bath, during Winter after he has had a shower-bath, it is beneficial.

" A person should not accustom himself to constant blood-letting ; he should only be cupped in a case of great urgency. He should not undergo it either in Summer or Winter, but a little during the days of Nisan and a little in the days of Tishri.39 After fifty years of age one should not submit to blood-letting. Nor should a person have cupping and enter the bath on the same day, nor cup and go on a journey, nor have it on the day he returns from a journey. On the day he has blood-letting he should eat and drink less than usual ; he should rest on that day, not tire himself, nor do exercise and walking.

" Whoever conducts himself according to the rules we have prescribed, I guarantee that he will not be afflicted with illness all his days until he reaches advanced age and dies. He will not need a physician, but always enjoy good health, unless he was physically weak from birth, or gave way to evil habits from early

youth, or some plague or drought befall the world "
(*Yad, Déot* IV, 1-18, 20).

§6. *Correct Living* (*Moral*). In general, man's life
should be motived, and his actions guided, by three
God-like qualities, viz., *ḥésed* " kindness ", *tsedakah*
" righteousness " and *mishpat* " judgment ". Maimonides gives the following definition of the terms :

" *Ḥésed* is especially used of extraordinary kindness. Lovingkindness is practised in two ways : first,
we show kindness to those who have no claim whatever upon us ; secondly, we are kind to those to whom
it is due, in a greater measure than is due to them. . . .

" The term *tsedakah* is derived from *tsédek*
' righteousness ' ; it denotes the act of giving every
one his due, and of showing kindness to every being
according as it deserves. In Scripture, however, the
expression *tsedakah* is not used in the first sense, and
does not apply to the payment of what we owe to
others. When we therefore give the hired labourer
his wages, or pay a debt, we do not perform an act of
tsedakah. But we do perform an act of *tsedakah* when
we fulfil those duties towards our fellow-men which
our moral conscience imposes upon us ; e.g., when we
heal the wound of the sufferer. Thus Scripture says,
in reference to the returning of the pledge to the poor
debtor, ' It shall be *tsedakah* unto thee ' (Deut. xxiv.
13). When we walk in the way of virtue, we act
righteously towards our intellectual faculty and pay
what is due unto it ; and because every virtue is thus
tsedakah, Scripture applies the term to the virtue of
faith in God. Comp. ' And he believed in the Lord,
and He accounted it to him for *tsedakah* ' (Gen. xv. 6).

" The noun *mishpat* ' judgment ' denotes the act
of deciding upon a certain action in accordance

with justice which may demand either mercy or punishment.

" We have thus shown that *ḥésed* denotes pure charity ; *tsedakah* kindness, prompted by a certain moral conscience in man, and being a means of attaining perfection for his soul ; whilst *mishpat* may in some cases find expression in revenge, in other cases in mercy " (*Guide* III, 53).

Maimonides in the passage just cited restricts his definition of *tsedakah* to its connotation in the Scriptures. In Rabbinic Hebrew it acquired the meaning of " benevolence ". This quality must be a conspicuous feature of the moral life.

" The law of the Torah commanded us to practise *tsedakah*, support the needy and help them financially. The command in connection with this duty occurs in various expressions ; e.g., ' Thou shalt surely open thy hand unto him ' (Deut. xv. 8), ' Thou shalt uphold him ; as a stranger and a settler shall he live with thee ' (Lev. xxv. 35). The intention in these passages is identical, viz., that we should console the poor man and support him to the extent of sufficiency. . . . The saying has come down to us that even if he were a poor man who is maintained by charity, this duty, viz., of *tsedakah*, is obligatory upon him, whether it be to one who is worse off than he or in a similar state to himself, though it be with a trifling amount " (*Mitswot*, Command. CXCV).

After detailing the laws regulating the giving of alms to the poor, he concludes :

" We are in duty bound to be more careful with the fulfilment of the commandment relating to alms than all the other commandments, for almsgiving is the characteristic of the righteous man of the seed of Abraham, our father ; as it is said, ' For I know him to the end that he command his children and his household after him, that they may keep the way of the Lord, to do *tsedakah* ' (Gen. xviii. 19). Nor can the throne of Israel be firmly established and the true Faith stand by any other means than *tsedakah* ; as it is said, ' In *tsedakah* shalt thou be established ' (Isa. liv. 14). Further, Israel will only be redeemed by the same virtue ; as it is said, ' Zion shall be redeemed with justice, and they that return of her with *tsedakah* ' (*ibid*. i. 27).⁴⁰

" A man is never impoverished through almsgiving, nor is evil or injury ever caused through it ; as it is said, ' The work of *tsedakah* shall be peace ' (*ibid*. xxxii. 17). Who displays mercy shall have mercy displayed towards him ; as it is said, ' And show thee mercy and have compassion upon thee, and multiply thee ' (Deut. xiii. 18). Whoever is hardhearted and merciless gives cause for suspecting his pure Israelite descent, because hardheartedness is only found among gentiles ; as it is said, ' They are cruel and have no compassion ' (Jer. vi. 23). Whereas all Israel and those who ally themselves to them are like brothers ; as it is said, ' Ye are children of the Lord your God ' (Deut. xiv. 1), and if brother is not merciful to brother, who should be merciful to him ! To whom, then, should the poor of Israel raise their eyes in pleading ? To the gentiles who hate and persecute them ! Surely their eyes can only be raised to their brethren.

" Whoever closes his eyes against charity is called, like the idol-worshipper, impious. . . . Whoever gives alms to the poor with bad grace and downcast looks, though he bestow a thousand gold pieces, all the merit of his action is lost ; but he must give with good grace, gladly, sympathising with the poor man in his trouble. If a poor man solicit alms of you and you have nothing to give him, console him with words ; and it is forbidden to upbraid the poor or raise the voice against him, since his heart is broken and crushed. . . . Woe, then, to the person who shames the poor man ! Be to him, rather, like a parent whether in compassion or in kindly words. . . .

" There are eight degrees in alms-giving, one higher than the other : Supreme above all is to give assistance to a co-religionist who has fallen on evil times by presenting him with a gift or loan, or entering into a partnership with him, or procuring him work, thereby helping him to become self-supporting.

" Inferior to this is giving charity to the poor in such a way that the giver and recipient are unknown to each other. This is, indeed, the performance of a commandment from disinterested motives ; and it is exemplified by the Institution of the Chamber of the Silent which existed in the Temple, where the righteous secretly deposited their alms and the respectable poor were secretly assisted.[41]

" Next in order is the donation of money to the charitable fund of the Community, to which no contribution should be made without the donors feeling confident that the administration is honest, prudent and capable of proper management.

" Below this degree is the instance where the donor is aware to whom he is giving the alms but the recipient is unaware from whom he received them ; as, e.g., the great Sages who used to go about secretly throwing money through the doors of the poor.[42] This is quite a proper course to adopt and a great virtue where the administrators of a charitable fund are not acting fairly.

" Inferior to this degree is the case where the recipient knows the identity of the donor, but not *vice versa* ; as, e.g., the great Sages who used to tie sums of money in linen bundles and throw them behind their backs for poor men to pick up, so that they should not feel shame[43].

" The next four degrees in their order are : the man who gives money to the poor before he is asked ; the man who gives money to the poor after he is asked ; the man who gives less than he should, but does it with good grace ; and lastly, he who gives grudgingly " (*Yad, Mattenot Aniyyim* X, 1-14).

Another important virtue of the moral life is chastity.

" It is proper for a man to practise self-control and exercise himself in additional holiness and pure thought and correct morals to be saved from going astray. He must guard against intimacy which is the great cause of sinning. He should likewise accustom himself to keep far from levity, intemperance and erotic subjects, because these are important factors which conduce to immorality. Nor should he live unwedded ; since marriage tends to purity. But above all this, advised the Rabbis, let him turn himself and his thoughts to the study of the Torah and enlarge his mind with wisdom[44] ; for lustful desire only prevails in a heart which is empty of wisdom " (*Yad, Issuré Biah* XXII, 20f).

A forgiving disposition is likewise advocated. " It is forbidden a man to be hard and unrelenting. He should, on the contrary, be easily appeased and hard to provoke ; and when the offender begs his pardon, he should forgive wholeheartedly and willingly. Even though the man may have grievously injured or offended him, he ought not to avenge himself nor bear a grudge, this being the characteristic of the seed of Israel and their uprightness of heart " (*Yad, Teshubah* II, 10).

Another moral virtue is the correct use of the power of speech.

" A fence to wisdom is silence.45 A man should therefore not be hasty in replying, nor talk too much. He should teach his pupils in a quiet and pleasant manner, without shouting and without prolixity. As Solomon said, ' The words of the wise are spoken in quiet ' (Eccles. ix. 17).

" It is forbidden a man to accustom himself to words of flattery or seduction ; nor should he be otherwise in his speech than he is in his heart, but alike within as without, so that what is in his heart is identical with the words in his mouth.

" It is forbidden to deceive one's fellow-creatures, even a gentile. For instance, a man should not sell to a gentile the flesh of a beast which died of itself as the flesh of a slaughtered beast, or a shoe made of the hide of a beast which died of itself as the shoe made of the hide of a slaughtered beast. He may not press his friend to eat with him when he knows that he will not eat with him, nor continue to urge gifts on him when he knows that he will not accept them ; nor open casks for him which he is obliged to open for the purpose of sale, in order to deceive him that it was in his honour that he had opened them ; and so on. Even a single word of seduction or deception is prohibited. Instead there should be truthful speech, an upright spirit, and a heart pure from treachery and mischief " (*Yad, Déot* II, 5f).

Maimonides draws a detailed picture of the manner of living to which the " wise " man should conform. He, first of all, rigorously submits to the rules of correct physical living. He also adopts the following outward characteristics :

" A wise man should not shout or be noisy when

he speaks, like animals, nor should he raise his voice too high ; but his speech with all people should be quiet. When speaking in a quiet tone, he must take care not to exaggerate, so as to appear as one talking haughtily. He also anticipates every man with his greeting, so that all are favourably disposed towards him.[46] He judges every man leniently,[47] recounts the praise of his friend but on no account says whatever is discreditable. He loves peace and pursues it.[48] If he perceives that his words are helpful and listened to he gives utterance to them, otherwise he keeps silent. For instance, he will never attempt to pacify his neighbour whilst the latter is angry, or question him concerning his vow at the time he made it, but waits until his mind has grown calm and composed. He does not comfort the mourner while the dead body still lies in his presence, because the mourner is too overcome before the burial; and so on. He does not enter the presence of his friend at the time of the latter's disgrace, but averts his eyes from him.[49] He does not depart from his word, neither adding to it nor subtracting from it, except when peace is involved.[50] In general, he only speaks on scholarly subjects or to practise benevolence. He does not converse with a woman in a public place, even if it be his wife, sister or daughter.[51]

" A wise man should not walk with a haughty demeanour ; nor should he walk with slow and measured gait like women and proud people ; nor run about in public roads like madmen ; nor stoop like a hunchback ; but he should gaze downwards as though standing in prayer, and walk in the street like a man occupied in business. From the manner of a man's walking, it may be perceived whether he is wise and intellectual or foolish and ignorant.[52]

" The dress of a wise man should be suitable and clean. It is forbidden that stains or grease-marks should be found on his garment.53 He should not wear the apparel of princes, e.g., garments of gold and purple, to attract the attention of people, nor the clothes of paupers which bring disrespect on the wearer ; but his garments should be of a medium character and suitable for him. His flesh should not be visible through his apparel, like the very fine linen garments made in Egypt ; nor should his dress drag along the ground like that of the haughty, but should only reach to the heel and the sleeves to the tips of the fingers. He should not wear his *Tallit*54 conspicuously long because it appears like haughtiness, except on Sabbath if he has no other in its place. He should not wear patched shoes in Summer, but if he is a poor man he may wear them in Winter.55 He should not go out into the street perfumed, nor with scented garments, nor use any perfume for his hair, but it is allowable if he anointed his body with perfume to remove the bad odour.56 He should not go out alone at night unless there be a fixed time when it is his habit to go out to attend to his study.57 All these rules are intended to avoid suspicion.

" A wise man measures his words with judgment, eats and drinks and supports his household according to his means and prosperity, and does not encumber himself with unnecessary burdens. . . . The Sages recommended that a man should spend upon food less than his means, upon dress up to his means, and expend in honour of his wife and children more than his means.58

" The course adopted by a man of intelligence is first to determine upon an occupation to maintain himself, then to purchase a dwelling-house and then to marry.59 . . . But fools first marry, then if they can afford it acquire a dwelling-house, and afterwards when advanced in years go about to find a trade or have to be supported from charity. . . .

" All transactions of the wise man must be in truth and integrity.60 His nay should be nay, his yea yea. In financial calculations he must be strict with himself but generous with others.61 He pays the purchase-money immediately62 ; he does not make himself a surety or responsible for others, nor undertake the liability of a power of attorney.63 He does not enter in the course of business into such obligations as the Torah has not imposed upon him, so that he may abide by his word and not depart from it. If others are legally indebted to him, he grants them an extension to pay, is forgiving and lends graciously. He does not interfere with the business of his neighbours, and never acts harshly towards anybody. In general, he is rather of the persecuted than of the persecutors, of the offended not of the offenders "64 (*Yad*, *Déot* V, 7-13).

The highest incentive to correct moral living is the consciousness of being always in the presence of God.

" We do not sit, move and occupy ourselves when we are alone and at home, in the same manner as we do in the presence of a great king ; we speak and open our mouth as we please when we are with the people of our own household and with our relatives, but not so when we are in a royal assembly. If we therefore desire to attain human perfection, and to be truly men of God, we must awake from our sleep, and bear in mind that the great King that is over us, and is always joined to us, is greater than any earthly king, greater than David and Solomon. The King that cleaves to us and embraces us is the Intellect that influences us, and forms the link between us and God.

We perceive God by means of that light that He sends down unto us, wherefore the Psalmist says, ' In Thy light do we see light ' (Ps. xxxvi. 10) ; so God looks down upon us through that same light, and is always with us beholding and watching us on account of this light.

" When the perfect bear this in mind, they will be filled with fear of God, humility and piety, with true, not apparent, reverence and respect of God, in such a manner that their conduct, even when alone with their wives or in the bath, will be as modest as they are in public intercourse with other people " (*Guide* III, 52).

§7. *Social Life.* Like Aristotle who described man as a " social animal ", Maimonides declares of him that he " is naturally a social being, that by virtue of his nature he seeks to form communities ; man is therefore different from other living beings that are not compelled to combine into communities " (*Guide* II, 40).

" It is well known that man requires friends all his lifetime. . . . When man is in good health and prosperous, he enjoys the company of his friends ; in time of trouble he is in need of them ; in old age, when his body is weak, he is assisted by them. This love is more frequent and more intense between parents and children, and among other relations. Perfect love, brotherhood, and mutual assistance are only found among those near to each other by relationship. The members of a family united by common descent from the same grandfather, or even from some more distant ancestor, have towards each other a certain feeling of love, help each other, and sympathise with each other. To effect this is one of the chief purposes of the Torah " (*Guide* III, 49).

It is the duty of man to take his place in the social

life around him and contribute his share towards its well-being. To live idly and depend on charity is a degradation to man.

" A man should ever suffer the deepest privations rather than have recourse to his fellowmen or throw himself upon the Community. Thus the Sages exhorted, ' Make thy (living on the) Sabbath as on a week-day, and be not dependent upon thy fellow-men '.[65] Even if he be wise and honoured, should he grow poor he must engage in a trade, however lowly, rather than have recourse to charity. ' Flay a carcass in the street and earn a living, and say not, " I am a great man and the work is below my dignity " ! '[66] Some of the great Sages were hewers of wood, carriers of logs, drawers of water for the gardens, metal-workers, smiths ; but they asked nothing from the community and refused whatever was offered to them "[67] (*Yad, Mattenot Aniyyim* X, 18).

To the question, Why did not God create all men lovers of knowledge and highly endowed intellectually ? Maimonides gave this answer :

" If all men were seekers of wisdom and philosophy, the social order would be destroyed and the human race quickly disappear from the world ; because man is very helpless and needs many things. Consequently it would be necessary for him to learn ploughing, reaping, threshing, grinding, baking and how to fashion implements for these tasks, for the purpose of securing his food-supply. Similarly he would have to learn spinning and weaving to clothe himself, the building art to provide a shelter, and to fashion tools for all these works.

" But the life of Methuselah would not be sufficiently long to learn all these occupations which are indispensable to human existence. When, in these conditions, would he find leisure to study and acquire wisdom ? Consequently, there is necessity for other types of men to follow these occupations which are essential in a city, so that the student may have his wants provided, the land may be inhabited and wisdom found among men " (C.M., Introduction).

He denounced gambling as an anti-social act, because no advantage accrued from it to the advancement of civilisation ; and he continued : " It is a fundamental teaching of the Torah that a man should properly only occupy himself in this world with one of two things : either in Torah for the purpose of perfecting his soul in its wisdom ; or in an occupation which helps him to gain a regular living, or in trade and commerce. But it is right to decrease the time spent in obtaining a livelihood and increase the time devoted to Torah " (C.M., *Sanhedrin* III, 3).

On social relationship with a man's neighbours Maimonides writes :

" It is a commandment upon each man to love his brother-Israelite like himself.[68] A man ought therefore to recount his neighbour's praise and be scrupulous with his money as with his own, and be concerned for his honour as he is concerned with his personal honour.[69] Whoever glories in the shame of his fellowman has no share in the world to come.[70]

" Love of the stranger who comes and enters beneath the wings of the *Shechinah*[71] is ordained in two commandments : First, because the stranger is included in the definition of ' neighbour ' (Lev. xix. 18) ; and secondly, because as a stranger he is included in the command ' Love ye therefore the stranger ' (Deut. x. 19). . . .

" Anyone who hates his fellow-Israelite in his heart transgresses a prohibition ; for it is said, ' Thou

shalt not hate thy brother in thine heart ' (Lev. xix.
17). . . . If a man is injured by another, he
should not bear hatred towards him in silence ; but
he is commanded to acquaint him with his grievance
and say to him, Why have you done so to me ? Why
have you injured me by such a thing ? And if the
other repent and ask his pardon, he must forgive him
and not be hard.[72]

"Whoever sees his fellowmen commit a sin, or
walk in the way which is not good, is under the
obligation to bring him back to the proper way and to
make known to him that by his wicked actions he sins
against himself. He who rebukes his fellow, whether
in matters between man and man or between man and
God, should rebuke him in private, talk to him quietly
and in gentle language, and let him know that he is
only telling him this for his own good, for the purpose
of bringing him to the life of the world to come. If
the other listen to him, well and good ; but if not,
he should rebuke him a second and a third time ; and
so he must rebuke him continually until the offender
strikes him and says, I will not listen. But he in
whose power it is to prevent others from sinning, but
does not do so, becomes himself responsible for the
iniquity, because it was possible for him to have
prevented them.[73]

" He who rebukes his fellow should not at first
talk to him harshly so as to put him to shame. . . .
It is forbidden a man to put an Israelite to shame, least
of all in public ; for although shaming a fellowman is
not an offence punishable by flagellation, it is nevertheless a great sin. Thus the Sages declare, ' He who
puts his fellowman to shame in public has no share
in the world to come '.[74] Consequently a man should
be very careful not to shame his neighbour publicly,

whether he be an inportant person or insignificant. He must not call him by any name of which he is ashamed, nor relate in his presence anything of which he may be ashamed.75

" This, however, applies only to matters between man and man ; but as regards matters relating to God, if he does not recant as the result of private rebuke, we may put him to shame publicly, proclaim his sin, reprove him in his presence, disgrace and denounce him until he amend, in the manner that the Prophets acted against Israel.

" If a person has been injured by his fellow and does not wish to reprove him, or mention it at all, because the offender is too vulgar a person or of disordered mind, but pardons him in his heart without hating or reproaching him, behold this is the degree of saintliness76 " (Yad, Déot VI, 3-9).

§8. *The Purpose of Life.* Maimonides devotes attention to the question for what purpose man exists. The answer to this question must be the basis of the ultimate problem of Ethics, viz., What should be the goal of human endeavour. His answer is based on the assertion, " Man is not endowed with perfection at the beginning, but at first possesses perfection *in potentia*, not in fact " (*Guide* I, 34). His purpose is therefore to convert potentiality into actuality.

" When the philosophers discovered that the end of all things in the Universe was to provide for the existence of man, they were compelled to continue their investigation and determine why man exists and what is the reason for his creation. After long research into this problem, they found that man possessed numerous activities, whereas all other animals and plants possessed only one or two directed to one end. We, e.g., see that the palm has no other activity than to produce dates, and similarly with the other trees. Likewise with animals, we find that some only spin, like the spider ; some build, like the swallow which constructs nests in Summer ; others store up food on which to subsist, like the ant.

" Man, on the other hand, performs many activities of a varied nature. The philosophers, accordingly, investigated all his activities seriatim to discover from them the purpose of his creation. They found that his purpose resolved itself into one function only on account of which he was created, and the rest of his activities were merely to maintain his stability so that he may thereby fulfil that one function—which is, to formulate in his soul concepts of the intellectual mysteries and to ascertain the exact truths. For it is self-evident how utterly false it is that the purpose of man should be eating, drinking and cohabiting, or building a wall or being a king ; because all these occurrences happen to him without developing his inner power, and also in these matters he is allied to most creatures. But it is wisdom which develops his inner power and removes him from a lowly to a dignified status, since he was only man *in potentia*, but has become man in reality" (C.M., Introduction).

" It was impossible, according to the wisdom of God, that substance should exist without form, or any of the forms of the bodies without substance, and it was necessary that the very noble form of man, which is the image and likeness of God, should be joined to the substance of dust and darkness, the source of all defect and loss. For these reasons the Creator gave to the form of man power, rule and dominion over the substance ; the form can subdue the substance, refuse the fulfilment of its desires, and reduce them, as far as possible, to a just and proper measure.

" The station of man varies according to the exercise of this power. Some persons constantly strive to choose that which is noble, and to seek perpetuation in accordance with the direction of their nobler part—their form ; their thoughts are engaged in the formation of ideas, the acquisition of true knowledge about everything, and the union with the divine intellect which flows down upon them, and which is the source of man's form. Whenever they are led by the wants of the body to that which is low and avowedly disgraceful, they are grieved at their position, they feel ashamed and confounded at their situation. They try with all their might to diminish this disgrace, and to guard against it in every possible way. . . .

" Some consider all wants of the body as shame, disgrace, and defect to which they are compelled to attend ; this is chiefly the case with the sense of touch, which is a disgrace to us according to Aristotle, and which is the cause of our desire for eating, drinking and sensuality. Intelligent persons must, as much as possible, reduce these wants, guard against them, feel grieved when satisfying them, abstain from speaking of them, discussing them, and attending to them in company with others. Man must have control over all these desires, reduce them as much as possible, and only retain of them as much as is indispensable. His aim must be the aim of man as man, viz., the formulation of ideas, and nothing else " (*Guide* III, 8).

On this view, the world is man's training-ground in spiritual development, and only when it is regarded as such are the opportunities it offers rightly used.

" After death there is no opportunity for man to attain perfection or increase of virtue ; he can only do so in this world. Solomon hints at this when he says, ' There is no work, nor device, nor knowledge, nor wisdom in the grave whither thou goest ' (Eccles. ix. 10) ; but these objects, which a man should pursue, remain for him so long as he lives. Therefore it is obligatory that he should strive for them during his brief span of life and not waste his time in the acquisition of anything but the virtues ; because his loss is great if he neglects his opportunities, since he can never repair it.

" When the saints perceived this, they took care not to spend their life except in acquiring wisdom and increase of the virtues, and devoted all their time to following the path of truth, and squandered none of it in the pursuit of material things, apart from the very minimum which necessity demanded. Others, however, spent all their time on material things only, and left this world as they entered it, thereby incurring eternal loss. But the masses invert the truth in this connection and maintain that the former class (the saints) wasted their life in this world, while the latter made the most of it. The contrary is the truth, as we have declared ; for these men make darkness for light and light for darkness. Woe to them who destroy the truth ! " (C.M., *Abot* IV, 22).

§9. *The Ultimate Goal of Living.* All that has been prescribed to guide man in the right way of life, physically and morally, is but the means to an end. These rules of conduct are the necessary preparation for the attempt to reach an ultimate goal which must be man's constant ideal throughout his life.

" It is possible for one to shape one's conduct entirely from the point of view of utility, as we have stated, with no aim beyond that of maintaining the health of the body, or guarding against disease. Such a one does not deserve to be called virtuous, for, just as he strives for the enjoyment of good health, another like him may have as his aim the gratification of eating, or of sexual intercourse, none of which actions leads towards the true goal. The real duty of man is, that in adopting whatever measures he may for his well-being, and the preservation of his existence in good health, he should do so with the object of maintaining a perfect condition of the instruments of the soul, which are the limbs of the body, so that his soul may be unhampered, and he may busy himself in acquiring the moral and mental virtues.

" So it is with all the sciences and knowledge man may learn. Concerning those which lead directly to this goal, there is naturally no question ; but such subjects as Mathematics, etc., which do not tend directly towards that goal, should be studied for the purpose of sharpening the mind, and training the mental faculties by scientific investigations, so that man may acquire intellectual ability to distinguish demonstrative proofs from others, whereby he will be enabled to comprehend the essence of God " (C.M., *Eight Chapters* V).

" Man ought to direct his heart and all his actions solely towards knowing God, blessed be He ! so that his sitting down, and his rising up, and his conversation should altogether tend to this goal. For instance, when he engages in business transactions or manual labour for remuneration, the intention in his heart should not be merely to accumulate money ; but he ought to do these things with the view of providing for his physical wants, such as food, drink, a home and marriage. Similarly, when he eats or drinks or cohabits, his purpose should not simply be physical gratification, so that he does not eat or drink except what is pleasant to the palate . . .; but he sets as his purpose when eating or drinking nothing else than the preservation of his body and limbs in good health. . . .

" He who conducts himself according to medical regulations, if he make it his object merely that his whole body and his limbs be perfect and that he should have sons to do his work and labour for his requirements, this is not the right way. He must intend that his body should be perfect and strong to the end that his soul may be fit to know the Lord ; because it is impossible for him to reflect and study the sciences when he is hungry, or ill, or any one of his limbs aches. He must likewise intend to have a son in the hope that he will be wise and a great man in Israel. Consequently, he who walks in this way throughout his life serves the Lord continually, even at the time when he is engaged in commerce, even when performing his marital duties ; because his object in all this is to provide his needs, so that his body may be perfect to serve the Lord. Even at the time when he sleeps—provided he sleeps that both his mind and body may enjoy rest, so that he may not become ill and be unable to serve the Lord when he is unwell—his very sleep will be found to be a service of the Omnipresent, blessed be He ! In this respect the Sages have commanded, ' Let all thine acts be for the sake of God '.77 And this is likewise what Solomon said in his wisdom, ' In all thy ways acknowledge Him, and He will direct thy paths' (Prov. iii. 6) " (*Yad, Déot* III, 2f).

Maimonides sums up his whole teaching in the concluding chapter of the *Guide*, where he enumerates four types of perfection and argues that the fourth is the true one after which man should aspire :

" The ancient and the modern philosophers have

shown that man can acquire four kinds of perfection. The first kind, the lowest, in the acquisition of which people spend their days, is perfection as regards property—the possession of money, garments, furniture, servants, land, and the like ; the possession of the title of a great king belongs to this class. There is no close connection between this possession and its possessor ; it is a perfectly imaginary relation when on account of the great advantage a person derives from these possessions, he says, This is my house, this is my servant, this is my money, and these are my hosts and armies. For when he examines himself he will find that all these things are external, and their qualities are entirely independent of the possessor. When, therefore, that relation ceases, he that has been a great king may one morning find that there is no difference between him and the lowest person, and yet no change has taken place in the things which were ascribed to him. The philosophers have shown that he whose sole aim in all his exertions and endeavours is the possession of this kind of perfection, only seeks perfectly imaginary and transient things ; and even if these remain his property all his lifetime, they do not give him any perfection.

" The second kind is more closely related to man's body than the first. It includes the perfection of the shape, constitution, and form of man's body ; the utmost evenness of temperaments, and the proper order and strength of his limbs. This kind of perfection must likewise be excluded from forming our chief aim ; because it is a perfection of the body, and man does not possess it as a man, but as a living being ; he has this property besides in common with the lowest animal ; and even if a person possesses the greatest possible strength, he could not be as strong as a mule, much less can he be as strong as a lion or an elephant ; he, therefore, can at the utmost have strength that might enable him to carry a heavy burden, or break a thick substance, or do similar things, in which there is no great profit for the body. The soul derives no profit from this kind of perfection.

" The third kind of perfection is more closely connected with man himself than the second perfection. It includes moral perfection, the highest degree of excellency in man's character. Most of the precepts aim at producing this perfection ; but even this kind is only a preparation for another perfection, and is not sought for its own sake. For all moral principles concern the relation of man to his neighbour ; the perfection of man's moral principles is, as it were, given to man for the benefit of mankind. Imagine a person living alone, and having no connection whatever with any other person ; all his good moral principles are at rest, they are not required, and give man no perfection whatever. These principles are only necessary and useful when man comes in contact with others.

" The fourth kind of perfection is the true perfection of man ; the possession of the highest intellectual faculties ; the possession of such notions which lead to true metaphysical opinions as regards God. With this perfection man has obtained his final object ; it gives him true human perfection ; it remains to him alone ; it gives him immortality,[78] and on its account he is called man. Examine the first three kinds of perfection; you will find that, if you possess them, they are not your property, but the property of others ; according to the ordinary view, however, they belong to you and to others. But the last kind of perfection is exclusively yours ; no one else owns any part of it, ' They shall be only thine own, and not strangers' with thee' (Prov. v. 17). Your aim must therefore be to attain this fourth perfection that is exclusively yours, and you ought not to continue to work and weary yourself for that which belongs to others, whilst neglecting your soul till it has lost entirely its original purity through the dominion of the bodily powers over it. . . .

" The Prophets have likewise explained unto us these things, and have expressed the same opinion on them as the philosophers. They say distinctly that perfection in property, in health, or in character, is not a perfection worthy to be sought as a cause of pride and glory for us ; that the knowledge of God, i.e., true wisdom, is the only perfection which we should seek and in which we should glorify ourselves. Jeremiah, referring to these four kinds of perfection, says : ' Thus saith the Lord, Let not the wise man glory in his wisdom,[79] neither let the mighty man glory in his might, let not the rich man glory in his riches ; but let him that glorieth glory in this, that he understandeth and knoweth Me that I am the Lord Who exercise lovingkindness, judgment and righteousness in the earth ; for in these things I delight, saith the Lord ' (Jer. ix. 22f). . . .

" The object of the above passage is to declare that the perfection, in which man can truly glory, is attained by him when he has acquired—as far as this is possible for man—the knowledge of God, the knowledge of His Providence, and of the manner in which it influences His creatures in their production and continued existence. Having acquired this knowledge he will then be determined always to seek lovingkindness, judgment and righteousness, and thus to imitate the ways of God.".[80]

On this exalted note the *Guide* ends. It is the culminating point of Maimonides' system of teaching.

CHAPTER XII

SOME *OBITER DICTA*

WHEN I have a difficult subject before me—when I find the road narrow, and can see no other way of teaching a well-established truth except by pleasing one intelligent man and displeasing ten thousand fools —I prefer to address myself to the one man and to take no notice whatever of the condemnation of the multitude (*Guide*, Introd.).

A truth, once established by proof, does neither gain force nor certainty by the consent of all scholars, nor lose by the general dissent (*ibid.* II, 15).

The fact that a certain proposition has been proved by a dialectical argument will never induce me to accept that proposition, but, on the contrary, will weaken my faith in it and cause me to doubt it. For when we understand the fallacy of a proof, our faith in the proposition itself is shaken (*ibid.* II, 16).

If a person studies too much and exhausts his reflective powers, he will be confused, and will not be able to apprehend even that which had been within the power of his apprehension (*ibid.* I, 32).

TEACHINGS OF MAIMONIDES

It is in fact ignorance or a kind of madness to weary our minds with finding out things which are beyond our reach, without having the means of approaching them (*ibid.* II, 24).

He who has studied insufficiently, and teaches and acts according to his defective knowledge, is to be considered as if he sinned knowingly (*ibid.* III, 41).

Do not consider a thing as proof because you find it written in books; for just as a liar will deceive with his tongue, he will not be deterred from doing the same thing with his pen. They are utter fools who accept a thing as convincing proof because it is in writing (*Iggéret Téman, Responsa* II, 5d).

The truth of a thing does not become greater by its frequent repetition, nor is it lessened by lack of repetition (*Tehiyyat ha-Métim, Responsa* II, 9d).

Whenever the words of a person can be interpreted in such a manner that they agree with fully established facts, it is the duty of every educated and honest man so to interpret them (*Guide* III, 14).

It is through the intellect that the human being has the capacity of honouring God (C.M., *Hagigah* II,1).

The heart is the tabernacle of the human intellect (*Ethical Will, Responsa* II, 39c).

The wise man is a greater asset to a nation than is a king (C.M., *Horayot* III, end).

A man should never cast his intellect behind him ; his eyes are in front, not behind (*Responsa* II, 26b).

Wisdom is the consciousness of self (*Guide* I, 53).

Let the truth and right by which you are apparently the loser be preferable to you to the falsehood and wrong by which you are apparently the gainer (*Ethical Will, Responsa* II, 38c).

Moral conduct is a preparation for intellectual progress, and only a man whose character is pure, calm and steadfast can attain to intellectual perfection —that is, acquire correct conceptions (*Guide* I, 34).

A miracle cannot prove that which is impossible ; it is useful only as a confirmation of that which is possible (*ibid* III, 24).

Make matter subject to the intellect, i.e. the body to the soul ; for this subjection is your freedom in this world and the world to come (*Ethical Will, Responsa* II, 38d).

It is of great advantage that man should know his station, and not erroneously imagine that the whole Universe exists only for him (*Guide* III, 12).

The multitude does not estimate man by his true form, but by the perfection of his bodily limbs and the beauty of his garments (*ibid.* III, 45).

It is to be feared that those who become great in riches and comfort generally fall into the vices of insolence and haughtiness, and abandon all good principles (*ibid.* III, 39).

It is in the nature of man to strive to gain money and to increase it ; and his great desire to add to his wealth and honour is the chief source of misery for man (*ibid. loc. cit*).

Ease destroys bravery, whilst trouble and care for food create strength (*ibid.* III, 24).

It is a natural phenomenon that we find consolation in our misfortune when the same misfortune or a greater one has befallen another person (*ibid.* III, 40).

It is indeed a fact that the transition from trouble to ease gives more pleasure than continual ease (*ibid.* III, 24).

When we continually see an object, however sublime it may be, our regard for that object will be lessened, and the impression we have received of it will be weakened (*ibid.* III, 47).

The sight of that to which a person has been accustomed for a long time does not produce such an ardent desire for its enjoyment as is produced by objects new in form and character (*ibid.* III, 49).

NOTES

INTRODUCTION

[1] See *Encyclopædia of Religion and Ethics*, IX, p. 873.

[2] Cf. Radin, *Jews among the Greeks and Romans*.

[3] See *Contra Apionem* I, 22.

[4] E.g., j. Betsah II, 5, 61c (a philosopher and Bar Kappara), Abodah Zarah 54b (philosophers in Rome and the Rabbis), Genesis Rabba XI, 6 (a philosopher and Rabbi Hoshayah).

[5] See Delitzsch, *Biblical Psychology*, pp. 292ff.

[6] Abot I, 17 (*Authorised Prayer Book*, ed. Singer, p. 186).

[7] Hagigah 14b.

[8] Literally " another ", the nickname given to Elisha ben Abuyah when he " cut the plants ", i.e., abandoned Judaism. He was then considered as having become a different person.

[9] Abot III, 19 (Singer, p. 194).

[10] Even Maimonides comments in a similar strain on this verse : " God alone has a perfect and true knowledge of the heavens, their nature, their essence, their form, their motions and their causes ; but He gave man power to know the things which are under the heavens ; here is man's world, here is his home, into which he has been placed, and of which he is himself a portion " (*Guide* II, 24). In one of his letters he states : " Whatever is beyond Nature no *savant* or philosopher is able to establish with clear proof, but whatever is in Nature is not hidden from his eyes " (*Responsa* II, 24b). If Maimonides had been charged with inconsistency in holding such an opinion and yet indulging in philosophical speculation, his answer would probably have been as follows : I admit the limited range of which the human intellect is capable and I have pointed out in my works (cf. Chap. X, §5) that it is idle to attempt to penetrate the mysteries of God. All I have done is to extract from His revealed word the utmost it contains and applied my intellect to the fullest possible development of its teachings.

[11] Maimonides writes of Aristotle that his intellect reached the highest plane of perfection attainable by man, apart from the Prophets who had been directly inspired by God (*Responsa* II, 28d).

[12] Only the briefest outline of the subject could be given in this Introduction. The story of the Jewish philosophers is fully told in Husik, *History of Medieval Jewish Philosophy*.

[13] For a fuller account of his biography, the reader is referred to the excellent monograph by David Yellin and Israel Abrahams.

[14] Literally " judge ", i.e., member of a Rabbinic court.

[15] In the *Guide* II, 9 he mentions " Ibn Aflaḥ of Seville with whose son I was acquainted . . . also the excellent philosopher Abu-Bekr ibn Alzaig, one of whose pupils was my fellow-student."

[16] The question is examined by Friedländer in the preface to his translation of the *Guide* (3 vol. edition, I, p. XXXIII) and Margoliouth in the *Jewish Quarterly Review* (old series), vol. XIII. They both give their decision in favour of Maimonides.

[17] *Nom de plume* of Asher Ginzberg, one of the foremost of modern Jewish writers. See his fine essay, " The Supremacy of Reason " in *Essays on Zionism and Judaism*, especially pp. 198ff.

[18] See p. 115.

[19] See Chap. IV, §5.

[20] The first of the six Orders into which the Mishnah is divided.

[21] It is in fourteen books, hence the name *Yad* which in Hebrew has the numerical value of fourteen.

[22] *History of the Jews* (American edition) III, pp. 466f.

[23] See p. 320, note 5.

[24] See p. 51.

[25] An interesting essay by Israel Friedländer on the way Maimonides' style reflects the character of the man is contained in the memorial work *Moses ben Maimon*, I, pp. 429ff.

[26] Kohler, *Jewish Theology*, p. 30.

[27] Lazarus, *Ethics of Judaism*, I, pp. 274f.

[28] Jowett, *Dialogues of Plato*, III, pp. 415f.

[29] Roth, *Spinoza Descartes and Maimonides*, p. 77.

[30] Paulsen, *Introduction to Philosophy*, p. 282.

[31] Jowett, III, p. 470.

[32] Husik, *op. cit.*, p. 236.

[33] Joel, *Die Religionsphilosophie des Maimonides*, p. 4.

[34] An account of this intellectual warfare is given by Schechter, *Studies in Judaism* (first series), pp. 199ff.

[35] Cf. Singer's edition, pp. 2f. and 89f.

[36] Abrahams, *Jewish Life in the Middle Ages*, p. 371.

[37] Roth, *Spinoza Descartes and Maimonides*.

[38] This great genius, one of the finest exponents of Kant's philosophy, was a Lithuanian Jew, born in 1754 and later migrated to Germany. A sympathetic sketch of him is given by Zangwill in *Dreamers of the Ghetto*. Out of admiration for the author of the *Guide* he assumed the name of Maimon. He states in his autobiography : " My reverence for this great teacher went so far that I regarded him as the ideal of a perfect man, and looked upon his teachings as if they had been inspired with Divine Wisdom " ; *Lebensgeschichte* II, p. 3.

[39] He studied the *Guide* in his boyhood. See *Jewish Encyc.*, VIII, p. 479.

[40] Two Latin translations were published, one by Justinianus in 1520 based on an earlier version, the other by the younger Buxtorf in 1629.

[41] Yellin and Abrahams, p. 157.

[42] Husik, p. 306.

NOTES

CHAPTER I

[1] An explanation of this term will be given below in §5.

[2] On the Intelligences or Angels and the Spheres, see Chap. II.

[3] Maimonides reads into the Hebrew word *emét* " truth " its later philosophical connotation, viz., reality.

[4] In its narrower sense, Torah (lit. teaching, direction) denotes the Five Books of Moses as distinct from the rest of the Scriptures. In its wider sense, it signifies the whole corpus of Jewish law and doctrine which is based on the Pentateuch.

[5] The ordinances of the Torah are divided into two classes : (i.) commandments of Do, i.e., positive commands, and (ii.) commandments of Do not, i.e., negative commands or prohibitions. The former number 248, the latter 365.

[6] For a discussion of this point where Maimonides disagreed with Aristotle, see below §8.

[7] The Propositions are too long, and the argument which Maimonides bases upon them too intricate, to be quoted *in extenso*. The reader will find a good summary in Husik, *Medieval Jewish Philosophy*, pp. 254ff.

[8] This deduction follows from Prop. VII : " Things which are changeable are at the same time divisible. Hence everything that moves is divisible and consequently corporeal ; but that which is indivisible cannot move and cannot therefore be corporeal " ; and from Prop. V : " Motion implies change and transition from potentiality to actuality." The reason why changeability implies divisibility is that the change is not instantaneous over the entire object. There must be a moment when part is changed and part unchanged ; therefore the object is capable of division. Motion is a form of change.

[9] Prop. XVI states : " Incorporeal bodies can only be numbered when they are forces situated in a body ; the several forces must then be counted together with substances or objects in which they exist. Hence purely spiritual beings, which are neither corporeal nor forces situated in corporeal objects, cannot be counted, except when considered as causes and effects." If, then, there be two gods, i.e., two incorporeal and infinite beings, only one of them can be regarded as the First Cause, because one can only be distinguished from the other by the relationship of cause and effect. One must, in fact, have brought the other into existence.

[10] This is a deduction from Prop. XV : " Time is an accident that is related and joined to motion in such a manner that the one is never found without the other. Motion is only possible in time, and the idea of time cannot be conceived otherwise than in connection with motion ; things which do not move have no relation to time ".

[11] Prop. VIII states : " A thing that moves accidentally must come to rest, because it does not move of its own accord ; hence accidental motion cannot continue for ever ". A material body can only have accidental motion, because it

does not move unless something or somebody sets it in motion. Since its motion is accidental, it cannot be perpetual. Similarly a force within a body can only cause accidental motion, since it can only move with the motion of the body, which consequently cannot be perpetual. Therefore if the heavenly Spheres have perpetual motion, the cause cannot be a body or a force within a body. The cause must be incorporeal.

[12] By an " absolute " Being is meant a Being independent of all cause and accident.

[13] By the *agens* is meant what the philosophers called *causa efficiens*, the " efficient ", or producing, cause. Aristotle (*Physics* II, 7) describes the four causes as matter, form, that which moves, and that for the sake of which a thing subsists.

[14] For the meaning of " form ", see the Introduction, p. 21. The sense in which God is spoken of as the form of the Universe is explained in the next §.

[15] It is essential to regard God as both " cause " and Creator. If He were only the Creator, it would be possible to believe that the Universe could exist without Him, in the same way that a building can continue in existence when the builder dies. But if God is the " cause " which includes the " form " of the Universe, His non-existence must also involve its non-existence.

[16] Defined in §5.

[17] Daniel xii. 7. There the phrase is usually rendered " He that liveth for ever." Cf. also Prayer Book, ed. Singer, pp. 17, 36.

[18] The root-meaning of *Faid* in Arabic and *Shéfa'* in Hebrew is rather of " abundance ", and when applied to a water-spring it describes its overflow rather than its flow.

[19] Cf. line 6 of the Prayer Book version of his Principles of Faith (ed. Singer, p. 3) : " The *Shéfa'* of His Prophecy He gave unto the men of His choice ".

[20] Several sayings to this effect are, e.g., found in Gabirol's *Choice of Pearls*. Cf. Nos. 510, 536f., 556. Plato likewise declares : " We acknowledge the world to be full of many goods and also of evils, and of more evils than goods "; *Laws* X, Jowett, V, p. 293.

[21] See Chap. II.

[22] See Chap. XI, §5.

[23] He means that they are not evil in themselves, but only in respect to the absence of good.

[24] See Introduction, p. 21.

[25] See below §10.

[26] See Midrash *ad loc.*

[27] And yet we believe in the incorporeality of God, because it is possible to interpret these expressions in such a manner that they do not conflict with that doctrine.

[28] By the words " such as they are ", he means in their present state as consisting of form and matter. God not only created the form but also the basic substance.

29 Plato also taught that time was created. He wrote in the *Timæus* : " There were no days and nights and months and years before the heaven was created, but when he constructed the heaven he created them also . . . Time, then, and the heaven came into being at the same instant in order that, having been created together, if ever there was to be a dissolution of them, they might be dissolved together ". Jowett III, pp. 456f.

30 The philosophical term " accident " is defined by Maimonides as follows : " A peculiarity which is found in many of a species or a few of it, and does not constitute it as a species, is called an accident. . . . Accidents are of two kinds : (i.) inseparable from the object, as, e.g., the blackness of pitch, the whiteness of snow, the heat of fire ; (ii.) separable, as, e.g., standing or sitting in the case of a person, the heat of iron and stone " (*Millot*, Chap. X). With this may be compared Aristotle's definition. He also distinguishes two kinds : (i.) " that which attaches to something and can be truly asserted, but neither of necessity nor usually " ; (ii.) " what attaches to each thing in virtue of itself but is not in its essence " (*Metaphysics* V, 30).

31 Just as whiteness cannot exist as an abstraction apart from matter, so time could not exist as an abstraction. Consequently if there were time before the Creation, there must also have been matter and motion.

32 The Hebrew word *'olam* means " Universe " and also " eternity ". Maimonides gives it the latter signification in this verse.

33 The meaning seems to be that by creating the *materia prima* which is the basic substance of the entire Universe, the Creation of the beings above and the things below became possible.

34 This refers to the apparent daily motion of the heavenly bodies from east to west, ascribed to the motion of the outermost Sphere in this direction (Friedländer).

35 The Sphere of Mercury, according to the opinion of the ancient astronomers, was above that of the Sun, and yet the Sun moves with greater velocity than Mercury. Maimonides' own opinion was that the Sphere of the Sun is above that of Mercury (see p. 71) (Friedländer).

36 Maimonides refers here to the Sphere of the Sun and that of Venus which complete their course in the circle of the Zodiac in about the same time (Friedländer). According to Plato : " Three planets (Sun, Mercury and Venus) he made to move with equal swiftness, and the remaining four (Moon, Saturn, Mars and Jupiter) to move with unequal swiftness to the three and to one another, but in due proportion " (*Timæus*, trans. Jowett III, p. 455).

37 i.e., the theory of the Creation and that of the eternity of the Universe.

38 Those who assume the eternity of the Universe recognise only changes in the individual members of each species, and

TEACHINGS OF MAIMONIDES

can consistently only inquire into the object of these changes. They rest content when these are satisfactorily explained by the perpetuation of the species and the production of the most perfect form in each species. It would be inconsistent with their theory of the eternity and stability of the species and the whole Universe to ask for the purpose of these permanent beings (Friedländer).

[39] This passage occurs in the concluding service of the Day of Atonement. See Prayer Book, p. 267. There are variants in the readings.

[40] i.e., are descriptive of His deeds, e.g., King, Judge, Merciful, etc. They are not used exclusively of God.

[41] This phrase means " the name which is set apart ", i.e., reserved for God and applied to none but Him.

[42] Sotah VII, 6, Tamid VII, 2.

[43] Yoma VI, 2.

[44] i.e., a point in the letter to double its sound. Gutturals and an initial could not have the *dagesh*, so the only letter possible of reduplication would be the third, and the word pronounced Yehavveh.

[45] Kiddushin 71a. The translation of *shabua'* by " seven years " is more correct than " week " given in the *Jewish Encyc.* XI, p. 263. It is so rendered in Vol. IX, p. 162.

[46] The name consisting of twelve letters is not specified in the Talmud (Kiddushin 71a). Maimonides therefore conjectures that it did not consist of a single word but of an entire phrase. Narboni in his commentary on the *Guide* is surprised that Maimonides ignored the form of the name which is mentioned in the *Séfer ha-Bahir* (a mystical work) in the name of R. Nehunyah ben Hakanah, and consisted of the Tetragrammaton pronounced in three different ways, viz., YiHVoH, YaHVeH, YaHaVaH (Friedländer).

[47] The priests discontinued the use of the Tetragrammaton forty years before the destruction of the Second Temple (Yoma 39b).

[48] Kiddushin 71a. What these letters were is not known with certainty. For the Kabbalistic form of the name of forty-two letters, see *Jewish Encyc.* IX, p. 164.

CHAPTER II

[1] A similar idea is found in Plato. See *Timæus*, Jowett, III, pp. 460f.

[2] The Cherubim, Exod. xxv. 18ff.

[3] These, the *Ophannim* and Cherubim occur in Ezekiel's visions (Chap. i. and x.). The *Hayyot ha-kodesh* and *Ophannim* are mentioned together in an old liturgical poem ; see Prayer Book, p. 129 bot.

[4] Derived from the Hebrew word occurring in Isa. xxxiii. 7. Its use to designate Angels must have been fairly early, because when Rabbi Judah the Prince died, about 200 C.E., the dirge was uttered over him, " The *Erelim* and mortals struggled

for the divine ark (i.e., the Rabbi), but the former were the victors " ; Ketubot 104a.

5 The word denotes a glittering substance and occurs in Ezek. i. 4, 27. On the basis fo the word *Ḥashmal*, these Angels have been defined in the Talmud (Hagigah 13a) as *ḤAyyot eSH meMALlelot*, i.e., " creatures of fire which speak ", or *'ittim ḤASHot 'ittim meMALlelot*, i.e., " sometimes they are silent and sometimes speak ".

6 Cf. Isa. vi. 2, 6.

7 The Common Biblical word for Angel.

8 The word is so interpreted in Ps. xcvii. 7. But Maimonides probably has in mind the phrase *elohé elohim* " God of gods " in Deut. x. 17, which some commentators explained as " God of the angelic host " (see Ibn Ezra on Gen. i. 1).

9 Cf. Job i. 6, ii. 1, xxxviii. 7.

10 This definition of the word is given in the Talmud, Ḥagigah 13b.

11 This term for Angels is not found in Biblical and Rabbinic literature. Maimonides is possibly thinking of Biblical passages where the Angel is called *Ish* "man"; e.g., Gen. xviii. 2, xxxii. 25 ; Josh. v. 13 ; Ezek. ix. 3, x. 2 ; Dan. x. 5.

12 See Chap. I, §5.

13 Through the Intelligences the human being derives his intellect *in potentia*, but through the influence of the Active Intellect that potentiality is converted into actuality.

14 The reference is to the *Ishim*, the lowest of the ten degrees of Angels.

15 It is not certain what Maimonides means. He is perhaps thinking of the narratives (e.g., Gen. xviii. Judg. xiii.) where an Angel announces the birth of a son to a barren woman.

16 Sanhedrin 38b ; cf. Genesis Rabba VIII, 8. In both passages the word used is " consulting " not " contemplating ". Maimonides often quotes loosely (probably from memory) from Talmud and Midrash.

17 It is doubtful whether Maimonides is actually quoting Plato. It has been plausibly suggested that Arab writers often confused Plato with Plotinus, and attributed ideas to the former which belong to the Neo-platonists. The idea Maimonides expounds here is found in Philo : " God having determined to found a mighty state, first of all conceived its form in His mind, according to which form He made a world perceptible only by the intellect, and then completed one visible to the external senses, using the first one as a model " (*On the Creation of the World*, IV).

18 Sanhedrin 38b.

19 Kohélet Rabba *ad loc.*, Genesis Rabba XII, 1. The word " king " in the verse is applied to God.

20 LI, 2.

21 Cf. Yebamot 16b, Ḥullin 60a.

[22] Actually the moon is about one-fiftieth the size of the earth ; but Maimonides underestimates the immensity of the sun as compared with the earth.

[23] This is a thought borrowed from the Greek philosophers. Plato described the planets as " living creatures having bodies fastened by vital chains " (*Timæus*, Jowett, III, p. 457). Aristotle speaks of the heaven as being " animated " (*On the Heavens*, II 2). He adds that we must " consider (the Spheres) as participating in action and life " (*ibid.* II, 12), and " it is necessary to think that the action of the stars is similar to that of animals and plants " (*loc. cit*).

[24] Two kinds of intellect were assumed in the explanation of the perpetual motion of the Spheres ; the intellect which the Spheres possess, i.e., the faculty of forming ideas, and the Intellect or Intelligence which is purely spiritual, separate from the Spheres. The former alone could not produce perpetual motion, according to Prop. VIII (quoted on p. 315, note 11), because it participates accidentally in the motion of the Spheres. The cause of the perpetual motion of the Sphere must be a purely spiritual being that does not participate in the motion of the Sphere (Friedländer).

[25] The reference is to *Metaphysics* XII, 6 : " If there is something which is capable of moving things or acting on them, but is not actually doing so, there will not necessarily be movement ; for that which has a potency need not exercise it " (trans. Ross).

[26] The ancient physicians thought that there were in the human being four humours, coloured respectively red, white, green, black ; and his disposition varied according to the colour which predominated.

[27] In one of his medical treatises Maimonides wrote : " What the medical men call ' spirits ' are vapours which exist in the bodies of animals. . . The vapours in the blood of the liver and the veins which issue from it are called the physical spirit ; in the heart and the arteries they are called the vital spirit ; in the inner part of the brains and in the canals of the nerves they are called animal spirit " (Friedländer).

[28] For the proof of the Unity of God based on the oneness of the Universe, see Chap. III, §5.

CHAPTER III

[1] Part I, Chap. 46f, 51-60.

[2] A Rabbinic aphorism (Berachot 31b) which Maimonides is fond of quoting when treating of anthropomorphisms in the Scriptures.

[3] See Chap. V, §3.

[4] " Soles " are mentioned in Ezek. xliii. 7.

[5] A homonym is defined as " a noun used with several significations " (*Millot*, chap. XIII). The opening chapters of the *Guide* are devoted to the discussion of the homonyms used in the Bible as applied to God.

⁶ See p. 317, note 30.

⁷ In the *Guide* I, 52, he argues that definition by means of *affirmative* attributes is impossible with God.

⁸ If we ascribe to God a positive attribute, it must have existed eternally together with His essence. But it is the very basis of the monotheistic creed that nothing existed eternally apart from God's essence.

⁹ This is reminiscent of Philo's teaching that we know that He is, but cannot know what He is. Cf. Drummond, *Philo Judæus*, II, pp. 18ff.

¹⁰ The expression " receive upon oneself the yoke, etc." is commonly used to denote the reading of the *Shema'*, the declaration of faith in the Unity. Cf. Berachot 13b.

¹¹ This follows from Prop. XIX : " A thing which owes its existence to certain causes has in itself merely the possibility of existence ; for only if these causes exist, the thing likewise exists. It does not exist if the causes do not exist at all, or if they have ceased to exist, or if there has been a change in the relation which implies the existence of that thing as a necessary consequence of those causes."

¹² See Chap. II, §5.

¹³ It would then follow that time preceded the existence of the deities or co-existed with them eternally. But philosophers agree that time was created. See Chap. I, §8.

¹⁴ Consequently their existence would not be absolute ; but if God exists at all His existence must be absolute. Cf. Chap. I, §2.

¹⁵ Based on Prop. XX : " A thing which has in itself the necessity of existence cannot have for its existence any cause whatever ".

¹⁶ A mantle of wool with " fringes " at the four corners, worn at the time of prayer. God is depicted as wrapped in the *Tallit* in Rosh Hashanah 17b.

¹⁷ Prop. XXII states : " Material objects are always composed of two elements, and are without exception subject to accidents. The two component elements of all bodies are substance and form. The accidents attributed to material objects are quantity, geometrical form and position ".

¹⁸ The idea of expressing motion by number is illustrated by a cinematograph film. The moving object in passing from point to point is represented in a series of pictures which can be numbered. Time is called an accident of motion because it is inseparable from it although not forming part of its essence.

¹⁹ Space is an accident of a physical body. If God is incorporeal, the idea of space is inapplicable to Him.

²⁰ Cf. Genesis Rabba V, 5.

²¹ Because each of these qualities would have had to be co-existent with God and therefore eternal.

²² i.e., the intellect, the being exercising intelligence and the idea formed by the intellect.

23 Since the ideas formed by the intellect are identical with the intellect, and since the action by which the idea is formed is also identical with the intellect, it follows that the intellect is identical with its action.

24 If the essence of intellect is comprehension and God comprehends constantly and He and the things comprehended are one and the same, the conclusion is that He is intellect, the Being exercising intellect and the idea formed by the intellect.

25 What is true of God is true also of the human being when his intellect is functioning. With man, however, the intellect is not always in action, as, e.g., during times of unconsciousness.

26 Maimonides confesses, " How God rules the Universe and provides for it is a complete mystery ; man is unable to solve it " (*Guide* I, 72).

CHAPTER IV

1 He contraverts this view in Chap. VII, §4.

2 An attitude based on the action of Hezekiah (Isa. xxxviii. 2 ; 2 Kings xx. 2). The Talmud accordingly teaches that nothing should intervene between one who prays and the wall (Berachot 5b).

3 The *Shema'* is the daily affirmation of belief in God's Unity. See Prayer Book, pp. 42ff. The *Tefillah*, or " prayer ", is a collection of benedictions which forms the central part of the daily devotions (Prayer Book, pp. 44-54).

4 According to the Rabbinic decision, the law is fulfilled if only the first verse of the *Shema'* is uttered with *Kawwanah*, i.e., with the deliberate intention of performing the religious duty of recital, and with concentration of mind (Berachot 13b). Maimonides declares that the requirement of the law must be exceeded in this matter.

5 When it is read in the Synagogue in the course of the Service on Sabbaths, Festivals, Mondays and Thursdays.

6 The Maimonidean authorship of this small treatise has been questioned by the historian Graetz ; but see Bacher's defence in the *Jewish Quarterly Review* (old series), vol. IX.

7 i.e., he loses consciousness of his body and its physical senses which pull the soul away from the purely spiritual beings, the Intelligences, with which it is akin, so that it is enabled to merge itself in them.

8 Cf. Sifré to Deut. vi. 5 : " Make Him loved by all His creatures, as did the Patriarch Abraham ".

9 He alludes to them again in *Guide* III, 25 as being among the " ignoble remnants of the nations left in the remote corners of the earth ". Friedländer suggests that he has in mind Ezek. xxxviii. 6, " the house of Togarmah in the uttermost parts of the north ".

10 The Ethiopians.

11 Ahad Ha'am comments on this passage : " We of the present day feel our moral sense particularly outraged by

his cruel treatment of the second class—' those who happen to hold false doctrines '— though we can understand that a logical thinker like Maimonides, who always went the whole length of his convictions, was bound to draw this conclusion from his philosophical system. For that system regards ' true opinions ' as something much more than ' opinions ' : it attributes to them the wonderful power of turning the reasoning faculty into a separate and eternal being, and sees therefore in the opposite opinions a danger to life in the most real sense. But in Maimonides' day the persecution of men for holding false opinions was a common thing (though it was done in the name of religion, not of philosophy) ; and even this piece of philosophic ruthlessness created no stir and aroused no contemporary protest ". *Essays on Zionism and Judaism*, p. 193.

[12] Abot II, 6 (Singer's Prayer Book, p. 187).

[13] They were the medieval successors of the Sadducees and denied the authority of the Rabbinic code of law.

[14] The passage is quoted in full in Chap. IX, §2.

[15] The reference is to the Kaabeh or " black stone " at Mecca, around which the Moslem pilgrims walk seven times and kiss the stone in each round.

[16] The point of the words " even on the Sabbath " is that the law only permits this in the case of an Israelite. Maimonides is therefore willing to recognise the Karaite who does not openly deride Rabbinism as a brother-Jew.

[17] The ancestors of the proselyte having been, of course, heathens.

[18] Maimonides explains that the command to love the *Gér* (proselyte) is specifically mentioned in the Torah although he is included in the general precept " love thy neighbour as thyself ", because additional love must be shown to him (*Mitswot*, Command. CCVII).

[19] Sanhedrin 106b.

[20] Tosifta Sanhedrin XIII, 2.

[21] Sifra, Aḥaré Mot, §143. Our texts read " who performs " not " who occupies himself with ".

[22] The son of Seth (Gen. v. 6).

[22a] Lecky, *Rationalism in Europe* (1910 ed. II, p. 282, note) remarks, " Maimonides wrote a letter on the vanity of astrology which two popes applauded ". It is quoted below.

[23] In the passage preceding this quotation he describes certain practices connected with witchcraft.

[24] In Maimonides' psychology, one of the intellectual virtues is " sagacity and intellectual cleverness " (see p. 246), and Aristotle regarded sagacity as " a species of happy conjecture" (*Eth. Nic.* VI, 10). This faculty, if strongly developed, " enables some persons to foretell important coming events " (*Guide* II, 38).

[25] From the description that follows one gathers that the procedure induced auto-hypnosis.

[26] A case, containing a piece of parchment on which is inscribed Deut. vi. 4-9, xi. 13-21, affixed to the door-post.

TEACHINGS OF MAIMONIDES

CHAPTER V

1 See Chap. I, §5.

2 Maimonides himself makes a somewhat similar statement in his *Ma'amar ha-Yiḥud*, Chap. II. " Know that it is one of the cardinal principles of this Torah that thou shouldest be aware that the Creator confers the prophetic gift on whomsoever He wishes and speaks to whomsoever He chooses of the children of men, only that Prophecy alights on one who is worthy of it." He continues to urge that, according to the Rabbis, it is a condition that the man should possess mental and moral virtues.

3 viz., the Aristotelians.

4 These philosophers taught that nothing could be possible with a class without at least one member of that class achieving it.

5 The idea that study is an essential pre-requisite of Prophecy is also found in Rabbinic teaching. " If there were no children, there would be no pupils ; without pupils there would be no Sages ; without Sages there would be no Elders ; without Elders there would be no Prophets " (Genesis Rabba XLII, 3).

6 See Chap. X, §1.

7 Berachot 57b.

8 Genesis Rabba XVII, 5.

9 This is evidently an allusion to the imperialistic ambitions of Mohammed.

10 This is an important point. According to Maimonides, one of the great purposes of the Torah is the improvement of the social relationship between man and man (see Chap. VI, §2). A true Prophet cannot act contrary to the teachings of the Torah. Therefore if a man, claiming to be a prophet, by his doctrines creates dissension between men, he cannot be a true prophet.

11 But this is something impossible of achievement. Says Maimonides elsewhere, " How God rules the Universe and provides for it is a complete mystery ; man is unable to solve it " (*Guide* I, 72).

12 This qualifying clause is necessary, because " there is not a righteous man upon earth that doeth good and sinneth not " (Eccles. VII, 20).

13 Pesaḥim 66b.

14 The Aramaic translation of the Pentateuch which embodies the Rabbinic exegesis.

15 Shabbat 30b, Pesaḥim 117a. The Talmudic text reads " Shechinah " in place of " spirit of Prophecy ".

16 By " ordinary Prophets " he means all with the exception of Moses of whom it is recorded, " his eye was not dim, nor his natural force abated " (Deut. xxxiv, 7).

17 These and similar expressions are often found in the Book of Judges (cf. ii. 18, vi. 34, xiv. 6).

18 Referring to the assistance he gave to Jethro's daughters against the shepherds (Exod. ii. 17).

324

[19] 1 Sam. xvi. 13.

[20] Megillah 7a.

[21] Cf. 1 Kings xi. 29ff, xii. 15, xiv. 2ff.

[22] In the Greek version, the Septuagint, Daniel is placed between Ezekiel and Hosea ; but the Talmud (Baba Batra 14b) inserts it between Lamentations and Esther.

[23] Genesis Rabba XLIV, 17.

[24] Maimonides depreciates the value of miracles as a sign of the prophet's claim because such evidence was used both by Christians and Mohammedans in support of Jesus and Mohammed respectively. He could not prove that they had not performed the wonders credited to them, and was therefore compelled to deny the validity of this criterion. He was further influenced by the teaching of the Torah in Deut. xiii. 2. See Introduction, pp. 9f.

[25] Cf. Deut. xviii. 21f.

[26] Maimonides admits this as a possibility. Cf. Chap. IV, §7.

[27] 1 Sam. ix. 6ff.

[28] Clearly a hint at the activities of Jesus and Mohammed.

[29] A Rabbinic dictum ; Berachot 7a.

[30] Sifra *ad loc.*

[31] Yebamot 49b.

[32] Maimonides explains that *see* " refers to perception by the intellect, and by no means to perception with the eye as in its literal meaning " (*Guide* I, 4).

[33] Cf. *Guide* III, 9, "The corporeal element in man is a large screen and partition that prevents him from perfectly perceiving abstract ideals ".

CHAPTER VI

[1] See Nicholson, *Literary History of the Arabs*, pp. 163, 368.

[1a] Deut. xxxiii. 21. The Targum renders by " Moses the great *scribe* of Israel ".

[2] Ps. xix. 8, 10.

[3] Sanhedrin 99b.

[4] Mishnah Sanhedrin X, 1 ; Sanhedrin 99a.

[5] The Biblical passages where these are ordained (Lev. xxiii. 42 ; *ibid.*, *v.* 40 ; *ibid.*, *v.* 24 ; Num. xv. 38 ; Deut. vi. 8) give no detailed account how these commandments are to be carried out. The manner of their observance is traditional and, according to the Rabbis, was explained to Moses on Mt. Sinai.

[6] " Assyrian script ", viz., the form of the alphabet in which the Scroll of the Law is written. It is also known as *ketab merubba'* " square script ".

[7] " Hebrew script ", i.e., the old Hebrew form of the characters which was preserved by the Samaritans. There is a statement in the Talmud (Sanhedrin 21b) to the effect : " Originally the Torah was given to Israel in the *ketab 'ibri* and Hebrew language ; it was retransmitted to them in the days of Ezra in the *ketab ashuri* and Aramaic language ".

[8] The Jews who traced their descent from the community in Spain. Other Jews also have adopted a different script for secular use.

[9] See Chap. XI. §7.

[10] viz., his spiritual and intellectual perfection.

[11] viz., the physical, since excess is harmful.

[12] See Chap. V, §6.

[13] Sanhedrin 90a.

[14] Sanhedrin, loc. cit.

[15] Abot I, 1 (Singer's Prayer Book, p. 184).

[16] Sanhedrin XI, 2.

[17] There are thirteen such rules, and they will be found in the Prayer Book, pp. 13f.

[18] Peah I, 1 (Prayer Book, p. 5).

[19] To I, 1, §8.

[20] See p. 188.

[21] Exod. xxii. 6-14.

[22] A silver coin worth 96 issar, the Roman as. In the Midrash (Shir, loc. cit.) the text reads " gold coin ".

[23] The doctrine associated with ma'aseh beréshit " the work of creation " formed a branch of the occult lore.

[24] Prov. ii. 16ff. Maimonides' interpretation is doubtless suggested by the Platonic comparison of matter to woman and form to man. See Introduction p. 22.

[25] Prov. xxxi. 10.

[26] The offence of using for a private purpose what had been donated to the Sanctuary. See Lev. v. 15ff.

[27] This was the opinion of the orthodox school of Mohammedan theologians, the Ash'ariyah. Cf. Chapter VII, §3, Third Theory. A similar conception is sometimes found in Rabbinic literature. E.g., " Why do we silence a man who says in his prayer ' To a bird's nest do Thy mercies extend ' ? Because he makes the ordinances of the Holy One, blessed be He, to be simply acts of mercy, whereas they are injunctions " (not necessarily with a purpose) ; Berachot 33b.

[28] Maimonides offers explanations for all of these.

[29] Yoma 67b, Numbers Rabba XIX, 5.

[30] He however suggests a reason for this below.

[31] Such an opinion is held by Saadya, Emunot III, 10.

[32] If Maimonides is thinking only of the physical sign, his argument loses force owing to the fact that other peoples, e.g., the Mohammedans, also practise circumcision.

[33] But it is known that among the Mohammedans circumcision is usually performed when the boy is five or six years old, and among the peasants not infrequently at the age of twelve or even fourteen. See Lane, Modern Egyptians, Chap. II. The real reason why the Bible ordains that it should be done on the eighth day is that for the first seven days the child, or young of an animal, was not regarded as having an independent existence. Cf. Exod. xxii. 30 (Heb. 29), Lev. xxii. 27.

[34] Kiddushin 29a.

35 This was a work on magic translated into Arabic from an Indian original. Maimonides refers to it three times in the *Guide*.

36 The people of Saba or Sheba in S.W. Arabia. He intends the heathen Arabs of pre-Mohammedan times.

37 The same idea is found among the ancient Greeks. Cf. *Odyssey* XI where the blood of a slain sheep is poured into a trench to attract the spirits of the dead.

38 Cf. Frazer, *Folklore in Old Testament*, III, pp. 299ff.

39 See Deut. xxiii. 13f.

40 *al-Ifrang*, orginally the French, but generally applied to all Europeans who do not belong to the Turkish Empire. The Mohammedans do not eat swine's flesh.

41 Berachot 25a.

42 This is not explicitly commanded in the Torah, but the Rabbis derived it from Deut. xii. 23 (Ḥullin 101b). The prohibition is one of the " seven commandments of the sons of Noah " (Sanhedrin 56a).

43 See Robertson Smith, *Religion of the Semites*, p. 343.

44 Exod. xxiii. 19, xxxiv. 26 ; Deut. xiv. 21. Radin in *American Journal of Semitic Languages*, XL, pp. 209-218, associates the practice with the Orphic-Dionysiac mysteries.

45 No description of the method of slaughter is given in the Pentateuch, but the Rabbis inferred that instructions had been given orally to Moses on Mt. Sinai from the statement, " thou shalt kill of thy herd and of thy flock . . . as I have commanded thee " (Deut. xii. 21), the last words being understood in the sense, " according to the method I commanded " (Ḥullin 28a).

46 Lev. xix. 27.

47 He repeats that explanation in *Yad*, *Akum* XII, 7. Herodotus (III, 8) reports of certain Arab tribes that they "cut their hair in a ring away from the temples" in honour of their god. Numerous superstitions are associated with cutting the hair ; cf. Frazer, *Folklore in Old Testament*, III, Part IV, Chap. IV, and Smith, *Religion of the Semites*, pp. 323ff.

48 Lev. xix. 19 ; Deut. xxii. 11.

49 Elsewhere he declared, " This is a well known practice to-day among the Coptic monks in Egypt " (*Mitswot*, Prohib. XLII).

50 The traditional Jewish interpretation of " that which pertaineth unto a man " is armour. See the Targum and Nazir 59a where it is explained that women may not fight in the ranks of an army. In the Talmudic passage it is also suggested that the purpose of the enactment is to check lust.

51 Kiddushin 31a.

52 The theory that the purpose of the sacrificial system was to divert the Israelites from the worship of idols is found in Leviticus Rabba XXII, 5.

53 Ḥagigah 19a.

54 The changes of the moon are marked by periods of seven days. A leper was examined each seventh day (Lev. xiii.) as a turning-point in the progress of the disease.

55 E.g., the Sabbath, Passover and Tabernacles. Cf. also Lev. xii. 2.

56 Lev. xxiii. 15.

57 The ram's horn.

58 This is according to Rabbinic tradition. The Revelation occurred on Sivan 6th ; Moses stayed on the Mount forty days and descended on Tammuz 17th when he broke the tables. He then spent forty days in prayer on behalf of Israel, ascending the Mount for the second tables on Ellul 1st and descending on Tishri 10th.

59 These were the words used by the High Priest in the confession he made on that day (Yoma III, 8).

60 The passage Maimonides cites occurs at the end of the eighth Book of the *Ethics* and reads : " For the ancient festivals and assemblies seem to take place after the gathering in of the harvest, being of the nature of a dedication of the first fruits, as it was at these seasons that people had most leisure ".

61 Used in the *lulab*, Lev. xxiii. 40.

CHAPTER VII

1 Cf. Chap. I, §6.

2 He expounds this view as held by Mohammedan thinkers in the *Guide* I, 73, First Proposition.

3 *Physics* II, 5f., *Metaphysics* XI, 8. Aristotle contends that there cannot be a science of the accidental, i.e., of what exists by chance.

4 The term Providence in the philosophical system of Aristotle has not the same meaning as it has in theology. Whilst in the latter it is chiefly to the changes and vicissitudes in human life that the term is applied, in the system of Aristotle Providence is the cause of the continual existence of everything that is either permanent or changes in accordance with certain constant laws (Friedländer).

5 1 Kings xiii. 24. Note especially *v.* 26, " the Lord hath delivered him unto the lion ".

6 Aristotle admits that Providence watches over men who are worthy, because he declares, " The wise man is the most beloved of heaven and therefore the happiest " (*Eth. Nic.* X, 8).

7 A sect of theologians founded by al-Ash'ari. They held the doctrine of Predestination and denied the reality of free will. " They believe that when a man has the will to do a thing and, as he believes, does it, the will has been created for him, then the power to conform to the will, and lastly the act itself. The act is not accomplished by the power created in man ; for, in reality, no act can be ascribed to that power " (*Guide* I, 73, Sixth Proposition). Cf. Macdonald, *Muslim Theology*, p. 192.

8 Literally " secessionists ". They were the opponents of the Ash'ariyah and denied Predestination.

9 They " contend that man acts by virtue of the power which has been created in him " (*Guide, loc. cit.*). God, as

it were, created the free will for each act which man performed voluntarily.

¹⁰ i.e., the Jewish theory generally held. He advances views of his own which differ from those held by Jewish teachers.

¹¹ This is in contrast to the Mu'tazilite theory.

¹² The points on which Maimonides diverges from his Jewish predecessors are : (i.) Providence is restricted to human beings ; (ii.) it varies with human beings according to their state of perfection.

¹³ He goes on to point out that the Biblical passages which speak of God's mercy to animals (e.g., Ps. civ. 21, cxlv. 16, cxlvii. 9) do not contradict his theory, because they refer to species and not to individual animals.

¹⁴ This is precisely Aristotle's view. See p. 328, note 6.

CHAPTER VIII

¹ Tanḥuma, Kedoshim, §15 ; Ta'anit 25b; Sanhedrin 96a.

² This does not agree with the passage cited from C.M., Abot.

³ See Chap. IV, §3.

⁴ Bachya uses a similar illustration in his *Duties of the Heart*, Section IV, Chap. IV.

⁵ The Roman *denarius*, which was both a silver and gold coin. The silver *denarius* was about the size of a sixpence.

⁶ Abot IV, 7 (Singer's Prayer Book, p. 196).

⁷ Maimonides held strongly that one should not take pay for teaching the Torah (C.M., Abot IV, ·7).

⁸ Abot I, 3 (Prayer Book, p. 184).

⁹ He is held up by the Rabbis as the pattern of one who served God purely from love (Sotah 31a).

¹⁰ Pesaḥim 50b. In the Talmudic text it is " Torah and the commandments ", i.e., both study and practice.

¹¹ Abot IV, 2 (Prayer Book, p. 195).

¹² Sanhedrin 64b, 90b. According to the exegesis of the Rabbis there is not a superfluous word in the Torah. Therefore the addition of " surely " to " cut off " must have significance. The Hebrew is literally " cutting shall be cut off ", the word " cut " occuring twice. Hence there must be two excisions, viz., one in this world and the second in the world to come.

¹³ Abodah Zarah 3b, Nedarim 8b. The verse in Malachi concludes : " It shall leave them neither root nor branch ", on which the Talmud comments : " no root " in this world, " no branch " in the world to come.

¹⁴ Ta'anit 16a.

¹⁵ Berachot 56a.

¹⁵ᵃ That is how Maimonides explains the hardening of Pharaoh's heart by God. " Pharaoh and his followers,

already of their own free will, without any constraint whatever, had rebelled by oppressing the strangers who were in
their midst. . . The punishment which God then inflicted
upon them was that He withheld from them the power of
repentance, so that there should fall upon them that punishment which justice declared should be meted out to them "
(C.M., *Eight Chapters* VIII).

[16] The R.V. rendering is : " Out of the mouth of the Most
High cometh there not evil and good ? " and " evil " means
calamity.

[17] Abodah Zarah 54b.

[18] See Chap. VII, §3.

[19] Mo'ed Katon 18b ; see Abrahams, *Book of Delight*,
pp. 172ff.

[20] See Chap. III, §§2, 9.

[21] That analogy was used by R. Joshua ben Ḥanayah in
an argument with a Roman Emperor (Ḥullin 59b).

CHAPTER IX

[1] See below, §4.

[2] Sanhedrin 97b.

[3] In *Yad, Melachim* XI, 1, he writes : " The doctrine of
the coming of the Messiah is also mentioned in the Chapter
of Balaam, and there he prophesies concerning the two
Messiahs—the first being David who saved Israel from the
hand of his enemies, and the second being one who will arise
from among his descendants and save Israel. He declared,
' I see him, but not now ' (Num. xxiv. 17), i.e., David ;
' I behold him, but not nigh '—i.e., king Messiah. ' There
shall step forth a star out of Jacob '—i.e., David ; ' and a
sceptre shall rise out of Israel '—i.e., king Messiah."

[4] i.e., the section comprising Deut. xxix. 9-xxx. 20.
The verse he is referring to in particular is xxx. 3, " the
Lord thy God will turn thy captivity " etc., to which he
attaches a Messianic significance (*Yad, loc. cit.*).

[5] See Chap. V, §4.

[6] He is evidently thinking of Jesus ; see Luke xviii. 22.

[7] See Chap. XI, §4.

[8] These signs and marvels will not consist of miracles in
the ordinary sense of the term, since these are no valid proof
of a prophet's claim (see Chap. V, §6). The conclusive proof
of the truth of the Messiah will be seen in the effect of his
advent.

[9] " Armour-bearer " means supporter. Akiba hailed Bar
Koziba, or Bar Kochba, as the expected Messiah, and applied
to him the phrase, " There shall step forth a star out of Jacob "
(see above, note 3); j. Ta'anit IV, 68d.

[10] This is not quite accurate. The Talmud (*loc. cit.*)
records that when Akiba acclaimed Bar Kochba as the
Messiah, Rabbi Joḥanan ben Torta retorted, " Akiba, grass
will grow in thy cheeks and still the son of David will not
come ".

[11] i.e., Jesus.

[12] i.e., Mohammed.

[13] The allusion here is to the Christian and Mohammedan attitude towards the legislation of the Pentateuch.

[14] Berachot 34b, Shabbat 63a.

[15] Shabbat 30b.

[16] See Lev. xxv.

[16a] Maimonides defends this metaphorical interpretation against critics in his *Ma'amar Teḥiyyat ha-Métim* (*Responsa* II, 9d, 10a), and repeats it in the *Guide* III, 11.

[17] See §9 below.

[18] Sanhedrin 97b.

[19] Introduction to his translation, p. XXI. Kaufmann also pronounces the passage to be an interpolation (*Revue des Études Juives* XXIV, pp. 112ff).

[20] Tosifta Sanhedrin XIII, 2.

[21] Pesaḥim 50a.

[22] Maimonides adopts Aristotle's view that the human soul at birth is a *tabula rasa*. It is consequently only a potentiality. The knowledge acquired during life converts it into reality, and that reality survives death. See Introduction, pp. 24f.

[23] The *néphesh* and *ruaḥ*, the former being the vitality which ends with death and the latter the immortal element.

[24] viz.: the *ruaḥ*. In *Guide* I, 40, one of the meanings he gives to this term is " that which remains of man after his death and is not subject to destruction ". Cf. Eccles. xii. 7.

[25] See Introduction, pp. 21f.

[26] Explaining the word " image ", Maimonides remarks : " the term signifies ' the specific form ' of man, viz. his intellectual perception " (*Guide* I, 1).

[27] See Chap. X, §1.

[28] Since knowledge is the essential quality which constitutes the soul as a reality, it bears to it the same relationship that form does to matter.

[29] The source of the quotation is Ta'anit 7a.

[30] Berachot 18a.

[31] Berachot 17a ; cf. Matthew xxii. 30.

[31a] See Chap. I, §10.

[32] Berachot 17a.

[33] Kiddushin 39b, Ḥullin 142a.

[34] Compare the description of Paradise in the Koran (Sura LV), " They shall repose on couches, the linings of which shall be of thick silk interwoven with gold . . . Therein shall receive them beauteous damsels, refraining their eyes from beholding any besides their spouses . . . having complexions like rubies and pearls ".

CHAPTER X

[1] i.e., Hippocrates.

[2] This was Aristotle's view. He maintained " numerically they (viz., the vital principles) are one and the same part,

although in their mode of expression they are manifold and different " (*de Juventute* I).

3 In Aristotle's analysis he includes motion and omits imagination (*de Anima* II, 3). But Maimonides regarded motion as not a soul-faculty but " an accident pertaining to living things actuated by physical needs or the desire to escape what is injurious " (*Guide* I, 26).

4 See p. 320, note 5.

5 Literally " they who dispute ". They were scholastic theologians concerned with the philosophy of Mohammedanism.

6 See Chap. V, §3.

7 But there were men who denied free will (see pp. 194ff) and there were philosophers, e.g., Zeno, who denied the reality of motion (Aristotle, *Physics* VI, 2).

7a From ὕλη " matter ", because it is, as it were, the basic substance which receives the form from the Intelligences to produce ideas. See Introduction, p. 24.

8 i.e., premisses, conclusions and inferences.

9 i.e., his intellect possesses the capacity of comprehension. The possibility of comprehending the thing exists ; but the act of comprehension turns the possibility into actuality.

10 Through the activity of the mind, the comprehension has become identified with the intellect.

11 Cf. Chap. III, §9.

12 See above p. 247.

13 When the intellect performs the action of comprehending, it becomes something in reality, not merely in capacity.

14 Since the mind necessarily resides in a body.

15 The Sciences deal with physical objects and their study falls within the scope of the imaginative faculty which is a " faculty of the body . . . (and) depends on the condition of the organ by which the faculty acts " (*Guide* II, 36).

16 The reference is to the passage in the Talmud (Ḥagigah 14b) which relates that " four men went up into Paradise ". See Introduction, p. 4.

17 See Chap. V, §3.

18 In a letter to his pupil, Joseph ibn Aknin, prefaced to the *Guide*, he wrote : " Observing your great fondness for Mathematics, I let you study them more deeply . . . Afterwards I took you through a course of Logic . . . and I considered you fit to receive from me an exposition of the esoteric ideas contained in the prophetic books ". Elsewhere he declared : " Such subjects as Mathematics, the study of Conic Sections, Mechanics, the various problems of Geometry, Hydraulics, and many others of a similar nature . . . should be studied for the purpose of sharpening the mind, and training the mental faculties by scientific investigations so that man may acquire intellectual ability to distinguish demonstrative proofs from others, whereby he will be enabled to comprehend the essence of God " (C.M., *Eight Chapters* V).

Commenting on his parable of the king in his palace whose audience is sought by his subjects (see pp. 114f), he states : " When you understand Physics, you have entered the hall ; and when, after completing the study of Natural Philosophy, you master Metaphysics, you have entered the innermost court and are with the king in the same palace" (*Guide* III, 51).

¹⁹ See Chap. V, §4.

²⁰ Alexander of Aphrodisius (his birthplace) was the leading exponent of Aristotle's philosophy. He was the head of the Lyceum at Athens about 200 C.E.

CHAPTER XI

¹ It is with perfection as with intellect.   See Chap. X, §§2f.

² See Chap. VII, §3.

³ i.e., the intellectual faculty.

⁴ He is referring to Aristotle's *Eth. Nic.* VII.

⁵ Sukkah 52a.

⁶ Abot V, end (Singer's Prayer Book, p. 204).

⁷ Sifra to Lev. xx. 26.   The teacher's name is Eleazar ben Azariah not Simeon ben Gamaliel.

⁸ Yoma 67b.   The Jewish theologians, following the lead of Saadya (*Emunot* III, 2) classify the commandments into rational and revealed.   The latter may or may not have a rational basis, but they are only incumbent because they are commanded by God.

⁹ Cf. Chap. VIII, §1.

¹⁰ This would be the golden *denarius* worth twenty-four times the silver coin, about thirteen shillings.

¹¹ Cf. *Guide* III, 27 : " This second perfection (i.e., of the Intellect) certainly does not include any action or good conduct ".

¹² i.e., the Greek philosophers, as contrasted with the later Arab metaphysicians.

¹³ The principal passage in the Talmudic literature where the middle course is advocated is : " This Torah is comparable to two paths, one of fire, the other of snow.   Should a man turn aside to the former he will be consumed by the fire, and if to the latter he will perish from cold.   What, then, should he do ?   Walk in the middle way " (j. Ḥagigah II, 1, 77a).

¹⁴ Aristotle denies the existence of men insensible to pleasure.   He says : " We never find people whose love of pleasures is deficient, and whose delight in them is less than it ought to be.   Such insensibility to pleasures is not human " (*Eth. Nic.* III, 14).

¹⁵ Aristotle says of the man who fears nothing that he is either a madman or insensible to pain (*ibid.*, III, 10), and in the subsequent chapter he distinguishes five spurious forms of courage.

¹⁶ Sifré *ad loc.* ; ed. Friedmann, p. 85a.

¹⁷ The text of the Talmud (Ketubot 111b) reads " whoever gives his daughter in marriage to ".

[18] Aristotle held that avarice was incurable (*Eth. Nic* IV, 3).

[19] Abot IV, 4 (Singer's Prayer Book, p. 195).

[20] Sotah 4b.

[21] *Ibid.*, 5a.

[22] Nedarim 22a.

[23] Pesaḥim 66b.

[24] *Ibid.*, 113b.

[25] The mention of " wool " is probably meant as a reference to the Sufis, the Mohammedan ascetics.

[26] Usually worn by Christian ascetics.

[27] Sifra *ad loc.*

[28] Sotah III, 4.

[29] See, e.g., Lev. v. 7, 11.

[30] Shabbat 25b. It is also said, " Three things make the mind cheerful ; a beautiful home, a beautiful woman, beautiful utensils " (Berachot 57b).

[31] It causes dropsy and jaundice (Berachot 25a).

[32] This is at variance with Talmudic teaching, viz., " He who makes his food float in water will not suffer with indigestion " (*ibid.*, 40a).

[33] *Ibid.*, 23b.

[34] Lying on the back is actually denounced (*ibid.* 13b).

[35] The Talmud declares, " He who makes it a habit to eat lentils once in thirty days keeps croup away from his house ; but not every day. . . It is bad for the breath of the mouth " (*ibid.* 40a). Mustard should also be used sparingly because it is bad for a weak heart (*ibid.*). Cabbage is nourishing, but " woe to the body through which vegetables keep constantly passing " (*ibid* 44b).

[36] Dates are one of the things which " enter the body without its deriving any benefit therefrom " (*ibid.* 57b).

[37] As that term is defined in Abot IV, 1, (Prayer Book, p. 195) : " Who is mighty ? He who curbs his desire ".

[38] He refers to a vapour-bath.

[39] i.e., Spring and Autumn.

[40] In all these passages Maimonides gives the word *tsedakah* its later signification.

[41] Tosifta Shekalim II, 16. This system of charity was adopted outside the Temple in several Palestinian and Babylonian cities.

[42] Ketubot 67b.

[43] *loc. cit.*

[44] Cf. Abot II, 2 (Prayer Book, p. 187).

[45] Abot III, 17 (Prayer Book, p. 193).

[46] It is recorded of Rabban Joḥanan ben Zakkai that he never allowed anybody to greet him first, not even the heathen in the street (Berachot 17a).

[47] Abot I, 6 (Prayer Book, p. 185).

[48] *Ibid.*, I, 12 (Prayer Book, p. 185).

[49] *Ibid.*, IV, 23 (Prayer Book, pp. 197f).

[50] Yebamot 65b.

[51] Abot I, 5 (Prayer Book, p. 185), Berachot 43b.

52 Cf. Berachot 43b.
53 Shabbat 114a.
54 See p. 321, note 16.
55 Berachot 43b.
56 *Ibid.*
57 *Ibid.*
58 Cf. Baba Metsia' 52a. But in Genesis Rabba XX, 12, man is advised to spend according to his means on food, less on clothing, and more on his house.
59 Sotah 44a. In Abot V, 24 (Prayer Book, pp. 203f) there is a teaching which apparently contradicts this. The passage is usually translated, " At eighteen for marriage, at twenty for seeking a livelihood ". But Herford, in his edition, p. 144, renders, on the authority of Rashi, " at twenty for pursuit of righteousness."
60 Yoma 86a.
61 Cf. Megillah 28a.
62 Cf. Yoma 86a.
63 Yebamot 109a.
64 Baba Kama 93a, Sanhedrin 49a.
65 Shabbat 118a.
66 Pesaḥim 113a, Baba Batra 110a.
67 See p. 329, note 7.
68 Maimonides refers to Lev. xix. 18, " Thou shalt love thy neighbour as thyself ". He evidently understands " neighbour " to mean brother-Israelite, as many modern exegetes do. Although Jewish ethics stresses the duties of the Jew to his coreligionist, it emphatically declares that those obligations extend to all men (Gittin 61a).
69 Abot II, 17, 15 (Prayer Book, p. 189).
70 j. Ḥagigah II, 1, 77c.
71 i.e., proselytes. See Chap. IV, §5.
72 Baba Kama VIII, 7.
73 Arachin 16b.
74 Baba Metsia' 59a.
75 *Ibid.*, 59b.
76 Cf. Arachin 16b.
77 Abot II, 17 (Prayer Book, p. 189).
78 Since it is the rational soul that survives. See Chap. IX, §7.
79 For the definition of " wisdom " see Chap. X, §2.
80 The " imitation of God " is the eighth commandment in his *Mitswot*.

INDEX

Abraham, 52, 119, 122, 141, 207
Abraham ibn Daud, 27, 129
" Accident," 317
Ahad Ha'am, 8ff., 322
Aher (Elisha ben Abuyah) 4, 252
Akiba, Rabbi, 4, 223, 252, 330
Albertus Magnus, 29
Alexander Aphrodisius, 256, 333
Almohades, 7
Angels, s.v. Intelligences
Anger, 274
Anthropomorphisms, 97f.
Apostates, 203
Aquinas, 29
Aristotle, 1, 3, 5, 6, 8, 17, 19, 21, 33, 50, 55, 57f., 68, 75, 187, 192ff., 241, 313, 316, 317, 323, 328, 331, 332, 333, 334
Asceticism, 274ff.
Ash'ariyah, 195, 326, 328
Astrology, 123f., 260
Atonement, day of, 186

Bachya, 329
Balaam, 164
Behaviour, correct, 290ff., 296ff.
Blood, eating the, 174f., 327
Body, care of, 283f.

Charity, 222, 286ff.
Chastity, 289
Christians, attitude towards, 117
Circumcision, 172ff., 326
Comfort, value of, 277
Commandments, purpose of, 167ff.
Confession, 187, 213
Conic Sections, 332

Creation, from nothing, 50ff.; purpose of, 56ff. ; Biblical account of, 163

Daniel, 140
David, 139f., 166f., 220
Design in Universe, 54ff.
Determinism, 217ff.
Dietary laws, 175f.
Dietetic rules, 278ff.
Divination, 125ff., 144
Dress, correct, 292

Eden, garden of, 228
Emanation, 37ff., 132
Epicurus, 192
Evil, problem of, 39ff., 198
Evil spirits, 123
Error, sources of, 256

" Fence " to the Torah, 159
Festivals, the, 183f.
Forgiveness, 289
" Form," 21f., 36, 164f.
Free will, 4, 40, 196ff., 214ff.
Future, foretelling the, 134, 143f., 175, 249

Gabirol, 316
Gehinnom, 211
Geometry, 332
God, knowledge of, 18f., 227 ; attributes of, 21, 83ff. ; existence, 31ff. ; unity, 33, 93ff. ; cause of the Universe, 34f. ; " form " of the Universe, 36 ; not cause of evil, 39ff. ; His work purposeful, 46ff. ; existed before the Universe, 51ff. ; names of, 62 ff.; incorporeality, 96ff. ; eternity, 98ff. ; omnipresence, 100f. ; His

INDEX

knowledge, 102ff., 218f.; love and fear of, 110ff., 204ff.; revealed the Torah, 152ff.; cognisant of man, 189ff.; Divine Providence, 192ff.; justice of, 202f.; withholds power of repentance, 213f.; consciousness of, 293f.; imitation of, 306, 335

Ḥasdai Crescas, 6, 27
Heart, in primitive psychology, 2f.
Hebrew language, 62; script, 154, 325
Herodotus, 327
Hippocrates, 331
Homer, 3, 327
Homonym, 320
Humility, 273
Hydraulics, 332

Idolatry, 120ff., 158, 169, 177
Imagination, 132, 242ff.
Imitation of God, 306, 335
Immortality, 233f.
Intellect, 245ff., 249ff., 255f., 308f.; the Active, 129, 130, 136
Intelligences, the, 31, 39, 40, 65ff., 238, 319
Interpretation of Scripture, 161ff.
Isaiah, 140

Jacob, 137, 164
Jeremiah, 140
Jesus, 117, 224, 325, 330
Job, 164
Josephus, 1
Joshua, 145, 164
Judah Halevi, 6
Judaism, 116f.

Karaites, 11, 116, 118
Kindness, 285
Knowledge, sources of, 133f., 253f.
Koran, 148, 152, 331

Labour, 295
Levi ben Gerson, 27
Life, purpose of, 298ff.; goal of, 301ff.
Logic, 254, 332
Lulab, 188

Man, 40ff., 49f., 58ff., 113, 155, 245ff., 258ff., 310
Marriage, 217, 293
Martyrdom, 232
Mathematics, 254, 302, 332
Materia prima, 76, 193, 317
Matter, eternity of, 17, 50ff.; constitution of, 76ff.
" Mean," the, 19, 267ff.
Mechanics, 332
Messiah, 220ff.
Metaphysics, 64, 137, 253, 254, 333
Miracles, 9, 54, 101, 223, 309
Mohammed, 8ff., 117, 224, 324, 325
Mohammedans, 118, 239, 323, 325, 326
Moses, 9f., 17, 139, 143, 145, 146ff., 152, 221
Mutakallimun, 243, 255
Mu'tazila, 196f.

Nature, 43, 46, 49, 55f., 60, 101
New Year, 185f.

Passover, 185, 187
Perfection, kinds of, 304ff.
Philo, 319, 321
Physics, 34f., 37, 333
Plato, 22, 69, 316, 317, 318, 319, 320, 326
Predestination, 4, 217ff.
Prescience and determinism, 217ff.
Prophets and Prophecy, 9f., 12, 38, 49, 68, 69, 85, 129ff., 157f., 221f., 254, 324f.
Proselytes, 118f., 296, 323
Providence, 189ff.
Pythagoras, 3